Life is meant to be a

Sacred Journey

Life is meant to be a

Sacred Journey

WARD TANNEBERG
AUTHOR OF REDEEMING GRACE

FORWARD BY
MISSY BUCHANAN

Copyright © 2016 Ward Tanneberg

All rights reserved. No part of this publication may be reproduced, stored in a retrieval system, or transmitted in any form or by any means—electronic, mechanical, photocopy, recording, or any other—except for brief quotations in printed reviews, without the prior permission of the publisher.

Unless otherwise indicated, Scripture references are from the Holy Bible, English Standard Version (ESV). Copyright © 2001 by Crossway, a publishing ministry of Good News Publishers. ESV Text Edition: 2011.

This work is a memoir which details the journey the author and his wife took through her illness. The author is not a doctor and medical information in this book is to illustrate their journey and should not be construed as medical advice.

Quotation from Dr. JoAnn Dahlkoetter used with permission.

Cover Photo: Dixie at Iona Abbey on the Isle of Iona, West Coast of Scotland

*Dedicated
to all who knew her as
~ Dixie, Dix, Mom, Gramma, GG ~
Her life became her message.*

*Looking for her Father
she took us with her on her journey.*

Dixie Lee Tanneberg 1935–2015

What people are saying about *Sacred Journey*:

Some love stories just need to be told—even the final pages of that story. Maybe especially those final pages. In the beautiful memoir, **Sacred Journey**, author Ward Tanneberg writes with a poignant tenderness about the life journey he and his beloved wife, Dixie, walked together. The path was not always easy, but in their story, we find hope for ours.
Dr. Jodi Detrick, Speaker,
former columnist for The Seattle Times
Author of The Jesus-Hearted Woman

Poignant, heartwarming and incredibly uplifting. In *Sacred Journey*, Ward tells the story of Dixie's well-lived life, from meager beginnings, to touching and impacting thousands of lives. You will laugh, cry and be forever changed. If you read one book this year—read *Sacred Journey*.
Dr. Chuck Stecker, President
A Chosen Generation.

An unwanted child. An angry mother. An abusive and absent father. An unpromising start in what life is meant to be. *Sacred Journey* is Dixie Tanneberg's true story of perseverance and faith in God; of dreams lost and love unexpected by the toss of a coin; of a woman's strength and courage in her final determination not to waste her cancer. Her story challenges and reaches out to us through each thoughtful word and page.

Wes Wick, Director
YES! Young Enough to Serve

Occasionally, I care for a patient that moves me to reflection, tenderness, and admiration. Dixie was that kind of person. A woman I was blessed to know. A direct gaze. No nonsense. A woman of love, with devoted daughter and husband by her side. She is ready to be well, but this cancer will not cooperate. Hard times come with precious ones. Who is this strong, amazing woman?
Lucille Marchand, MD, BSN, FAAHPM, Professor
Stuart J Farber, MD and Annalu Farber Endowed Faculty Fellow in Palliative Care Education
Department of Family Medicine, Section Chief of Palliative Care
Director Palliative Care Program—UW Medical Center
University of Washington School of Medicine

For more of what people are saying, please turn to that section in the back of the book.

Acknowledgements

There are many people who are part of this true story. The list is far too long to be recited here. You know who you are. Thank you so much for being in her life and in mine. Thank you to the church families we have served and that have been there for us in return; to our many friends, neighbors, and those of you we have yet to meet in person, who prayed for us, shared simple acts of kindness, and offered words of encouragement during the final months of Dixie's sacred journey.

A special thanks to our children Michele and Stephen, and their spouses, Mark and Nancy, who joined with Susan Harper and Dr. Lucille Marchand as readers and consultants, helping to ensure accuracy and clarity of content. Your corrections and suggestions were so valuable to this writer. Thanks to Robert Burger and Michele Peterson for creating the *Sacred Journey Discussion Guide,* thus enabling the reader's personal review, as well as couples, book clubs and small groups; turning thoughtful interactive discussion toward our own sacred journeys.

A shout out to my good friend, literary agent and president of Hartline Literary Agency, Joyce Hart, who keeps on being my writing advocate and encourager; and to Elizabeth-Anne Kim at Hartline, who has faithfully guided this project to completion. I told you you were really going to like working with me, Elizabeth. And you were courageous enough to believe it. So the next time I'm in Pittsburgh, dinner is on me.

Contents

Acknowledgements · iv
Photographs · xiv
Forward · xvi
Introduction ·1

1 Calm before Storm ·5
2 Valentine's Day · 10
3 Options Are Good · 16
4 Looking for Signposts ·21
5 Song Sparrows and Hummingbirds · · · · · · · · · · · · · · · · · 28
6 The Warmest Room · 36
7 Regrets... There Are a Few · 44
8 Looking for My Father ·50
9 The Numbers Game · 55
10 Waiting and Watching ·62
11 Love Unexpected · 68
12 A New Normal ·75
13 Yielding · 80
14 Questioning ·88
15 The "What if" Question ·91
16 The Restless Years ·98
17 Success and Sadness ·108

18	Full Circle	120
19	Farewell for Awhile	127
20	Any Port in a Storm	135
21	Always a Bride	139
22	Why Do You Think You're Here?	143
23	Where Help Comes From	148
24	Left Alone	152
25	Satisfied... Not Settling	157
26	Seeing with the Eyes of God	162
27	Against the Wind	167
28	Lifting Weary Hands	173
29	Ring That Bell!	177
30	Selah	187
31	Perspective	191
32	When Setbacks Come	195
33	Uncharted Territory	199
34	Midcourse Check	204
35	My Journey Through the Valley of Shadows	210
36	Road Trips	216
37	The Bad Week	222
38	The Thousand-Year Day	225
39	Doctors Treat... Jesus Heals	229
40	Merry Christmas!	232
41	The Greatest Small Gift	236
42	When Rights Are Not Always Right	242
43	It's Not Over 'til It's Over	247
44	The Thing Between God and Us	250
45	Happy Valentine's Day	256
46	Our Family in Christ	259
47	Don't Breathe	263
48	It Takes a Village!	266

49	"Beam Me up, Scotty"	269
50	Traits of the Long Distance Runner	273
51	More Traits…	276
52	Chemotherapy Round 4	280
53	Icons of Aging	283
54	Attitude and Tenacity	291
55	The Tipping Point	299
56	What I Learned from Dixie	303
57	The Most Important Thing	306
58	The Journey Ends	314

A Postscript for Dixie	319
The Beginning	325
Life is meant to be a Sacred Journey	333
More of What People Are Saying About Sacred Journey	345
About the Author	351

Photographs

	Dixie Lee Tanneberg 1935–2015	v
1	Desert	6
2	Barbee family ~ Sam and Edna Barbee; Don, Dixie, Darvin	16
3	Dixie's childhood home in Claremore, OK	36
4	Fun and faithful: Nancy (behind), L-R Bev, Carolyn, Dixie	64
5	Dixie went fishing once - the only fish she ever caught - 115 lbs!	112
6	Mom and Michele were never far apart.	121
7	The wedding - L-R Wanda, Dixie, Ward, Clyde	139
8	Dixie wears her wedding dress on her 50th anniversary.	142
9	Dixie teaching Women's Bible Study	162
10	Dixie rings the bell.	180
11	The radiation team joins in celebration	181
12	Michele with step granddaughters: Karen, Amy, Jody, Becky and Dixie	184
13	Our son, Stephen, Nancy and Jesse	184
14	Our granddaughter, Jessica	185
15	Our daughter, Michele, and Mark	185
16	(L-R) Our Granddaughter, Katy, Finnigan, Geoff, and Corbin	186
17	The SR520 Lake Washington Floating Bridge	199
18	Dixie finds still waters.	211

19	Dixie waits for the plane at Budapest Ferenc Liszt International Airport	216
20	GG and great-grandson, Corbin	234
21	Dixie stays warm while waiting for treatment to get underway.	251
22	A proton therapy treatment bay	271
23	Dixie with the Charles River and Boston in background	284
24	Dixie's mountain	307
25	Postscript to a love story	323
26	Song sparrow	326
27	Hummingbird	331

Forward

I didn't want Ward to write this book. Not *this* book. I wanted him to write an inspiring story of Dixie's amazing triumph against the Enemy Cancer. A story that ends with Dixie and Ward strolling hand-in-hand on a beach with their boodle of grandkids and great-grands laughing up ahead.

Like so many others who knew and loved Dixie, I desperately wanted her cancer to be annihilated. Zapped. Totally obliterated. I wished for the next high-tech treatment to work when the last one didn't. I repeatedly asked God for an out-of-the-ballpark miracle, a Red Sea moment in her wilderness experience. But that miracle did not come.

When I first met Dixie some years ago, I was immediately drawn to her engaging smile and the lyrical way she carried herself, both confident and gentle. We were in southern California for a leadership conference hosted by CASA—Christian Association Serving Adults. Since I have a special affinity for older adults who are growing frail, I was asked to speak on how to help the oldest old discover a renewed sense of purpose even as they age.

Over the years, mature saints have taught me many things, but most importantly, they have encouraged me not to gloss over the hard realities of aging in a flimsy attempt to be positive and upbeat. From them I have learned the power of trust and hope amid the trials that often accompany this season of change and loss.

Following my session that day, Dixie took my hand in hers, looked deep into my eyes, and quietly said something that is etched in my mind. "You are a true gift for older adults," she said. "We need your message of enduring hope and perseverance in difficult times, even when it's hard to hear."

Dixie seemed to understand how some adults, particularly Boomers, shy away from talking about the tough challenges of aging. They don't want to think about physical decline or loss of independence. Her generous words of affirmation that day made me feel as though I had known her for decades instead of hours. Then a couple of years later, we had the opportunity to share fellowship and conversation at another conference, affirming what I already knew. Dixie was the real deal. An authentic, humble servant of God. It wasn't until recently that I even wondered if there was a story about how this gracious woman from Washington State had been given a southern name like Dixie.

My heart ached when I first learned of Dixie's diagnosis. I anxiously awaited Ward's weekly posts with updates on her journey. I read about the ups and downs of her treatments and celebrated the moments of unexpected grace. Each week I discovered a palpable hope woven into the texture of Ward's words, a hope that only comes from unwavering trust in an almighty God. Even friends of mine who had never met Ward and Dixie began to follow along on their intimate yet sacred journey.

Reading about the medical procedures, trial programs and medications brought to mind an image of Dixie's beloved Pacific Northwest where I had visited just a few years earlier. I pictured the rugged coastline where frigid waves pound the rocky shore, causing white spray to explode like fireworks. I knew there had to be days when Dixie felt like those boulders, sustaining the brunt force of the sea. Yet, like the huge rocks, she remained steadfast in faith.

I thought, too, about how the ocean waves are much like aging. There is no stopping the white-capped waves. They are relentless, constantly pushing their way upon the shore, just as God designed them to do. Yet when I stood before this scene of nature, I was moved in an inexplicable way by the stunning spectacle of perseverance and power before me. Like Dixie's life, a majestic, awe-inspiring beauty that is best understood in the spiritual realm.

I am grateful that Ward resisted the urge to gloss over the tough realities of Dixie's journey. There are moments we may be tempted to close our eyes to the pain and suffering, but without them, the significance of her obedience, courage and hope are diminished. Ward tenderly invites us into the darkness so we can fully experience the fragrance of grace and the light of hope, giving witness to a mature faith.

I have had the honor of holding the timeworn hands of many older adults in their last days on earth. Their lives have been like glimmering gold threads stitched into my life, making me stronger for having witnessed their faith. And as I look back, I can see their golden threads trailing behind their earthly lives. A lasting legacy for others to see.

I thank God for the golden thread of Dixie Tanneberg who so unselfishly stitched into countless lives over the years, making each of us stronger by her faithful witness. This is the book that needed to be written. It is Dixie's *message of enduring hope and perseverance in difficult times, even when it's hard to hear.*

Missy Buchanan
Author of ***Voices of Aging*** and other books
www.missybuchanan.com.

My self is given to me far more than it is formed by me.
~ *Pierre Teilhard de Chardin, The Divine Milieu*

The *now* is only a thin slice of who I am; isolated from the rich deposits of *before*, it cannot be understood.
The *before* is the root system of the visible *now*.
~ *Eugene Peterson, Run with the Horses*

Introduction

IN THE BEGINNING

The world was in trouble the year I was born, as was the family of my birth. It was the middle of the Great Depression; the economic world was in shambles and unemployment rampant. The turmoil within my family was intensified by persistent, prevailing winds sweeping clean the soil that produced the food they ate; and more bad news, another baby was on the way. My birth was not a joyous occasion. I was the only girl in a family of boys, but I was not welcomed. I was another mouth to feed, another body to clothe, another strain on an already emotionally depleted marriage. ~ DLT, diary, 2015

AT THE ENDING
79 years and 39 weeks later.

When news of her death is posted on the Internet, word spreads quickly. Thousands visit the announcement to see her picture, to grieve over the loss of one who has left her mark in one way or another on each of them and on a world that at first had not welcomed her coming, but in the end was a better place for her having been here. What drew so many men and women to her during her lifetime?

An ordinary child, born on 5 November 1935, into a poor farmer's family in Carnegie, Oklahoma, she grew to womanhood in the city. Her first paying job was dressing windows in a Tulsa, Oklahoma, department store. She never went to college, never did the things that usually precede greatness. Never followed youthful dreams of singing in the opera. Married young. Had two children. Was not wealthy. She was a working mother, a grandmother, a great-grandmother. Never wrote a book. Never had a Facebook or LinkedIn or Pinterest account and never once Tweeted.

In her favorite Bible are two blank pages now filled with handwritten quotes from Eugene Peterson, a Protestant pastor, theologian, author; Henri Nouwen, a Catholic priest, professor and writer; and Irenaeus, a disciple of the Apostle John. Following these quotes, on a page by itself, are these words, audacious and bold, brave, almost defiant, written by the same feminine hand, "My limitations do not keep God from doing His work through me."

A private woman, she lived a public life. Not by choice, but by calling. She read broadly and deeply. She challenged others to be the best they could be. Those who knew her described her as a role model, mentor and friend, kind and warm. These and other such descriptors were meant to encourage her, to acknowledge her worth and value, but were hard for her to accept. Affirming words are difficult to acknowledge as true if not heard while growing up at home.

There is one descriptor often used by those who knew her best. It is the word "extra." She refused to let this adjective linger as something well deserved, but passed it on to others whom she touched and believed in, especially those struggling with destructive feelings of unworthiness or the crippling lack of being valued by those important to their wellbeing. She was certain that extra could happen for them as it had for her, as each person comes to understand how God intends their ordinary, everyday life to become an *extra*ordinary sacred journey, with the amazing pursuit of *knowing God* as its highest endeavor.

Had she realized so many would stop what they were doing to view her picture and mention her name or shed tears of sadness at the end, she would have said, "Whoa, this is way too much exposure!" She was not comfortable in front of large groups or crowds, though she often taught or was a guest speaker. She was more at home listening to and encouraging people one-to-one on their sacred journeys. In the end, her children, grandchildren, great-grandchildren, and thousands more loved her for that very reason.

Sacred Journey is a true love story, framed in the final eighteen months of her life. Simple, vulnerable and transparent, written as a reminder to older men and women with lines of experience carved into their countenance; as a legacy to adult children and their children who dream of attaching lasting meaning to their lives; as a thank you note to those who knew and loved her on her journey; and as an invitation to the reader who would like to know someone who believes God's intention is for *extra* to belong to every *ordinary* human soul. A story of two people in love, filled with dreams and disappointments, hope and hopelessness, emotional pain and physical suffering, and a Light in a valley of dark shadows. A story you can identify with, in many ways as being very much your own.

I knew her better than anyone. I often introduced her to strangers as "This is my wife, Dixie." Then after living a few years together as husband and wife, I came to realize she was never meant to be mine in the possessive, ownership sense of the word. She was on loan to me, to help mold and shape me into a man that God might actually want to hang out with and use someday. Like Paul of old, she was "not called by any group or agency. (Her) call is from Jesus Christ himself and from God the Father who raised him from the dead" (Galatians 1:1 *TLB*).

She offered me and countless others the most precious gifts any person can give; a lifetime of presence, time and energy, encouragement and wisdom. Courage. A mind that listened and love regardless. She was good here. She is perfect there. She is experiencing the completion of a promise made to every Christ follower. If anyone is in Christ, he/she is a new creation. The old has passed away; behold, the new has come (2 Corinthians 5:17).

Life is meant to be a Sacred Journey is her story. It became *our* story. We understand our own stories best sometimes by seeing us in someone else. Perhaps this will happen for you and Dixie. I know it has for me.

I can't wait to meet her again one day for the very first time!

1

Calm before Storm

The year was 1935. The stock market had crashed six years before, causing a domino effect of bank failures, unemployment, disintegrated fortunes and homes lost to foreclosures, leaving people feeling helpless and fearful. Many lived in despair, while others reached for strong inner resources and fought their despair with hope. And some just gave up on life, choosing death by their own devices. Still others existed in a living death of fear and anger, my parents included. My family were farmers in Oklahoma, and probably not greatly affected by bank failures and stock market demise. They lost their land! The lack of rain and fury of winds and irreparable farming practices collided in mid-America, creating the perfect storm for soil erosion as farms literally blew away. ~ DLT diary, 2015

⁓

There is no doubt. Loss brings with it its own demons. And when crises subside, the demons are not gone with the winds. They settle in with no intention of going away. ~ WT

Early in January, after two long travel days driving south from our home in Bellevue, Washington, we arrive in Indio, California, exhausted and wondering why we left the comforts and conveniences of home to accept the inconveniences and less comfortable circumstances of a hotel situated in the middle of a desert.

1 Desert

This is a different kind of desert however; an oasis made beautiful by money and water. Oh yes, and sun. Well, there is that! When rain is normal and seeing the sun in January a rare event, this might be enough. But there is more.

A different place helps me gather up life's fringes and draw them into my center. To focus and think. To plan and pray. It can happen almost anywhere, but there is something for me that is truly restorative about the desert. The warmth and sun, the barren hills and jagged mountains. I grew up in the high desert of eastern Washington state. This could be part of it. Or maybe it's because so much of what happens in the Bible, what Jesus did, how God reveals himself to us, takes place in the desert.

It's about roots. The desert has a way of speaking to us. The trees, the barrenness, sudden rain-flooded streams and dry river beds. When you plant something here and water and nurture it, it grows quickly, leafs out, bears fruit, becomes a beautiful thing. I like that. It shouldn't happen, but it does. A stick turns into an orange or lemon or grapefruit tree almost overnight it seems. A little water and the desert blooms. It's extraordinary!

Life, I think, is like this. Even in January.

Dixie and I spend the entire month of days here in this desert where once we lived for four years. In the early morning sunshine, we stretch our legs by walking a 2.8-mile route before preparing a breakfast we enjoy outdoors on the deck. Later I go for a swim, then sit by the pool and read. I am preparing to go to Russia in a few weeks to teach in a seminary extension program. Dixie prefers the quiet of our room to do some catch up reading and meditation.

We do not tell acquaintances in the area we are here. We want to be together, but alone. Just the two of us. Something we need, especially since I will be leaving soon. Each day is a pleasant repeat of the one before. Evenings are warm and quiet and meals are simple. We enjoy desert sunsets, more beautiful, we agree, than anywhere else in the world. At least we feel that way right now.

The final day comes at last as we knew it would. Reluctantly we leave this desert hideaway to resume our real life. As we drive north on I-5, we are unaware we have just completed our last major trip together.

The day following our arrival home is Super Bowl Sunday. Seattle and Denver square off against one another. In a few hours, we are ecstatic over Seattle winning its first Super Bowl victory ever! Dixie doesn't watch the game. She spends most of the day upstairs lying down with a recurrence of headaches and dizziness. She is not feeling well. In the following days her discomfort increases.

On Tuesday, Dixie participates in a breast exam at nine o'clock and an MRI at eleven. At one-thirty we meet with a neurosurgeon who assures us nothing untoward has been found. He points to a small spot shown in the X-ray that is likely nothing at all. It should be re-examined in a year. She goes for a haircut the following day. The day after is First Thursday, and a night out with our daughter, Michele. On each month's first Thursday, Michele meets me for Starbucks coffee at 5 o'clock in the morning, before going off to work. It's her Father's Day gift. This way Dad gets to celebrate Father's Day twelve times a year. In the evening she and Mom spend time together.

On Friday, I fly to the Bay Area for an Assist International board meeting. On Saturday, Dixie speaks at a Presbyterian women's retreat in Tacoma. Life goes on as usual. But life is about to change. When I return home on Sunday early afternoon, I find Dixie feeling even more under the weather.

The following Tuesday, I go for my annual physical checkup. I have jotted down a list of questions to ask. On completion of my exam, I remind Dr. Anne Bankson, "We haven't talked about this item that's at the top of my list. Dixie's not here today, but she is really sick and I am concerned. Since last October it seems like she's had every exam possible. Nothing has been found, yet I know she is not well. Her pain has increased since we came home from the desert. She has an appointment to see a naturopathic physician to discuss dietary options. Her digestive system seems out of sync. It's not doing its job. She's even beginning to look jaundiced."

When I say the word, "jaundiced," Dr. Anne jumps to her feet.

"She doesn't need to go to a naturopath," she declares emphatically, turning to her computer. "It's not dietary."

"It's not?" I question, startled by her sudden response. "So what then?"

"I'm sending her to gastroenterology," she says, continuing to type.

"But she's had a colonoscopy and an endoscopy not very long ago. And she just had an MRI."

"This is different," she said. "I don't know for sure, but we need to take a look."

When I return home with news that the doctor's office will call us with an appointment for another exam, Dixie listens, taking it in, then turns away without a word. What is she thinking? When she is quiet like this one can only guess. I am cautious about probing further. If she wants to tell me something she will without me pressing the point. Besides, I'm not sure I want to go there right now. Something unsettling is hovering. Our amazing respite in the desert seems like a distant memory. Storm clouds are building. Today the sun is not shining.

2

Valentine's Day

Love is our true destiny. We do not find the meaning of life by ourselves alone ~ we find it with another. ~ Thomas Merton

⌒

"I'm leaving. I won't be long." Dixie is standing at the door with hat and coat on.

"Where are you headed?"

"Doctor's appointment."

"I'm going with you," I say, pushing away from the desk and reaching for my jacket.

"Why? He is just going to give me the results of the test."

"I'm going with you," I repeat.

She says nothing further.

We head out together, locking the door behind us.

Thirty minutes later we sit quietly in the doctor's office. We are alone. The reception desk is unoccupied. There is an opaque glass door on the left side of the room and I see the blurred outlines of people behind the door, their voices unintelligible, but obviously discussing something. I think this is taking longer than it should. I don't have a good feeling. I glance at Dixie. Her hands are folded together in her lap. I place mine on hers. Hers are often cold and this morning is no exception.

When the door finally opens, Dr. Wohlman enters followed by his nurse assistant. They greet us and seat themselves across from us. There is a long silence as I watch the doctor shuffle the papers in his hands. The nurse's face is turned toward him and looking down, her eyes on what I assume is a report of medical findings. I think to myself, this can't be good. At last the doctor speaks, gazing steadily at Dixie.

"I'm afraid the news is not good," he begins carefully. "From the samples we have taken, we are ninety-five percent certain you have pancreatic cancer."

The words are surreal, brief, matter-of-fact, to the point. A mixture of fact and incredulity. It's as though the world has suddenly stopped. My hand remains on hers. We sit staring at each other, waiting for... what? This cannot be happening. Is he going to say anything more? At last he does. "We need to confirm our findings so I am going to schedule you in the hospital for additional scrapings in the suspected area in order to make a final determination."

My mind is swimming, trying to absorb what we've just heard. Cancer? Okay. But not just any cancer. This is the worst kind. Isn't it? Pancreatic cancer!

"So how should I feel about this diagnosis?" Dixie asks at last. I glance at her. She has not moved, yet looks smaller somehow, as though bracing herself against the impact of what we've just heard.

The doctor pauses, appearing unsure how to answer a question so direct. At last he says simply, "Nervous?"

Minutes later we are outside, walking hand in hand down the hall leading to the parking lot elevator. We cover the short distance home in a matter of minutes, living only two miles away from the hospital. The drive time is quiet, as if the weight of words spoken might shatter the last remaining evidence of something no longer existing for us, the surety of what is coming next. I cover her hand with mine, breaking our silence at last and say, "I am so sorry."

"Me, too," she answers.

It's Valentine's Day. A day to celebrate love and happiness. Chocolates and romantic cards and dinner out. None of these things are happening for us today.

⌒

Two days later, alone with her thoughts, Dixie writes in her diary.

When we first heard the diagnosis "cancer," it was a surreal moment. I was numb. I had no other immediate emotion or reaction. I even asked the doctor how I should feel about this diagnosis. His response was a one-word question. "Nervous?"

I do not feel nervous. Instead, I seem to be wrapped in a cocoon of peace. That peace remains with me as I move along a pathway that leads me to the shadows of biopsies and scans and surgery and chemotherapy. Jesus' words in John 14:27, "Peace I leave with you; my peace I give to you," take on new meaning for me. All the peace Jesus exhibited while here on earth, he gives to me now. His peace feels warm and comforting, like the blankets caring nurses wrap around me.

"Even though I walk through the valley of the shadow of death, I will fear no evil for you are with me" ~ Psalm 23:4. Oh, how blessed to know that truth. Thank you, Lord!

Watching a tiny hummingbird outside my window reminds me that you know all the birds of the air and not one falls without your knowing. You are aware of me and what the next days will hold. Thank you for holding me during this part of my journey. I ask for strength through these days, however long it takes. Please give Ward and my family peace and strength. Their journey is different than mine. Theirs much more difficult. Hold them in your care. ~ DLT diary, February 2014

The following Wednesday, at 12 noon, we return to Overlake Medical Center for an endoscopic biopsy. We hold hands and kiss goodbye and she is wheeled away from me by strangers to the operating room.

Two hours later, Dr. Selinger enters the room where I have begun the first of what is destined to be hundreds of waiting hours in five regional medical centers. Her evaluation is forthright and cautious.

"Dixie is fine and in recovery," she says. "We will come get you when she is fully awake. We X-rayed the ducts that carry bile from the liver to the gallbladder and from the gallbladder to the small intestine. This is where the blockage is that's causing the extreme discomfort and the jaundice. It's what is making food difficult for her to digest, and contributes to her weight loss. Once the esophageal insertion reached the blocked area, we inserted a stent and left it in place to keep the duct open and hopefully provide Dixie some much needed relief. Tissue samples are already on their way to a pathology lab."

She pauses briefly before continuing. "We have confirmed she has pancreatic cancer, Stage II. I'm referring her to Seattle Cancer Care Alliance. They are the best. They'll take a look at what we've found and make a treatment recommendation. A team of doctors and medical specialists from SCCA and University of Washington Medical Center meet every Friday morning to go over their cases and make recommendations. It's Wednesday afternoon and I'm told their case load is full so they will not get to Dixie until a week from Friday. Sorry."

I thank her as she leaves and resume my seat, trying to assimilate the dreaded news. Stage II. What does that mean? I look up stages of cancer on the Internet. I already know there are four, but now I am looking for reassurance, something that will tell me Stage II is manageable, maybe even curable. I am aware more than ever at just how little I really know about this illness, even less about the journey on which we are embarking. I am already on a quest to fix this terrible thing that is happening, to somehow change the course we are on. I send up arrow prayers. Then I look for the phone number and place a call to SCCA myself.

I explain the reason for my call to the person answering. She transfers me to someone called a scheduler. I explain our circumstance again and ask, if possible, that Dixie be included in this Friday's agenda, even though I understand it is filled already. I am given little encouragement but assured my request will be passed along. Meanwhile Dixie is transferred to a private hospital room. Our daughter, Michele, joins us. Late in the evening Dixie is released and we arrive back home at 9 o'clock.

The following day she is drained of energy, although she decides to make some real chicken soup (as opposed to the hospital version), so we're in for a tasty treat for dinner. Being active in the kitchen seems therapeutic. The soup, coupled with cornbread she may or may not be able to eat, represents comfort food, though taste is not coming easily for her. She is quite sore throughout the esophageal area today and her gut hurts too. It is a quiet day. No word on pathology outcomes.

GG (Great Gramma) braces herself for a love attack from the little dude, Corbin, our 2–1/2-year-old great-grandson whom we haven't seen since Christmas. Gramma Michele is bringing him by after work.

Late that evening, I answer the telephone to hear a woman's voice telling me that if we are still interested, Dixie will be included in tomorrow's SCCA medical team agenda. Of course we are interested. Dixie is growing weaker, unable to absorb anything beyond sipping an occasional Boost, a little soup, some soda crackers and water. This is an answer to prayer. I love it when things happen the way I want them to. She proceeds to give us instructions as to where and when to arrive and what to expect.

Early the next morning we pray and prepare. At seven-thirty we are engulfed in Seattle's Mercer Street exit traffic mess as we get off I-5, something we soon learn is an everyday, sometimes all-day occurrence. By 8 o'clock we have navigated underground parking where spaces are the size of wheelchairs and gray cement pillars are eager to befriend your car. We take an elevator to F1 and stand in line at the Seattle Cancer Center Alliance admissions desk, ready to begin whatever is next, but with apprehension rising. This is a scary time in which life has suddenly gone off course. How much of what is happening to us is random and how much is being guided by an Unseen Hand? If we ever were in control it is certain we are not now!

3

Options Are Good

The farm was not the first agonizing loss for Samuel and Edna Anne Francis Barbee, my parents. Their firstborn child, Franklin, died in my mother's arms at the age of thirteen months, death by choking from food

2 Barbee family ~ Sam and Edna Barbee; Don, Dixie, Darvin

she had given him to eat. The doctor could not help. How they grieved their loss, or if they grieved at all, I will never know. The wounds from their losses, however, were etched deeply into their own lives and embedded lifetime scars in my two brothers, Pete and Don, and me as well. Confronting and conquering the torment that inflicted those scars has been for me, a precarious adventure.

Someone once said in essence, "Whatever doesn't kill you can only make you stronger." I've often wondered why some people faced with overwhelming circumstances are resilient and durable, while others wither in the heat of turmoil. Can one's attitude determine the outcome? I have come to believe it does. My parents exhibited disparate attitudes; both equally destructive to their own wellbeing and ultimately crippling to their progeny.

Their marriage relationship disintegrated into an emotional battlefield. Dad retreated into an interior, private place, emotionally withdrawn from family while his outward demeanor with others was friendly and engaging. His actions were confusing to me. Mom was often angry and hostile at home, but her friends all believed her to be a paragon of kindness and Christian love. Mom's actions were bewildering and unsafe. I was never sure what to expect.

Separating seemed to be the way they dealt with conflict. If not physical separation, certainly being emotionally aloof, refusing to talk to one another for days, sometimes weeks. Those times were agony for my brothers and me. The atmosphere inside the walls of our house felt as cold as an igloo in winter; my fears hung like icicles on their silence. ~ DLT diary, 2015

I've always told our children, when making important decisions, "Keep your options open as long as you can. Think things through carefully. Options are good." Today is that kind of day. Only today, options are not our only issue. So is time. Every day we delay is a day our problem grows more deadly. We cannot put our options on hold this time.

There are myriad forms to fill out it seems, boxes to be checked, questions to be asked and answered to the best of our ability. And we wait. In the interim someone explains to us that the multi-disciplinary group discussing Dixie's and other patient cases consists of a surgeon, oncologist, radiologist, pathologist, pharmacist, nutritionist, researcher, social worker, chaplain and perhaps one or two others I have already forgotten. An amazing array of medical knowledge to say the least.

Early in the afternoon we are met by a physician who, we are told, "specializes in your disease." Also a nurse who manages patient care, a patient team coordinator who serves as scheduler, and a nutritionist. The physician is Dr. James O. Park, a surgeon whose specialty is colorectal, liver and pancreatic cancer care.

I first notice his hands as we greet one another. They are small, clean and soft. He is medium in height, hair jet black, glasses, wearing a dark blue suit, white shirt and tie. His voice exudes the confidence of a doctor in charge as he tells us the medical team has reviewed Dixie's data and agrees she qualifies as a candidate for surgery, if she concurs. On the back of a file folder he scribbles lines depicting his view of Dixie's internal organs, explaining as he goes what to him makes perfect sense. To us maybe not so much.

We listen intently anyway as he outlines what he calls the "Whipple surgical procedure." My iPad is open, but his explanation is in such rapid sequence taking notes is out of the question. Eventually he concludes by saying if we decide to go forward, surgery will of necessity be followed up by radiation and chemotherapy. Are there any questions? Are you kidding? Yes, there are hundreds. We just don't know what they are yet.

I ask the first one that comes to mind as I look at this doctor who seems way too young to be someone who knows what he is talking about. *Pancreaticoduodenectomy.* Seriously? Is this really a word? And the "Whipple procedure," as he calls it, turns out to be an extremely difficult surgery for both patient and surgeon. Dr. Park says it is in fact the "Cadillac of all surgeries," very big and very complicated, so I ask if he has ever done this before.

He offers a knowing smile, one suggesting he has heard this question at other times; then in a quiet but very confident voice he answers, "Yes, I have done over nine hundred Whipple surgeries to date. In fact, it is all I do."

Well, this is not quite the answer I had expected. I ask Dixie, "What do you think?"

"I think we should do it," she replies. "We have prayed for guidance and for healing. This seems to be a part of our answer."

University of Washington Medical Center is, of course, a teaching hospital. Dixie will undergo surgery with the attending physician being Dr. Park. We understand that a 5th year resident doctor will hone his present and future skills by working at the attending physician's side, along with a room full of other team members who are at varying stages in their medical studies. Maybe this is what is meant by doctors and nurses "practicing medicine."

Ever the mentor, even in this Dixie agrees to participate in both UWMC and the renowned Fred Hutchinson Cancer research programs connected with SCCA, aiding in research for better ways to diagnose and treat those who at a future time may be on this same journey. Her question of me throughout life as we make our way into and out of difficult seasons has always been, "What do you think God is teaching us now?"

We share with Dr. Park that we believe in, and have experienced in our lifetimes, the healing power of God. We are asking for a miracle of healing now, at the hand of God. Concurrently, we respect the mind, heart and hands of the physician, the practice of medicine, of medical science, and of the varied disciplines of medicine, naturopathic and spiritual healing. Our Creator and Redeemer works in many ways "his wonders to perform." As we have always done throughout life, above all else, we trust in our Lord's perfect will. God willing, the outcome Dixie and I look forward to includes many more productive and joyful years together!

And so at 5:30 on Friday morning, 7 March 2014, Pastor Gary is waiting when we arrive at the hospital. We huddle for words of comfort and prayer and then walk with Dixie to the staging area where she is admitted for surgery into the University of Washington Medical Center.

4

Looking for Signposts

Set up road markers for yourself;
make yourself guideposts;
consider well the highway,
the road by which you went.

~ Jeremiah 31:21

∼

Memory is a curious thing.

Like when a Reader's Digest *article awakens a poignant memory for me that, in turn, triggers an avalanche of childhood memories.*

In my early forties and with much of childhood still a virtual blank, a Christmas scene with vivid detail suddenly drops into my memory bank. The scene is our dining table, piled with special foods and presents, all gifts from Dad who is not living at home at the time. He separated from Mom a few months before. Although he is not here, nor is my deceased brother, Franklin, there are places set for them, both remaining empty. The only gift I can recall from that occasion is a silk robe for my mother. It is the most beautiful robe I have ever seen, a deep maroon red with big white flowers. I never saw her wear it.

I remember another incident when my parents are about to separate. I am around three years old and my mother is leaving, taking only me with her. I cry hard and long until I become ill. My Grandmother Barbee is crying, too, silently standing by the door, outside. I suspect she is the reason for my mother's rage. Mom deeply dislikes grandmother. My mother stays, my grandmother leaves, her return visits rare and only when other family members come with her.

That was then. This is now. Shadowy places can still be scary and dark. This new part of my life journey is all of that. Dark and scary. And lonely, too. Yet here in my Valley of Shadows, I have discovered what should have been obvious to me going in. Without light, there can be no shadows. Looking to the Light of my life has been my rod and staff that brings me comfort. The shadows are a reminder that my Light is always with me. Something I've not always known. ~ DLT diary, 2015

Friday 7 March. The hours pass slowly in the waiting area, a fairly large room with fifteen or twenty people coming and going at any given time. A male volunteer serves as coordinator who, every once in a while takes a phone message and then motions to someone, saying, "The doctor is ready to see you now." Those who've been called follow him and disappear from sight behind a door at the far side of the room. Moments later, the volunteer returns and resumes his place at his desk. At this point, I invariably look at the clock on the wall, asking silently, will we be next?

Michele has taken the day off to be with us; well, mostly with me as it turns out. Late in the afternoon one of our neighbors who works in another Seattle hospital drops by to check on how things are going. I am surprised to see her, but grateful.

She stays for a couple of hours until needing to catch her bus ride home. The volunteer continues to work the room; everyone else it seems, but not us. There is only a handful of people still waiting when at last he heads in our direction. He motions to us. We stand as we hear the familiar, "The doctor is ready to see you now." I look at the clock. More than six hours have come and gone since we first arrived in this room.

Michele and I follow the volunteer to the mysterious door we have been staring at all day. It opens into a small windowless room, with table and chairs, where we are greeted by Dr. Park. We gather close around the small table and listen carefully to every word as he states, very matter-of-factly, that Dixie's cancer tumor has been removed along with other no longer needed human parts and everything disassembled has been re-attached. Just another day's work. He assures us everything has gone well and we can now see her in recovery. She will be drowsy, but awake. He then excuses himself saying, "I have to go. I have another surgery."

"Another surgery? Right now?" I blurt out, incredulous at the thought.

"Yes."

"As complicated as this one?"

"The same. Another Whipple," he replies, reaching for the door. "I will check on Dixie tonight and see you later."

I look at Michele and shake my head with a sense of relief. "I'm glad we were the first." We walk out together and down the hall to the recovery room.

I should pause here, in case you may be wondering why so often in this narrative, I use "we" instead of "Dixie," or "she" or "her." When one you love deeply is going through cancer surgery or any other traumatic major happening in their life, it quickly becomes a "we" event. And while much of what happens is *hers* alone to bear, the truth is, *we* are all affected as well. *We* are on this journey together whether we want to be or not.

∽

Monday 9 March. It's 5 o'clock. We are forty-eight hours post-surgery now. Michele is sitting across the hospital room, knitting. Dixie is reading the Sunday Seattle Times, her favorite issue of our daily newspaper. And I am writing to the growing number of people from all around the world who have spread a blanket of prayer over us these last few days.

Our personal lives and ministry of late have been an emotional and spiritual storm. Like Elijah of old, we've had to believe God is somewhere in the storm and just ride it out until we can see him again. Only weeks ago Dixie and I were reviewing our life together, setting personal and ministry goals in a lovely, quiet setting in a desert we both find refreshing. Then our world turned upside down!

I have connected with seminary leadership in Kiev, notifying them of our situation and of the necessity to cancel my trip into Russia. Since I am scheduled to teach later this month, my not being available puts them in an awkward position. Fortunately, a brother from New Zealand is contacted to step in and take my place.

I also notify our immediate family and, as president/executive director of the CASA 50+ Network, apprise the organization's board members of what is taking place. It remains unclear to me at present, but I feel as though we may have just entered the most precious season of Dixie's and my sixty-year journey together since first we met.

As word of our circumstance spreads, hundreds of pastors and ministry colleagues, many friends and even total strangers stop whatever they are doing to begin praying for Dixie. This prayer covering of our Protestant, Catholic, Jewish and Muslim friends, combined with the best wishes of our non-religious friends, stretches around the world and is amazing to think about! We are humbled and strengthened by our Lord's peaceful attention to us here at storm center.

Dixie feels strong at this point. Less than twenty-four hours after surgery, she takes a first short walk, then sits for a few minutes in a chair. Today, she has taken two longer walks and plans one more before day's end. Little signs of progress are big on the path back from life's edge toward health and wellness.

When the doctor first said, "Ninety-five percent chance of pancreatic cancer," we were stunned silent. Twenty-four days later, post surgery, I am here with the woman I met for the very first time and fell in love with sixty years ago in Tulsa, Oklahoma. Twenty-four days of words like *nervous, tense, anxious, hopeless, lost.* Words dealt like cards of despair from the hand of a shady dealer.

Yet in these twenty-four days we have also been reminded of words like *peace, calm, trust, faith, hope;* words reassuring us we are never far from the Good Shepherd. None who trust in him ever are. We are not lost. We are found. Not only by the Shepherd, but by others, too. People are emerging from our past and present, bringing with them the Light of Hope and Joy, Peace and Love. It is what family is about. God's family, burning brightly for one another, candles pushing back the darkness surrounding us. During twenty-four dark days, with prayer and encouragement and acts of kindness, the family of God has been Light to us.

Each day I look for signposts giving direction on this part of our journey, telling us where we are, but there are few. Dixie shares with me, for the first time, an awareness she received in prayer months earlier, suggesting something major would soon be coming her way. She had said nothing, thinking it a premonition more about my health issues than any of her own, preparing her to deal with what might take place. Instead it has been the opposite.

We pray for healing and for obedience, confident in our asking, secure in his will. She speaks of a great peace in preparing for and coming through this major surgery, as though being embraced by the Holy Spirit in some unseen, yet beautiful way. And why not? She is the child of a Father strong and faithful. It is a battle, no doubt about it. It is a hard time. But she is uncomplaining and courageous in the face of our Enemy Cancer.

You have put more joy in my heart than they have when their grain and wine abound.

In peace I will both lie down and sleep; for you alone O LORD, make me dwell in safety.

~ Psalm 4:7,8

On Day 3, the remaining hospital spaghetti is removed, except for one line leading to the epidural located in her back. Doctors are smiling. Nurses are talking about "the woman in 4332."

After all she's been through and at her age they say her recovery is remarkable. She takes two walks today, sits in the chair for a few minutes and for the first time in several weeks, Dixie eats real food. You know, the kind you have to chew before swallowing?

Soup broth and an egg salad sandwich, of which only the bread does not make the trip. The egg salad is gone, though we are not sure where exactly, since her plumbing is pretty well rearranged down there. We find humor in imagining how the salad may be exploring new twists and turns right now, asking for directions on its intended mission. But whatever happens, it's down there for sure, breaking in new frontiers of assimilation.

A couple of hours later things are not going well. The food has created an upset. One of the resident physicians says, "No worries, we just have to go a bit slower reintroducing food to her system." The drink Boost is suggested. Unfortunately, the hospital doesn't have it available. She needs the calories and content to help restart the engines so I leave to find a nearby 24-hour Safeway and purchase a carton of Boost.

Tonight is the first night I return to our home. I've been sleeping on a makeshift bed on the floor in her hospital room. It is Dixie's first night away from Michele or me since arriving in the hospital. I think she is looking forward to it. As it turns out, there are two Code Blues during the night, together with the usual "I need to check your..." wake ups, so Dixie doesn't get much sleep.

5

Song Sparrows and Hummingbirds

I saw little of the Barbee side of the family. Grandfather Barbee was tall and robust with deeply tanned skin and beautiful white hair and mustache. He was a handsome man, as was my father and his older brother, Dick. Both his sons resembled him in looks. Grandmother Barbee was tall and dark skinned, her long smooth and shiny hair was dark as well with sprinkles of grey, worn with an elegant bun on the back of her head. I remember her as always being pleasant. Of her four daughters; two were tall, thin, attractive, and openly despised by my mother.

Mom had a particular distaste for Aunt Lettie. I can still hear her belittling words in my head which she repeated often to me: "You will turn out to be just like Lettie!" I knew it was not a compliment nor an endearing remark. I saw my Aunt Lettie at Dad's funeral and was shocked at my resemblance to her. Hindsight tells me that jealousy was a strong motivating factor for Mom's disparaging words. ~ DLT, 2015

∽

I sleep through the night in my own bed, finally getting up at 5 o'clock, stumbling around getting my bearings, an indicator of the stress I am feeling, but not owning. At last I realize I am an hour late for whatever the day has in store. None of our clocks have been changed over to Daylight Saving Time.

I walk into Starbucks on 8th Street, pausing to look for my cell phone, hoping it is on my person somewhere. It has my Starbucks app. It finally shows up in the last pocket while the guy behind me has to be wondering.

"Tough day already," I murmur, glancing up. "Couldn't find my phone. Had to be sure so I can order."

"What is making it so tough?" he asks.

I might pass off a question like this with some banal response were it not for the funk I started out with that I can't seem to shake.

"My wife is in the hospital."

"Is it something serious?" he asks, his eyes now expressing more than a casual interest.

"Yeah, pancreatic cancer," I reply, wondering why I am telling him this, while showing my phone app to the barista. "A blueberry scone and a *grandé latté,* please."

At the same time the guy is ordering from the other barista.

"No, no," she puts up her hand, pointing to the guy next to me as I push my phone toward her. "He already took care of it."

"Wait, no," I turn, stammering in my sudden surprise, "please, you didn't have to...well, thank you."

We move to one side waiting for our orders to be filled.

"Thank you," I say again. "What's your name?"

"Steve."

"I'm Ward."

"When was your wife's surgery?"

"Friday."

"What's her name?"

"Dixie."

"I'm going to pray for your wife," he said. "Actually, I belong to a group of guys at my church. I'm headed there now. We'll all pray for her. And for you, too."

"Thanks, Steve. What church do you attend?"

"It's called Overlake." The way he spoke, I was certain he had no idea I was a believer.

"I go to Westminster," I reply, certain he will recognize this sister Eastside church. I tell him since he is praying for Dixie and me, he might like to follow her story on Facebook or CaringBridge and give him the information he will need.

So, Steve I-didn't-think-to-get-your-last-name, if you happen to read this someday, thank you again. Your random act of kindness lifted a guy who was feeling his way through a monster depressing morning start. I think it's the kind of thing Jesus would do. Thanks for standing in for him!

When I finally arrive at UWMC, the "woman in 4332" has been sitting up in a chair for about an hour. Together we take the elevator and walk along the 3rd floor hall for a change. Turns out everything looks pretty much the same. Only the numbers on the doors are different. So we go back onto the 4th floor to her room. Later the pain team comes to remove the epidural from Dixie's back. The nurse finds a new arm vein for an IV port, so she is now a free woman for the first time since her arrival last Friday.

Getting all the new equipment synced with the old is an important task that walking is supposed to help. Her pain level is a 6 out of 10 at the moment, manageable with some help from OxyContin and aspirin. That's a good thing. She has suffered enough. As we walk, we pray for food digestion and no plumbing leaks.

Dad was a story teller. His audiences were most often visitors. He kept our family history alive by his retelling of stories. I had not noticed my absence in those stories until his wife, Alma died. (Dixie's father officially divorced her mother and remarried shortly before our wedding.) *Thinking he would need someone to help him, I stayed ten days beyond her funeral. When his friends dropped by, he told them stories. He recounted to me stories about people and events and often I had been there as the story had happened. "I was there, Dad, I remember," I would say to him. During my last dinner with him, he stopped mid-story and said to me, "You know, I don't remember you." The bitter truth of his confession ripped through me like a hot knife, opening embedded scars put there by his physical neglect and emotional absence. He had a relationship with both my brothers and I often wondered... why not me.*

The most logical answer to the question, "Why not me?" was, I concluded, "I'm not loved." A scene latently remembered, almost too painful to recount, reinforced the logic of this answer. I defied Dad's command to sit on a bench between my two brothers for dinner. Sitting between them was unacceptable for this four-year-old. To endure their teasing that no one else could hear, or wasn't paying attention to, was to be avoided at any cost. My typical reactions almost always got me into trouble. My answer to Dad's command was an emphatic "NO!" Three times I defied him and three times he hit me repeatedly with a razor strap.

A razor strap is a three-inch wide, three-foot long piece of leather used in those days by barbers to sharpen their razors. Razor straps made impressive instruments of punishment that left their victims with welts and bruises. I sat on the bench. The welts and bruises healed. My fear of him did not. For him, perhaps it was easier to withdraw physically and emotionally and lock me out of his memory than to face his shame for such abuse, or perhaps fear of a repeat performance. Don asked me a few years ago if I had any memory of that incident. Such traumatic events are not easily dulled by decades of time. ~ DLT diary, 2015

These stories and others Dixie would share with me, but not until months, even years had come and gone in our relationship. Even then they did not surface all at once, but rather bit by painful bit. I accepted them as a part of her history, not understanding or respecting their devastating impact at first. I know what it is to have been grounded at home and school, timed out, isolated alone on school days at recess and the noon hour, spanked by my parents.

Once my teacher spanked me in front of all the students. I was probably in the fifth grade. In preparation for the spanking, the older boys told me to laugh when she hit me and she would stop. I did. She didn't.

I broke a boy's nose in a fight on the playground (not the same incident for which I was spanked). Unfortunately, it was the teacher's son. I had my moments, deserved all I got, and was thankful I didn't get all I deserved.

I was spanked more than a few times, but never beaten. An adult never slapped me in the face. I was never whipped with a razor strap. I was never afraid of my parents. I knew I was loved. I deserved the occasional punishment I received. Breaking one's willfulness and one's spirit are two very different things. There was no question. Not in my mind or in the minds of those who punished. They meant it for all the right reasons. I realize spanking is no longer in vogue for disciplining a child. This is not intended as a defense of the practice. There are better ways. The takeaway here is that time passed before I recognized the significant difference between my experience and hers.

My parents taught me right from wrong in the best way they knew. I never doubted their love for me in the process. I was never left with physical wounds. I was never wronged by parents who did not understand or care about the outcome of their actions on my own sacred journey. I never lived with parents whom I could not trust, yet from whom I desperately needed both trust and love. This is the difference between my experience and hers.

It was a long time before Dixie was able to fully trust. Even though she believed in and accepted my love, her willingness to trust anyone close to her had been broken by her parents. If I was to gain her trust in our relationship, it would have to be earned.

In the early 1900s, Mr. and Mrs. Martin developed a friendship with the Doolittles of Elmira, New York. Mrs. Doolittle had been bedridden for twenty years and her husband was crippled, propelling himself to and from his work in a wheelchair. When asked the secret of their being so positive and hopeful, Mrs. Doolittle replied, "His eye is on the sparrow, and I know He watches me."

This single statement inspired two white people, Civilla D. Martin and Charles H. Gabriel, to write the words and music that today is best known as an African American hymn, made famous by Ethel Waters, "Why should I feel discouraged, why should the shadows come? Why should my heart be lonely, and long for heaven and home, When Jesus is my portion? My constant Friend is He: His eye is on the sparrow, and I know He watches me; I sing because I'm happy, I sing because I'm free, For

His eye is on the sparrow, and I know He watches me."[1] Words of a song lasting for generations.

Are not two sparrows sold for a penny? And not one of them will fall to the ground apart from your Father. But even the hairs of your head are all numbered. Fear not, therefore; you are of more value than many sparrows. ~ Matthew 10:29–31

Our home is located on the third floor of a low-rise condominium, surrounded by trees through which we look out onto the city. We feed hummingbirds that live in these nearby trees. A variety of other birds join the hummers with some regularity, not the least of which is the lowly and unpretentious song sparrow. Symbols that speak of safety, trust and human kindness. Reminders that God always loves, even when nests are cold. How appropriate that Jesus chose this bird to make his point, "Aren't two sparrows sold for a penny?"

Years ago, Neil Armstrong, on the moon's surface made famous the phrase, "The eagle has landed," an idiom indicating the completion of a mission or a purpose. While we do have eagles here in the Northwest, none live in our trees. Just humble little hummers. And the sparrow. When I am traveling and touch down safely somewhere, I text home the phrase, "Hummer landed." This way Dixie knows I've reached my destination safely. We will talk later when there's more time. If she is traveling without me, on her arrival it is, "Sparrow landed."

Why should discouragement rob us of our peace? Why should shadows of doubt be entertained? Why should we always

---

[1] *Published in 1905: writer Civilla D. Martin; Composer Charles H. Gagriel.*

be longing for something just beyond our reach? Jesus is our portion. We continue asking for a miracle of healing. He is our strength. Our constant and faithful Friend. We ask him in absolute faith and we trust him in his perfect will for us. There is no inconsistency in this. How could we not ask and trust in the same breath? His eye is on the sparrow. He sees us in the storm. He hears us as we call out to him.

Today, after five days at University of Washington Medical Center, the last release papers are signed, final instructions for caregiving listened to attentively, prescriptions filled. We load several gifted floral arrangements and the "woman who used to be in 4332" into the car.

"Will you be back today?" asks the Pavilion parking attendant as we pay the UWMC parking fee.

"No," I answer, "not today."

We drive out into an absolutely stunning day, make our way east across the SR 520 floating bridge, sunlight dancing on the water, snow-capped mountains glistening in every direction we can see. Familiar words singing in my heart.

Dixie is home tonight. The sparrow has landed. She is safely back in her nest.

6

The Warmest Room

A question was once asked in a small group setting, "What was the {emotionally} warmest room in your home when you were growing up?" My answer was, "My friend's house." The importance of that answer dawned on me much later after I had gained the fortitude to look at my parents as people; to strive to understand their struggles, not to hold them in judgment for their reactions to their painful life. ~ DLT diary, 2015

3 Dixie's childhood home in Claremore, OK

We begin the eighth day of the rest of our lives as usual, with devotional readings and prayer. It is a quiet morning. It has not been a good night. I glance at the nightstand by her bed. The pain meds that had been laid out the night before, just in case, are gone. Dixie is not feeling well. She does not complain. I wish she would. It would be easier to gauge how things are going for her. But she is strong. Always has been. Doesn't plan to stop anytime soon. She is also beautiful. Unique. And now, suddenly, very fragile.

As I conclude the last reading, she voices discouragement that her body is not responding to (her) plan. Eating is something she finds difficult to do. A few sips of smoothie, some water, and not much else. The very idea of eating is upsetting.

In the afternoon, we step out the 99th Avenue exit of our condominium complex for the first time since coming home from the hospital. Around to the front entrance on 100th. Not the 2.8-mile speed walk of a few weeks ago. A small exercise. A little fresh air. Two blocks. All good, but leaving her exhausted. One of our neighbors, a retired Naval officer, sees us from his window and sends word that if we are walking tomorrow he will hang out the flag. Can't buy that kind of support!

She is sleeping as I write these words. We are in a kind of holding pattern, where conflicting ideas and thought patterns and uncertainties await the next storm. We're not sure from what direction, but it is certain we are about to leave the peaceful center where we have been, and touch the other side of what we've just passed through.

Preserve me, O God, for in you I take refuge. I say to the LORD, "You are the Lord; I have no good apart from you." ~ Psalm 16:1,2

Sunday is better. Our spirits are up. Nothing appreciable has changed. We wait. No difference yet in body function. Still losing weight. Michele drops by today and we three walk the full circumference of about a square block around our condominium complex. A bit of yogurt. A scrambled egg. A half cup of coffee with milk and sugar. Linda drops off some chick flicks for Dixie and a slice of birthday cake for me. Wait. It's my birthday? Lisa drops off flowers. Dixie rests in between our measuring meds and pain pills and the daily shot. Oh yes, about the shot.

Every day for thirty days following surgery Dixie must have an evening shot in the belly. I have been informed by the nurse this will be my job. Our first night home I approach the belly in question, cleanse it with alcohol and proceed to stab her with the needle like I think I've seen it done on television. The surprised look on her face said my first attempt at a medical procedure needed serious improvement. It did evoke a great deal of laughter once she recovered, and its recounting was fodder for several good stories thereafter. And yes, I did refine my procedure.

Lots of cards and flowers for Dixie these past few days. And the amazing prayers of close friends and complete strangers around the world. Do we have God's ear? On the day of Dixie's surgery, we leave our home at 4:30 in the morning, heading for the hospital. At that very hour (we learn later from cards received), my 90 something-year-old-aunt in eastern Washington and a dear woman in our former pastorate in California, two saints who've never met in this life, are awakened from their sleep with a holy urgency to go to prayer on Dixie's behalf. They begin the day and are eventually joined by hundreds of others, covering her in prayer from that moment until now. It is this awareness of God at work that gives us hope.

⌒

I began to learn about God when I was in the third grade. My family attended church with friends, and to my recollection it was my first time ever in church. We became regular attenders, but eventually Dad quit going, which meant we had to walk to church. Dad was the only driver at the time. I liked the preacher when he talked to me one-to-one, but not when he preached. His message seemed more threatening than loving and God was painted in my mind as a powerful being who was watching, waiting for me to do something bad. The "bad" was an amorphous something which lingered in the shadows of my mind as God took on the persona of my parents.

Mom was always watching, always ready to punish with a slap in the face, a switch to the legs, the razor strap to the bottom or a look that said, "I'll take care of you later." Dad was absent or disengaged, at least with me. God was harsh, someone I needed to please, and if not, he would either punish me, ignore me, or leave me. It took many years to erase that opinion of God and to see him as someone who loves me, is pleased with me just as I am, who wants to be known for who he is. God is not like my parents.

Looking through a rear view mirror often clarifies one's vision on past life situations. Someone asked me once if I came to faith in God through a sense of His love or out of fear. God was not presented to me as a God of love, but as someone to be feared. He punished people for not living right. Fear and punishment were strong motivating factors. I was afraid of punishment. Punishment meant bodily pain. ~ DLT diary, 2015

When this day dawns, it is winter. Before morning ends, it is spring. High clouds, with sun. Crisp and cool. No rain. A good first Northwest spring day. And a breakthrough day for Dixie.

Tuesday, late afternoon we return to UWMC for our first post-op visit. We've been waiting to receive the pathology report. Dr. Park provides the news. Simply put, the operation was successful in removing the pancreatic mass and cancerous duodenum. The gallbladder removal and all margins (i.e., bile duct, distal pancreatic, etc.) in the area are negative. However, some peripancreatic lymph nodes tested positive for carcinoma, overall resulting in a kind of good news/bad news outcome. We do not yet fully understand the implications.

We had hoped for a complete and total victory, but this is not to be. Not yet. Like Old Testament Israelites, we give thanks for a major battle has been won. Just not the war. Now life's battle lines are shifting for us. Preparations must be made. But how? Has everything changed or is it all still the same as when we started at the beginning?

How does one prepare in the beginning...for childbirth?

Birth: any coming into existence; any act or instance of being born; the beginning.

When expecting your child, you learn about the birth process; choose a doctor for your baby; get both parents involved; talk to those who've been there and done that about birth and baby care; prepare older siblings—and pets; line up helpers for after the birth; know what to do when labor starts; decide who will attend the birth; pack your bag; plan what is needed for what comes after you go home and start the rest of your lives together.

Most of all, you must be especially concerned for your little one's body. Life is a miracle!

But there's more.

How does one prepare at the end...to finish well?

By first accepting all of one's life as sacred; to be lived with a sense of awe and reverence, set apart as unique, not to be violated or trespassed upon.

You decide about (re)dedicating your life to God; find a church where people are loved and the Bible is taught; single, married or single again, you get involved; connect with spiritual mentors (friends or relatives whose life journey and faith walk you admire); give your children good examples; nurture your own spiritual growth as a follower of Jesus and encourage others with whom you have influence to finish well.

You choose how you will be remembered. Life is meant to be a sacred journey!

And now, nearing the end of life, this is what we are doing. Creating a new chapter. Not simply an ending, but a fresh beginning. We must educate ourselves, choose doctors, get the immediate family involved, speak with others who've been through this themselves, decide what help will be needed, know what to do when treatments get underway, prepare for hospital stays and for what will be needed after you return home.

Our Enemy Cancer, is making an effort to infiltrate beyond the initial battleground and our assignment is to stop it in its diabolical tracks. Our primary weapons are prayer, the promises in his Word, and the rest and restoration one finds in "green pastures, beside still waters" (Psalm 23).

The days are hard for Dixie. Some parts in her body are beginning to stir again, ever so slowly and painfully. She likens it to giving birth. Her bodily functions continue to accelerate, and here is the real winner. For the first time since the end of January, she is eating (and digesting) real food!

When I ask what she wants for dinner this evening, she replies, "You know what sounds good to me? What I'd really like to eat? Some Kentucky fried chicken, dark meat, mashed potatoes and gravy." Then she blinks a big underfed and pathetic, brown-eyed look, and gives me the smile that has made me do anything she has ever wanted for sixty all too swiftly passing years. I am certain Dr. Park stirred up dormant southern cells while he was in there! So I get in the car, drive across town, order up, and bring the Colonel home. And she did it.

༄

The week begins quietly, with a church service. I stand as the choir and congregation sing. I want to sing with them, try to sing, but I cannot join in. My heart is heavy. The voices of others surround me, spilling over, leaking rivulets of worship into my dry, empty place; but I am alone in a crowd. Verses of a hymn and songs of praise, an offering lifted up to God by voices, some in tune, others off key, all singing nonetheless. All but me.

Why is this morning different from countless other mornings when we were apart while serving, teaching, preaching? I can't truly say. I am deciding how to slip out unobtrusively when I look up to see my daughter and her husband. They move into my row to be beside me. She nudges in close, puts her arm through mine and whispers, "I love you, Dad."

And all at once I am struck by the importance of the Church. "C" denoting not just the church local, but the larger all-encompassing body of Christ. The church (small "c") is painful for me just now. It is the music. It is the sermon I am not preaching; could not even if I wanted to. It is the feeling of being with people once broken, standing as one with those broken still. I am not sure anyone understands this, but I have always loved being with once broken and broken still people. They are my people. My family-in-Christ people. People who need to be touched by God through someone with flesh on. People like me.

Dixie's life and mine are fruit of the church vine. Our faith was birthed in the church. We found each other and grew together because of the church, answered a call to serve God in the Church, raised our children to believe in God and be active in the big "C" Church as well as in a small "c" local church. I learned about Jesus at an early age in a country Sunday school, accepted him as my Savior, was baptized, and later made a no turning back commitment of my life to God in a small town church. Dixie's faith was developed in a big city church. We've served the capitol "C" church with its many stripes, denominations and tribes all our lives. But this morning, the church, big "C" or little "c"... any church feels dissonant, out of harmony. It doesn't feel like my family anymore. Is this a foreshadowing? Is it that she is not here? Is this the way it's going to be?

She is there; resting alone at home. Getting ready for Monday. And I am here; grieving alone at church, twisted inward, way too vulnerable, and not at all ready for Monday.

7

Regrets ... There Are a Few

My best friend in elementary school had a great family. Their home was warm and welcoming. I liked being there. Her mother was gentle and when she smiled, her eyes smiled, too. She was kind and I liked being near her. She sewed beautiful clothes for my friend. I often witnessed fittings of her latest creations. Her father, a firefighter, frightened me a little. He was a big man with a big voice; but he often brought home neat gifts for my friend.

One of those gifts was a puppy that she named, "Dixie," which irked me not a little. However, the thoughtfulness of her father was impressive to me. I had to ask my father for everything I needed. It was not automatically provided for me as it was for my friend. In the years Dad was absent from home, I waited on the curb in front of the store where he would eventually arrive on his regular, weekly sales route, just to ask for money for a current need. My needs were as varied as any nine to twelve-year-old would have, but the process was humiliating. My friend rarely had to ask. Her needs and wants were anticipated and provided.

Dad was absent from my piano recitals, school talent shows, church performances, and graduations even when he lived with us. When he and Mom separated the last time, I had just graduated high school and was planning for college. He asked me if I wanted to live with him or with Mom. He had already made it very clear that he would not pay any financial support. I was a few months shy of eighteen and instinctively that Mom and I were on our own. College would have to wait.

I wanted to see where Dad was going to live, but it did not occur to me until in a counseling session twenty some years later that I could recall how his living arrangements looked when he took me to see his apartment. It was a studio apartment. He had made no provisions for me to live with him. It was just a rhetorical question. He had no intention to care for me. At the urging of the counselor, I wrote him a letter asking, among other things, about that day. I never mailed it. I was afraid to hear his answers. ~ DLT diary, 2015

The psychological push-pull of an extremely dysfunctional family may affect a child for a lifetime. Every child wants a parent who is really there for him or her, of whom they can be proud. We want our friends to "Get to know my Dad. He is a really cool guy." "Once you meet Mom, she will like you."

Desperately needing our parents to be something they are unable or unwilling to attain is a heartache for children. Covering up neglect, erratic behavior, emotional or physical abuse, is hurtful and embarrassing. It may result in feelings of shame or inadequacy, withdrawal or lashing out, or the need to measure up to someone else's standards or expectations in order to feel accepted. These are not the gifts we want to pass on to our children.

Monday is a day of first appointments. We begin with Dr. Kim and the team at UWMC Radiology, outlining what Dixie can expect from their services. Then a short drive to SCCA and an hour consultation with Dr. Kasser, specialist in medical nutrition therapy. Next, more nurses, assistants, and Dr. Chiorean, head of the oncology team, to review the proposed chemotherapy treatments.

Three appointments. A full day for anyone, especially when still recovering from what doctors all are calling the "Cadillac of surgeries" (I translate this as meaning the biggest and most expensive on the showroom floor). By the time we begin this final interview of the day, Dixie has had it. She is chilling, shaking uncontrollably, so we leave F4 for a few minutes to go to F2 and the Red Brick Cafe to order some hot tea. When we return to F4, we are met by a nurse who begins lecturing us for not being where we should have been when Dixie's name was called a few minutes before.

Her lectures continue as we follow her to the room where we are to wait for Dr. Chiorean. She just won't let it go that we were not in the right place at the right time. Finally, I hold up my hand and say, "Please stop. We hear you. We apologize. It's our first time and we didn't know the drill, but my wife is not well. Do you not see how she is chilling? This is her third appointment today, so give us a break here."

All at once it seems, the proverbial lights go on.

"Would you like a warm blanket?"

"Yes."

"Maybe two?"

The woman disappears and moments later returns with two heated blankets. We wrap them around Dixie as she leans into them, waiting for the doctor to appear. It is the only time we were not treated with polite dignity during any of her treatments. We did not say anything to anyone about it. We never saw this person again. A few minutes later we are introduced to Dr. Chiorean.

On Tuesday, Dixie is still not feeling well and shows a temperature high enough to suggest infection. Wednesday morning, SCCA calls and asks us to come in. By 10 o'clock, we are there. After a few tests, we are sent to ER at UWMC for further tests, cultures, a CT scan and X-ray. Then it's overnight at the hospital again, back on 4th floor SE Tower, where Dixie is greeted by nurses like an old friend, not just a patient they had served a few days before.

By Thursday, Dr. Park has been contacted. He is out of town at a cancer conference. He orders a procedure to remove a plastic stent that had been inserted during surgery. It is thought this may be the culprit causing fluctuating temperatures and a rise in liver counts. E-coli has also been identified, requiring treatment with antibiotics. It is apparent this is a "really big deal," and that maintaining the delicate healing balance on all levels is critical if we are to have a successful outcome.

Friday mid-afternoon, we walk out of the hospital to retrieve our car. Once again the parking attendant asks, "Will you be returning today?"

I am able to respond with a smile, "No, not today."

This time we drive through heavy rain and wind, crossing the SR 520 floating bridge to our home on the Eastside. From our condo underground parking we take the elevator to the third floor and our apartment, then up the stairs to bed and rest. After awhile, a friend comes to our door with chicken soup. Everyone knows chicken soup has been healing mankind for generations. We receive this gift with grateful hearts. God is on his throne tonight. I think he is smiling. At least I hope so. The sparrow is once more in her nest.

I have two lingering regrets where Dad is concerned. One is that I did not let him walk me down the aisle at my wedding. Mom had made it clear to me that if he did, she would not come. My embarrassment over their divorce and fear they would not be civil to each other, caused me to make the decision to have my family as guests only. What would Ward's parents think? I had not met them yet and I wanted them to like me. In reality, I was afraid they would not accept me if they knew the awful truth about my family. How would Mom act toward Dad and my new stepmother, Alma, whom I had just met? My moms had known each other many years before when they were teenagers. What would she do when she saw Grandmother Barbee who was also an invited guest? Would my two new stepsisters, ages 6 and 9, whom my dad seemed to enjoy, come, too? Perhaps it would have been easier to sort it out if I had talked with someone about it, but I kept it all bottled up inside, too afraid of being exposed. Our wedding pictures reveal the true story. Mom smiling is the only family member in the pictures. I walked the aisle on the arm of our youth pastor.

My other regret is not having the courage to resolve my issues with Dad before he died. I was still angry with him, even after seven years had separated my last visit with him and his death. His children and grandchildren were all together at Mom's funeral and we wondered why he didn't come just to connect with us. We had all been there for him when Alma died three years before.

He made no effort to sort me out in his empty memory bank nor did he attempt to keep in touch. All his worldly goods were willed to his stepdaughters and my brothers, except for his remaining bank balance. That was divided equally. In the end, I felt optional, nonessential to him, like a "sticky note" attached to his life. Looking now through the rear view mirror, I can thankfully acknowledge those issues have been settled; I have forgiven him, but a lingering sense of loss remains.

Admittedly, my parents' negative reactions were like manacles attached to my emotional wellbeing and I have carried them like iron weights through much of my adult life. I have had to examine my own lingering negative attitudes and discard the dead weights of an injured self-concept. Slowly, I'm finding the right keys to unlock the "real" me. I'm discovering the woman God created when He chose the strands of DNA and wove them together in my mother's womb.

I was not a mistake. I was planned by a loving God! ~ DLT diary, 2015

8

Looking for My Father

What comes into our minds when we think about God is the most important thing about us.

~ A. W. Tozer

In diaries written as a young adult, I find many notations of my desire to know God as Father. Jesus was my Friend, but I longed to know God as an attentive, loving, and caring Father. I've searched for him often in Scripture, and wept through many prayers to be worthy of his presence in my life.

Looking back over my journey, I see vividly how he has cared for me all through my life. I continue to be amazed at the intimacy of his presence. I will never be worthy, but I do not have to earn his love. He is my heavenly Father. He cares for me. He is attentive to me. He anticipates my need and everything I need for today is already provided by him. I don't need to be concerned about tomorrow. God is already in tomorrow and His provisions will be there, too. He teaches me consistently and continually to trust him. As I relinquish my preconceived notions about God and open my mind to really know him, my understanding of his actions in Scripture, his answers to my prayers, and his actions in our present culture has increased exponentially. I am humbled at his wisdom and patience with his creation. He teaches me carefully and wisely about himself. And I am a grateful and eager learner. ~ DLT diary, 2015

⁓

In his book, *A Shelter in the Time of Storm*[2], Paul David Tripp points up a great temptation: that in times of waiting for answers, instead of filling our thoughts with reminders of God's limitless power and growing stronger in faith, our tendency may be "to focus on the thing we are waiting for, *all the obstacles that are in our way*, (italics mine) our inability to make it happen, and all the other people who haven't seemed to have had to wait."

It will be this kind of week for us. One marked with waiting while "all the obstacles that are in our way" test our focus and our faith.

On Sunday, we host a family gathering in our home, consisting of our daughter, Michele, and her husband, Mark; Robin, a niece; Linda, who worked as my assistant in our California church and who now lives nearby; and Janine, a dear friend and prayer partner. All except Michele have in common the fact that immediate family members do not live close geographically or have already passed on.

Janine leads today's devotional with a collective reading about family, sharing how much the gathering represents family to her, a feeling quickly affirmed by everyone present. We share in holy communion. Next a luncheon to which everyone contributes something each time we meet. Hugs and kisses mark

---

[2] *A Shelter in the Time of Storm*, Paul David Tripp. Crossway Books 2009.

the end of a quality time in the presence of our Lord and with one another. Very New Testament.

On Wednesday the guys in our C3Leaders Forum[3] begin gathering at 7 o'clock for our weekly meeting. Soon the living room is comfortably filled. Everyone wants the latest on Dixie. Jerry leads a good what's-next discussion on leadership. Time to pray for one another. By 9:00 the last guy is out the door. A bite of breakfast for Dixie. A telephone conversation and a couple of callbacks. Then Dixie and I prepare for the afternoon at SCCA.

At SCCA, we listen as Drs. Chiorean and McClintock share disturbing findings. There appear to be abscesses in the liver area. What exactly they represent remains questionable. There are bits of good news scattered throughout the report as well, cloaked in medical mumbo jumbo; but all that is lost on the fact that something has been identified in the liver that should not be there.

I ask Dr. Chiorean, "Given everything you've outlined, just how nervous should we be?"

"You should be very nervous," is her reply, and the look in her eyes confirms her concern.

"...all the obstacles that are in our way..."

Thursday, we return to SCCA for another blood draw and CT scan. Driving to either SCCA or UWMC is 15–20 minutes each way across the SR 520 Lake Washington floating bridge. Tack on another 2–3 hours for the appointment and the afternoon is gone. Dixie is discouraged and, frankly, so am I. Once we are home, however, I try to put the best possible spin on the report. I interpret the look she gives me in response to mean, "Don't play me. I know what you're trying to do and it's not working." After fifty-eight married years, what should I expect?

---

3 *For information on C3Leaders, visit www.c3leaders.com*

This is First Thursday, and Michele is sitting with Mom in front of the fireplace, doing her best to help sell my futile attempts at encouragement, but we both can see we are failing. Mom is not buying. Tonight is not the best of nights. Dixie must begin a medical fast after a small bowl of soup, in preparation for an appointment with the Infectious Diseases medical unit. Infectious diseases? Dixie? What's this about? What is happening to us?

The following dreaded Infectious Diseases Day turns out to be not so bad. The doctors who meet with us are nice, efficient, apologize for making us wait, poke and push and pull and make Dixie say, "Ah," and ask, "In what countries have you traveled?" and other infectious diseases types of questions.

Eventually Doctor Deb says, "Let's not waste any more of our time. We are going to talk with Dr. Chiorean. Then we'll get an appointment with the radiology department to do a needle biopsy of the liver. In the meantime, we will send a couple of antibiotics prescriptions to your pharmacist. You'll begin taking these tonight. Get lots of rest over the weekend. We will find out for sure what is happening next week."

Don't you love it when someone just steps up and takes charge?

The remainder of the afternoon is spent in making new appointments, canceling old ones, and cautiously agreeing we feel more optimistic than we did twenty-four hours ago.

Saturday. Dixie is trying to eat more today and bring a halt to the weight skid. We walk around the block in a gentle rain. Katy and Geoff bring Corbin, "our little dude," by for a short visit with GG and Papa.

During Corbin's first year, GG cared for him five days a week while Katy was at work. He became too much for her during his second year because of his physical growth and her reduced stamina, so reluctantly she cut her care time to one day a week. When asked why she took on such a task at her age, when she could be traveling or doing things for herself and taking life easy, her response was, "I want to be sure Corbin always remembers who his great-grandmother is. I am busy creating memories."

For the remainder of the weekend her doctor's orders are to rest and wait—and remind ourselves that it is not *all the obstacles that are in our way* that will define the journey. As with Abraham of old, it is faith in the power and promises of a faithful God that saves the day.

༄

I have set the Lord always before me; because he is at my right hand, I shall not be shaken. Therefore my heart is glad and my whole being rejoices; my flesh also dwells secure. ~ Psalm 16:8,9

༄

9

The Numbers Game

Grade is only a number. We are greater than numbers. ~ Lailah Gifty Akita

∽

Saturday 12 April. Numbers tell stories, sometimes filled with mystery, stories we do not understand. I watch as her numbers decrease, sensing her avoidance, not wanting to answer when I ask what the numbers are as she grows smaller each day right before my eyes. I go to the numbers to remind myself, how long has it been? Seven weeks? Is that all? Seven weeks since Valentine's Day, when first we heard the words, "We're ninety-five percent certain it's pancreatic cancer?" Numbers...the rest of that day is blurred over, numbed by that dreaded word, cancer...and that awful number...ninety-five!

Seven sevens. Surely more numbers on the calendar have passed since that day than these. And the numbers keep changing. It's not ninety-five percent now. It's one hundred. It's Stage II. It's pancreatic cancer. No lymph node activity detected. A surgery called Whipple. What is that? Five days in the hospital. Pathology reports keep changing. It's not pancreatic cancer.

Then what? A rare carcinoma of the ampulla of vater. What? It's a rare *kind of* pancreatic cancer. Very aggressive. We must treat it as such. Four lymph nodes out of twelve show positive. Are we supposed to feel good about the eight that were negative? Home for recovery. Recurring fever. Two more days in the hospital. Another surgical procedure. Home. One more hospital day for a liver biopsy. It's not Stage II anymore. Now it is Stage IV.

Twenty pounds disappear from her body in a matter of weeks. Am I losing her? It feels that way. I wake up in the night and look for her. Is she still here? In the morning I watch her gaze out the window at the first signs of spring. A lone tulip blossoming. She planted it. The leafing of the trees. All the things she loves about this time of year. Does she wonder if this will be her last spring? This should not be happening, God. Are you listening? Of course you are. Then tell me, why does she suffer so?

We are, not metaphorically but in very truth, a Divine work of art, something that God is making, and therefore something with which He will not be satisfied until it has a certain character. Here again we come up against what I have called the "intolerable compliment." Over a sketch made idly to amuse a child, an artist may not take much trouble: he may be content to let it go even though it is not exactly as he meant it to be. But over the great picture of his life— the work which he loves, though in a different fashion, as intensely as a man loves a woman or a mother a child—he will take endless trouble—and would doubtless, thereby give endless trouble to the picture if it were sentient. One can imagine a sentient picture, after being rubbed and scraped and re-commenced for the tenth time, wishing that it were only a thumbnail sketch whose making was

over in a minute. In the same way, it is natural for us to wish that God had designed for us a less glorious and less arduous destiny; but then we are wishing not for more love but for less.
                    ~ C.S. Lewis, *The Problem of Pain*[4]

⁓

It is hard to see... to understand things from God's point of view. Impossible really. Except for what he lets us in on in the Old and New Testaments. And for what we see through glimpses of himself in one another.

I think she is perfect, but obviously, he does not. He's not satisfied yet. What is the matter with you, God? It's me who needs more work. I'm the one who's a mess. Can't you see what is happening to her?

But hers is not an ordinary sketch, is it? You have been at it, outlining, layering, contrasting colors and shades on the canvas of her life since before she was born.

For you formed my inward parts; you knitted me together in my mother's womb. ~ Psalm 139:13

This is the kind of work you love, isn't it, God? Displaying your image in the lives of your children. You choose whom you will choose to share the *extra*ordinary "intolerable compliment" of divine love's tender touch and terrifying passion. She is one. You knew her before she was known. You had in mind who and what she would be. So I am made to watch as with the intensity of each new color and the artistry of every brush stroke you continue to "rub and scrape and re-commence for the tenth time"

---
4   *The Problem of Pain*, C.S. Lewis. HarperCollins. 2009.

your passionate finale, while this living canvas on which you display your omniscient self struggles to hold steady against the unbearable weight of the Artist's scarred hand.

I long to cry out, to beg you to stop! Yet there is beauty in her struggle. An amazing courage. And a deep longing. She remains silent, uncomplaining beneath your touch.

Is this what it means "to put on the new self, (to be) created after the likeness of God in true righteousness and holiness" (Ephesians 4:24)? It is, isn't it? It's what you have been doing all along; your divine work of living art kept secret until now. "For you have died, and your life is hidden with Christ in God. When Christ who is your life appears, then you also will appear with him in glory" (Colossians 3:3,4). Is she the reason for these terrible scars on your hand? Am I?

I see a sketch of earthly beauty. You see a work of eternal perfection. Made perfect in suffering. Your head. Your hands. Your feet. Your side. *Your* suffering. *The Redeeming Artist and the living canvas.* You make possible the successful completion of every person's sacred journey.

For as we share abundantly in Christ's sufferings, so through Christ we share abundantly in comfort too. ~ 2 Corinthians 1:5

Oh my God, how deeply you must love!

Monday. We leave home in the early dawn to arrive at UWMC before 7 o'clock. First, we go to Blood Draw, then to Admitting, with its endlessly repetitive paper work. A walk to the Pacific Elevators, down one floor to F2 and Radiation. At 9:30 we kiss and say goodbye as Dixie is taken by gurney to the procedure room. An hour later, she is transported to F4 North, where in Room 425 she is placed on a bed and we begin post-op observation. Six hours. Checking for bleeding or any other untoward reaction to the just performed liver needle biopsy.

We know something is there. We've looked over the scans with doctors at SCCA. The question is, what? Two tiny spots, both small, one difficult even to discern with the naked eye, but there nonetheless. I wonder what person's trained eye first caught these tiny abscess cavities? Not knowing could have meant severe illness, even death. I wish I could thank you, whoever you are. Just for doing your ordinary job, but doing it so well. *Extra*ordinary. At the end of the day, this is what we all wish could be said for ourselves on our respective sacred journeys.

Is it an infection, more easily treated, yet necessary to deal with before anything further can be done? Or is it the Enemy Cancer having crept in, after our first major victory, to an area vital to her wellbeing? It is nearing five o'clock on a sunny afternoon as we leave the building. Merging into bumper to bumper traffic we make our way across the SR 520 bridge and home.

Tuesday. We return to UWMC for a routine follow-up appointment. Dr. Park is tracking with Dixie and the various other doctors involved in her wellness. We have known him only a few weeks. Our relationship, albeit a professional one, some might say is the luck of the draw. But we sense the Great Physician's involvement in the selection of this quiet, dedicated young doctor in his prime. After discussing her progress, the last thing Dr. Park does is check the computer screen again for any biopsy results. He shakes his head slowly. Nothing yet.

Wednesday through Friday. Life seems almost normal. C3 Leaders gather in our living room early today. I spend an hour at CASA 50+ Network's office. Some additional appointments. A delightful home visit with our pastor, Gary Gulbranson, and his wife, Jorie. These are colleagues in ministry and good friends. Gary reminds me of our first ever get acquainted breakfast at CoCo's in 1999, when we were then considering a possible role for me in pastoral care at Westminster Chapel.

I had been aware of the tragic death of their recently married daughter and it prompted my first question, one he told me later no one had ever asked. As we shook hands and sat across from each other, I said, "Gary, are you going to make it?" His honest answer let me know this was someone I could work with if he felt the same about me.

Now years later, here in our living room, he reminds me of that day. I am surprised he remembers. He says pointedly, "Now it's my turn to ask you the same thing." My answer is just as heartfelt and just as honest.

After a time, Jorie reads a passage of Scripture, then serves the bread and cup that expresses so beautifully the death of our suffering Savior. Gary leads us in receiving holy communion together. A short while later we say goodbye. I close the door and turn to Dixie, "So this is the way people feel when the pastor makes a call. How good was that?" Very, as it turns out. I hope and pray it has been just as good for the countless calls on others whom Jesus loves that Dixie and I have made together through the years.

Numbers. This is Dixie's best week in seven. She is eating small bits of solid food. Lots of liquids. Only one Tylenol in the last three days. Still, no pathology report. We think of some friends, who like us on a purely human level wish, "after being rubbed and scraped and re-commenced for the tenth time...that it were only a thumb-nail sketch whose making was over in a minute."

But it's not a minute.

God is taking his time.

Lewis was right: "... it is natural for us to wish that God has designed for us a less glorious and less arduous destiny; but that would be wishing not for more love but for less."

⸺

10

Waiting and Watching

My soul waits for the Lord more than watchmen for the morning, more than watchmen for the morning. ~ Psalm 130:6

While carrying a full academic load my second year in Bible college, I worked the night shift as a manifest clerk for a large trucking company, from eleven at night until seven the next morning, five days a week. For a few months, I washed cars in a car wash at 75 cents an hour. During my third college year, I worked days part time, hand-setting type in a Seattle print shop owned by two Christian brothers who taught me the skill with great patience.

In my final year of undergraduate studies, it was full time again at night for a music store, offloading crates from train boxcars, delivering pianos and organs to the store and to individual homeowners throughout the greater Seattle and Puget Sound area. I understand firsthand the watchers' waiting for morning's first light, signaling an ending to the dark toil of the night, in good weather or bad, grateful for the breaking of another dawn.

Here the psalmist seems to be saying, life is like this for one who is tired and thirsty, who is waiting for an end to what has become, in the words of 16th century monk, St John of the Cross, "the dark night of the soul," or at the very least, a season of waiting for things to get better.

By instinct, or perhaps it is something we are taught, we in the Western world are impatient. We do not do waiting well. Not for a bus, for dinner, for another person, for much of anything. We do not like to be kept waiting. Yet, in spite of our not liking it much, it is an oft-used word in our vocabulary. "Don't wait up for me," "I don't like waiting in lines," "Are you our waiter?"

Waiting suggests an interval of time, "I have a long wait between connecting flights." Or to supplying the wants and needs of someone as in, "Do you serve a meal on this flight?" Something several friends have done for us of late. Mercy meals on wheels. Homemade delicacies left hanging on our doorknob by neighbors. Beautiful acts of being waited on.

Recent days have been days of waiting. Waiting for change, for information, for answers. Waiting in lines at grocery stores, in banks, the post office, the pharmacy, and of course, the never ending lines at Starbucks. Days filled waiting for visitors from our church family, for relatives, for three women who live out of state, with whom Dixie has met every other year for many years, renewing relationships and listening to how each has grown spiritually during the interim.

Three women, married to a fireman, an engineer, and a scientist, respectively. All retired. Young mothers when first they met. Two were followers of Jesus, one an avowed agnostic. And Dixie, around whom their relationship formed. "Dixie explained the good news to me and nurtured my heart until my soul was

4 Fun and faithful: Nancy (behind), L-R Bev, Carolyn, Dixie

ready to embrace Jesus," says one. "She challenged us toward higher goals, winsomely beckoning us forward by casting the vision of a God-honoring life. She became our spiritual mother, mentor and friend."

Over the years, each growing in true faith and understanding.

Waiting.

And watching

In a strange, yet beautiful way, these three disparate friends symbolize the many others who through the years have been waiting and watching with Dixie, this woman who welcomes everyone into her world of deep, transforming faith and a passion to know her Father God; a world ever more real and inviting, not just by what she says or teaches, but by the manner in which she lives out her faith each day. Natural. Flawed. Beautiful.

Breakable. Touchable. Believable. Stirring within those she touches the desire to be and do the same.

⌒

Stacks of cards from these last two months continue piling up on the counter in the library, each sharing someone's personal note, telling stories of life change, of relationships restored. Thanking Dixie for the ways she reached out to them, loved and cared for them. Cards from people who may not remember exactly what she said to them, but who with clarity do remember what they felt and saw while with her that helped them overcome *all the obstacles that were in the way.*

Watchers with whom she took part in a new day dawning, and in doing so experienced new light on her own journey. Just the way it's supposed to work.

She hears from those who are in her present day and all the way back to the very beginnings of our ministry over fifty-five years ago. The detail can be amazingly vivid and unexpected. Like one who was a teenager in our first pastorate, now a missionary, who recently suffered the death of her husband. She writes: "I was thinking back to the first time I met you and Dixie. It was in Forks and you had just been voted in as our pastor. Leave it to me, but I remember what Dixie was wearing. A periwinkle blue dress with a periwinkle blue pill box hat. She was gorgeous! I remember something about you, too … it was your hair. A Princeton crew cut on top and long on the sides, combed back. Very handsome! You have blessed my life for many years! You are loved and I'm praying for you as you walk this latest adventure/ journey in your lives."

The things young minds absorb!

We were, in fact, the youngest pastors ever in this church and have fond memories of good times with those teens, not being that many years older than them ourselves. They babysat our children. We did Fort Flagler kids camps and teen camps every summer. We grew up together and that is the most wonderful thing anyone can say, really. We grew up in faith and trust in our Lord Jesus. Together. Pill box hat, Princeton haircut and all.

In some way or another we are all watchers, aren't we?

No one is sure who first said, "All good things come to those who wait," though it is generally attributed to President Abraham Lincoln. We do know the Scripture says, "The Lord is good to those who wait for him, to the soul who seeks him" (Lamentations 3:25).

And so we wait.

We wait to hear an official word from SCCA regarding the results of Dixie's liver biopsy. Unofficially, we've been informed the spots being evaluated are not cancer. Instead, they appear to be abscesses, usually treatable with antibiotics or surgical drainage, depending on their size, number, and complexity. She is taking antibiotics which, hopefully, are helping. What additional steps, if any, are unknown to us.

Dixie is having a good week, gaining strength and energy, though not regaining any of her lost weight. She says, with a smile, that shopping is in the near term because she has nothing to wear that fits. For once, shopping actually sounds good to me.

Our son, Stephen, flew in from Hong Kong yesterday. He and Nancy and their son, Jesse, now officially a teenager, have been living and working there as part of the administrative staff of Savannah College of Art and Design HK. He says you are never too old for a "Mommy fix," but is bunking at home with his sister and her husband, Michele and Mark, rather than on a floor in our apartment.

We are learning to live one day at a time, each day being precious in God's hands. We are goal-oriented people and, as such, we've accomplished a good deal in life, investing ourselves in our children and in thousands of others along our journey. And we are not done yet. But we also know we have missed some things along the way. We've at times been so focused on the next person or the next project that we've misplaced some of the amazing people and precious times in our past. Reminders come daily now of just how important we all are, to our Lord Jesus Christ, and to one another.

With our Creator, at the end of the day we can say, "We are pleased."

Even though I walk through the valley of the shadow of death, I will fear no evil, for you are with me; your rod and your staff, they comfort me. You prepare a table before me in the presence of my enemies; you anoint my head with oil; my cup overflows. ~ Psalm 23:4,5

11

Love Unexpected

Since God determined the time and exact places you would live (Acts 17:26), it's no accident which neighborhood you grew up in, who lived next door, who went to school with you, who was part of your church youth group, who was there to help you and pray for you. Our relationships were appointed by God, and there's every reason to believe they'll continue in Heaven.[5] ~ Randy Alcorn

Does every young woman dream about her future? Perhaps, if she believes it will be filled with something good. I can't recall ever dreaming specifically about marriage or career. However, I knew what I did not want. I would not marry the man my mother had chosen for me. This was one control issue with her I was determined to win.

The love of my life showed up quite unexpectedly. My introduction to Ward, in February of 1955, was an "accident" caused by a misunderstanding of who the "friends" were who were coming to meet us at Joan's house. I was expecting someone I knew from across town, not a male gospel quartet from Central Bible College. For Ward, who sang bass, our first meeting was an incidental part of a sightseeing tour of Tulsa, Oklahoma,

---

5   *Heaven*, Randy Alcorn. Tyndale House, 2004.

my home town. A means to an end. Having come from a very small town, he just wanted to see the biggest city he'd ever been in.

We met that night in Joan's driveway and since it was dark, I couldn't see his face, nor was I much interested. Meeting another man training for ministry from CBC was not the fulfillment of any potential dreams of mine. I was told (much later) that he and Geoff stood behind the car and flipped a coin to see where to sit. Right side was Jo, left side was me. Ward likens it now to the casting of lots in the Old Testament, when seeking divine direction. I'm not so sure. All I know is Joan, Carl, Brent and Clyde sat in the front seat. Ward sat next to me.

We four squeezed into the back seat of the small four-door 1954 Ford Fairlane and were off to tour the beautiful city I loved. Conversation with Ward was easy and humorous. He was straightforward with his answers to my questions and I liked him. He must have liked me, too, for a letter came the next week suggesting he could come again the following weekend. His school in Springfield, Missouri, was over two hundred miles from Tulsa, but weekend visits continued and so did the daily letters. ~ DLT diary, 2015

We toss the coin, but it is the Lord who controls its decision ~ Proverbs 16:33 TLB.

Love at first sight? I can't honestly say that. I may have blinked once. After all, I was a seventeen-year-old college freshman, two thousand miles from home. What did I really know about anything? But I came away interested, yes indeed. I had enjoyed sitting crushed together in the car with someone who, from all I could see in the flickering lights as we drove around the city, was very attractive. She spoke with pride about her city, words flowing across her lips with a soft southern accent as she described various sites and buildings, including the iconic *Art Deco* Philtower, where she worked.

And the way she laughed. You can tell a lot about a person by how they laugh. I liked the ease and unforced spontaneity in her laughter, leaving me with the feeling of laughing with, not at anyone. The time for getting acquainted with eight people crammed into a moving vehicle, talking, laughing, and innocently touching, passed quickly. Everyone seemed to be having a good time.

At our very conservative Christian college there was a well-intentioned item in the Code of Student Conduct loosely referred to as the "six-inch rule," which stated there should be no handholding or touching of the opposite sex in any way at any time. On this night in Tulsa, five guys and three girls, taking in the sights of the city while stuffed together in a small automobile, totally flunked that rule. Since we were off campus and conducted ourselves properly in every other way throughout the evening as befitted young Bible college students, we granted ourselves amnesty. I'm sure the dean of men would have been proud of us had he known. Wisely, we never told him.

Eventually we returned to Joan's home and went inside for some promised tea and cookies in a more spacious setting. It was my first opportunity to sit directly across from the young woman with whom I had just ridden around the city, side by side, for the past two hours. As conversation continued, with an ease young people in groups seem universally to possess, I couldn't stop glancing at her.

The person I'd been talking to, mostly in the dark, now sat in front of me in a well-lit living room. She wore a sleeveless patterned top, the colors were, I think, a light coral and gray, though with the passing of years I cannot be certain; her legs crossed beneath a long denim skirt, and hands folded neatly on her lap. The girls were dressed for a casual evening that had been interrupted by our unexpected appearance.

Yet somehow she had turned into this vivacious, dark-haired beauty with the most amazing brown eyes, and an infectious smile that could fill the room whenever she wanted to. I all at once found myself groping for words to fill in blank spaces; verbs and adjectives and nouns that had come so naturally such a short time ago were gone. I looked around at the others, reassuring myself I could hold my own with anyone else in the room. But this one across from me ... instinctively I knew the random flip of a coin had placed me next to a woman in a class all her own. A sophisticated city girl had just spent the evening with a country boy who knew deep down he was a long way from home!

But by the time I was back in my college dorm room and done describing this incredible person I had just met to my roommate, I worked up enough courage to write her a letter. The first of many that were to follow between us. Five hundred and eleven actually, all handwritten and all still tucked away for our children and grandchildren to one day discover and pore over; hopefully, by that time, having learned to laugh *with* and not *at* their elder lovers from another generation as they read.

I will tell you this much. The first letter was written in February 1955, and is no great loss to literary antiquity. After numerous letters back and forth in March of that year (postage stamps were only 3 cents; airmail 6 cents), Dixie signed off on April 7, using for the first time the word, "Love." When I saw it I was over the top with enthusiasm, taking this as a signal that our affections were headed in the right direction.

Why so many letters? Keep in mind the Bible college I attended was over two hundred miles one-way from Tulsa. I worked, sang in concerts, plus every Sunday night with *Revivaltime* choir on the ABC radio network, traveled with the King's Ambassadors quartet (the group responsible for Dixie's and my meeting in the first place), and carried a full academic load. Dixie worked full-time supporting both herself and her mother. We were busy! The actual amount of time spent together over the sixteen months of our courtship? About six weeks. And did I say we were very young?

A first meeting and first letter in February: *Dear Dixie... I had a lot of fun Saturday... Dear Ward... It was a nice surprise to get your letter today...* Revivaltime *was really good Sunday night. Joan and I were listening...*

More letters.

Numerous weekend concerts in churches in eastern Oklahoma.

More letters.

A spring *Revivaltime* Choir tour throughout the South.

More letters.

A summer concert tour with the King's Ambassadors Quartet.

Lots more letters!

"You know, one thing I've noticed the last two months is the closer to the Lord I get, the more I seem to love you. I never felt quite like this before. It's all so crazy and yet so wonderful. I've never been more contented in my life. Maybe this wonderful thing that has happened to me has just begun to dawn on me that it's really true. I'll be so glad when you get here. These last few days will probably drag by. I love you. I would give almost anything to see you tonight. But it won't be long now." ~ DLT letter, 7 August 1955

A first answer to "Darling, will you marry me?" came on a warm summer evening, 25 August, beneath the old oak tree in front of her home.

A first and last wedding date set for 2 June, the following year.

A young man and woman, with so much still to learn, tie their love together in handwritten letters filled with faith and hope and the anticipation of *forever after.*

The reason why so many letters.

⌒

For a twenty-year-old girl, planning my wedding should have been filled with excitement and anticipation. In reality, it was a time of inner turmoil and outward struggle. Mom refused to be involved in the planning. She also gave me an ultimatum; if Dad walked me down the aisle, she would not attend. I also worried about the future for both of us. I had taken on the support of Mom and for three years had provided for our needs. How would she live?

Ward's call to the ministry was troubling to me. I emphatically did not want to be a pastor's wife. I observed close up friends who had married into a life in ministry and was quite sure it was not for me. My desire was for a quiet life; besides I knew I would never fit in church ministry. Ward, however, had chosen to be a military chaplain, which meant many more years of school to qualify. We knew it would not be easy, but we were willing to work hard to achieve his goals. In reality it was a blind leap into the future.

"And they lived happily ever after" doesn't quite fit this narrative. After the wedding we traveled to our new home in Springfield, a tiny basement apartment which our mothers had already helped us settle into. I soon got a job working days. Ward already had a job working nights;

an arrangement that worked well with his school schedule, but not with a new bride. Pay was low and college bills loomed large. Ward would be a junior, but seminary would come after graduation. Reality hit like a thunderbolt.

It had taken less than six weeks. ~ DLT diary, 2015

12

A New Normal

In times of uncertainty, the easiest thing to do is revert to what you know. Ward knew he could get a job in the wheat harvests working to earn money for our immediate needs. He also knew Northwest College in Seattle to be a good alternative to Central Bible College in Springfield. So, we packed up a U-Haul trailer, took a detour through Tulsa to say goodbye to my family, and drove west. When calculating the cost of gasoline, we had not thought how the drag of our trailer would affect mileage through the Rocky Mountains, nor how far our picnic-type food would satisfy our hunger. It was nothing short of a miracle that the gas was sufficient, and our bellies, although not full, weren't empty. We arrived at Nadeen and Earl's house in the wee hours of the morning with an empty gas tank and grateful hearts. Wheat was ripe and Ward worked in the harvest fields for the rest of the summer. ~ DLT diary, 2015

Monday, 21 April. It is the beginning of a new week and of what is rapidly becoming our new normal. Blood draw is set for 3:30 today. We arrive at SCCA the requisite "15 minutes ahead of your appointment time, please." After the draw, there is an appointment at 4:30 with Dr. Chiorean. At 5 o'clock, we are getting restless. At 5:15, we're the only ones left in the waiting area. At twenty after, a nurse comes to lead us to an exam room. First, the usual "birthdate?" (still the same), "weight?" (gained a pound), "blood pressure?" (A *little* high?) Hello, with this much time waiting there's a reason for that!

"Doctor will be here shortly. She's running late" (don't say it).

At a quarter-to-six, I step out into the hall.

"Hello. Is anybody here?"

A lone face peeks around the corner.

"Just checking. Didn't want to think we'd been forgotten?"

I go back to the room where Dixie is sitting. And wait. A new person comes to explain that Dr. Chiorean is running late but will be here shortly. She has been working with a patient through an interpreter. Okay, a reason for lateness that I understand. I've taught in situations requiring interpreters and it takes extra time to get it done. Part of the new day of ethnic diversity in which we live in America.

Eventually, Dr. Chiorean opens the door and hurries in, with apologies.

Is it obvious that waiting is not my spiritual gift? I'm working on it as a *skill* (still a ways to go), but it is definitely not a gift. However, after all is said and done, it is hard to be upset with someone as nice as Dr. Chiorean. She is a special lady. Gabriela. Dr. Park refers to her affectionately as, Gabby. I usually move to a first name basis with people quickly, but for some reason with her, I do not. To me she is still Dr. Chiorean. Maybe someday. It is nearing 6:30 when Dixie asks about her accent. Romanian. I tell her I was in her homeland shortly after the revolution, at a time when my friend, Bob Pagett, founder and president of the then fledgling Assist International, and I went there to see what we could do to help.

We entered the country on a winter's night train from Belgrade; one with no heat and minimal lighting. As it happened, we were seated across from two women who turned out to be nurses. One of them spoke a little English. When we asked what was needed in Romania's medical world, they said medical supplies of any kind were desperately needed, starting with such basics as needles and surgical gloves.

Dr. Chiorean nods affirmatively as she listens, telling us that as a young woman, she practiced on her mother by giving shots repeatedly with needles they sterilized and reused, since few were available (both mothers *and* needles) at the time. I think how pleased she would be to know that one of Romania's orphan children, who found a loving home resulting from the seeds of our initial visit there, is now at University studying to become a doctor. The room is filled with a sense of renewed respect at what we have heard. Someone we may have helped fulfill a dream over twenty years ago is sitting across from us, preparing to help us with our dream today. And so we listen to the game plan.

Wednesday. Our schedule for the day. Chemo education at 10 o'clock on F2. First infusion at 11 o'clock on F5.

Our son, Stephen, joins us today at SCCA, listening as the nurse fills us in on what is about to happen. A long litany of common, less common, and finally rare side effects. She writes some prescriptions, designed to ameliorate the side effects of what we are about to do.

After listening to all the possibilities, I am eager to have these medicines in hand. That we have agreed to Dixie undergoing this treatment, willingly subjecting herself to these destructive chemicals, causes unspoken hesitation on my part, second thoughts. Doubt? Fear? For me at the very least, anxiety. What must Dixie be thinking? I don't ask. Right when the battle reaches a new level of intensity is not the time to show apprehension or misgiving. That boat has already sailed. Instead, I hurry off to the pharmacy on F5 and place the orders. *Your rod and your staff, Lord? I could use some reassurance right now.*

At 11:15, we step through double doors and enter that *darkest valley*. This time the valley morphs into a room at the end of one of two halls, lined with lookalike rooms on either side. As we walk, I'm thinking it takes a lot of people to require this kind of facility. Cancer is big business! At 11:30, the nurse inserts a saline drip line into Dixie's right forearm and steps out of the room. We are alone with our thoughts now, offering up silent prayers to God, who responds with equally silent answers.

In a few minutes the nurse reappears, dons an apron and slips on extra strength gloves. Stephen asks about the gloves. She explains that she and her coworkers deal so much with chemotherapy drugs, it is important to their own wellbeing to keep it away from inadvertently touching their clothes or skin. This answer is not comforting to me. I watch her remove the saline and attach the bag of *Gemcitabine* to the line in Dixie's forearm.

Another nurse comes in. One spells out Dixie's name and reads a series of chemo identity numbers that is confirmed by the other. He leaves with a parting, "Nice to meet you."

Seconds later the infusion is under way, and the battle against Enemy Cancer has been re-engaged! Thirty minutes? An hour? It doesn't take long to change one's world.

Thursday and Friday. Our children are in motion for two days while I am in Los Angeles helping plan for a CASA conference. I have let it be known to the board that my days as leader of this ministry are rapidly coming to a close. Stephen spends his last day with Mom before returning to Hong Kong. Michele takes Mom for a pedicure. The doctors say this is important to do before chemo begins in earnest, improving appearance, stimulating blood flow to the feet and legs, relaxation, and adding euphoric benefits that help focus, memory, mood and quality of life. Who knew? It actually sounds pretty good.

On Friday, Michele takes Mom "mercy shopping." At her new normal, 20 pounds lighter than when she began this part of her sacred journey, Dixie has nothing she can wear that doesn't hang or fall off altogether. Something new is not just an Easter frock, but a real life necessity.

Saturday. Wheels on the ground. A text to Dixie, "Hummer landed." When I arrive at home, I am met at the door by a beautiful woman with an infectious smile and killer eyes, dressed in a recently purchased blouse with pants that actually fit. Looking good. Actually, better than good. She looks like a young woman I met in Tulsa almost sixty years ago and she still knocks me out, just like she did then! It's good to be back home.

Sunday. It's a windy, sunny Sunday morning. I get up early to take Mark and Michele to the airport. They are flying to Hawaii to spend a few R&R days on Oahu with the wife of an Army helicopter pilot who is stationed there. The young mother is someone Michele served as a mentor during her high school days and the relationship with this young couple continues. Though quite different in their styles, both our adult children do one-to-one sharing of life well with others, as do their spouses. I guess the acorns did not fall as far from the tree as we had sometimes thought.

Dixie and I spend the rest of Sunday absorbing the quiet.

Just the two of us.

13

Yielding

If you cannot "cherish" what it is the Lord is doing in your life, at least do not "waste" what he is doing in your life. Lay down the self-pity, and with all the strength and grace that he allows you, yield to his work. ~ from the Aidan, bishop of Lindisfarne, series of daily readings

It took me longer than it should have to appreciate the complexity of Dixie's relationship with her parents. I didn't ask the questions I could have asked and she didn't volunteer the feelings she might have shared. I now know it was because she couldn't. She was too uncertain in our young days of marriage. Would I respect her? Would I love her still? If the dysfunctional years with her parents were exposed in its depth, what would her new family think? Everything was too new. It was too risky. It is a lesson for every man, I think, to tenderly open our hearts and minds to the feelings of our mate in ways we are not used to doing.

The signals were there in her letters. I was too self-centered, too much in-love to read them for what they were. Her comments about her mother and father were complimentary. She spoke of them in glowing terms at times, hiding the deep pain she felt in their relationship. Her mother was outwardly pleasant to me, and to others soft spoken and kind. Dixie wrote of times when her mom had been especially considerate and warm to her. Still, I knew things were not good. Not really.

Though I was not around her father for any length of time, when I was with him, he seemed gentle, respectful and complimentary in his attitude. A down-home farmer-in-the-city kind of guy. She wrote of borrowing his car or going to his home to prepare dinner together. The kinds of father/daughter things that say, "I love you." At no time did she refer disparagingly toward either of her parents.

When we were first engaged, she asked her dad to walk her down the aisle and give her away at our wedding. In spite of everything, she wanted this. Most brides do. However, when her mother refused to attend the wedding if this happened, her parent's bitter animosity proved impossible to cover up. Dixie was certain it was more than an idle threat. Her mother meant it. To avoid a wedding catastrophe, she caved to her pressure as being the lesser of two evils. She had tried to recreate her parents into what she desired and needed them to be. Parents like those her best friends had. In the end it was not to be.

My earning her trust was essential to her overcoming silent fears of being tainted somehow by the failures of her parents. I missed this at first because I wasn't listening well. I was too absorbed in what I was trying to be and do. Eventually, she risked sharing her hidden story. In the sharing she became stronger, and so did I. I was blown away by her inner strength and the courage of this beautiful creature I had married!

Our move to the West Coast put distance between them and us. Though it was not something we had thought through at first, it proved to be healthy in the long run. Like knowing the Grand Canyon is there, but not having to cross it every day. I am confident God had this in mind long before we understood its importance.

There were a couple of times she went back to Oklahoma alone and on a few occasions our whole family made the trek. Each time both parents received a visit, though they lived some distance from each other. Dixie's mom visited us three times before she passed away. Her father was never in our home. Even when he came to California, while we were pastors there, he made no attempt to come see us. On a visit back to Tulsa, given his awareness of Dixie's childhood and young adult years, her brother, Don, assured her our move to the West Coast was the best thing she could have done.

Meeting Ward's family was an experience like none I had ever had. He has aunts and uncles galore and cousins beyond counting, compared to this girl who hardly knew any extended family. I was a novelty for inspection at the Coulee City church, where the pastor's wife had already dubbed me from pictures she had seen as having "evil eyes." It is a small town, a small church. Where could I hide?

I sensed Ward's immediate family close ranks around me. His sister, Nadeen, was amazing! Nothing ruffled her. She included me in whatever she was doing, wherever she needed to go, and with such ease that I soon truly felt part of the family. By my observing, she taught me about being a mom and a wife. She was patient with me in the kitchen, performing the simplest of tasks that were totally new to me. Things an impatient mom had failed to teach me. Her capacity for patience and caring for her daughter, Candy, and husband, Earl, was with good humor that impressed me. This was quite a different family picture than I was accustomed to seeing.

Ward's brother, Doug, was a baby about eight months old. Ras and Luella, grandparents to six-year-old Candy, and a baby of their own, were likewise impressive. I was quite sure, however, I would never measure up to Luella's standards. She was Nadeen's opposite. Where Nadeen was relaxed in a room scattered with the debris of living, Luella was neat and tidy. If I was reading a book and put it down to go to the bathroom, the book was closed and put away on the shelf when I got back. Everything had a place and everything was in its place.

Ras, on the other hand was very warm from the first time we met. He was a "huggy bear." When I first met him, he didn't offer me his hand, or say, "Hello." He hugged me! I was shocked and first looked at Luella to see if this was an okay thing. And then I looked at my mother to see her disapproval. I don't recall my father ever hugging me growing up. Ras would engage me in conversation just to hear my "Oakie" accent. I didn't realize he enjoyed hearing it. I thought he was making fun of me. I wanted his approval so badly, I worked very hard to get rid of the accent, much to his disappointment. To this day, I can't easily pick up accents.

Luella and I sought for a comfortable place with each other. I eventually realized she was not judging me; she was giving me time to find a place to be. She invited me to tell her about myself and she shared her life with me. She became my dearest friend, a spiritual guide, a mentor, and a mother confidant who helped me through many perilous places in the years ahead. I still miss her. ~ DLT diary, 2015

Thursday. We are at Seattle Cancer Care Alliance, F4, admitting Dixie for her second chemo infusion. The view across Lake Union is the same in this waiting area as it is on any of SCCA's seven floors. Through long floor-to-ceiling walls of clear glass windows, one cannot help being mesmerized by the old/new Seattle scene.

Houseboats moored along the shore. A seaplane dropping onto the lake from the north. Construction cranes, like giant steel and cable obstetricians, signaling the birth of new office and condo buildings, while older buildings stand by silently absorbing the inevitability of it all. Change. Signs of the times.

Blue sky. Blue water. Queen Anne Hill, long a Seattle favorite, looming on the opposite shore. The bridge that crosses over to funky Fremont. The revival of old Wallingford and the University districts in the distance, where we lived our first years of married life together. *Yesterday*. We laughed here. We cried. We struggled. We dreamed here. *Yesterday*. We loved. We held new life in our arms here. We went away. *Yesterday*. And now years later, as ironic as it seems, we are here again. *Today*.

This could be a fine hotel, a gorgeous vacation spot. But it's not. That was *yesterday*. Not able to cherish this season but unwilling to waste it. This is *today*.

In her pre-check they say she's doing well, although the white cells need a boost. It's the neutrophils. Of course it is. We listen silently, as if we knew all along. She shows us the chart. There were 4000 before her first infusion; today 1100. The second chemo treatment will be administered as planned, but if these aggressive little fighters were to drop below 1000, Dixie's chemo treatment will come to a screeching halt. To correct the drop, she needs two shots to motivate bone marrow function. They must be administered right away. The first will be tomorrow, the second the day following.

And with that, the chemotherapy process gets underway a second time.

On the drive home, late in the afternoon, we stop by a local nursery to purchase a few small plants for our deck. And we choose an early Mother's Day hanging basket of flowers that will be seen the first thing every morning through our bedroom window. The beauty of color accomplishes something medicine cannot do. Yet by dinner time, she is feeling nauseous. The chemo is on its deadly mission. Her body is the battlefield. She eats some lactose-free ice cream with ginger ale poured over it. It's all she can manage for nourishment tonight.

Friday. We are back again at SCCA, awaiting yet another nurse, who, upon her arrival, mentions she came here some years before from a little town in Sweden. As she prepares to administer the neurogenic injection, she explains to us the "why" of what is happening.

Neutrophils are the most abundant white blood cells in humans. They play a key role in one's front-line defense against invading pathogens. A low white blood cell count, or "neutropenia," is a condition characterized by abnormally low levels of neutrophils in the circulating blood. Dixie's neutropenia is a side effect of the chemotherapy. Chemotherapy uses drugs to destroy cells that grow rapidly, like cancer cells. Unfortunately, as we are learning, chemotherapy also affects normal cells that grow rapidly, such as blood cells in the bone marrow, cells in hair follicles, or cells in the mouth and intestines.

These white blood cell defenders rush in to prevent and fight infections. As in the time-honored Bible story of Esther, they, like she, are created "for such a time as this." But as their numbers drop the risk of infection increases, resulting in the disruption of cancer treatment. Fortunately, the nurse tells us, neutropenia can be prevented by the injection of white blood cell growth factors, thereby reducing the risk of infection and hospitalization.

Reinforcements now appearing. Important to any cancer patient, but especially to those who are older and at greater risk of more severe infection and longer hospitalizations.

And so the neurogenic injection is given. Moments later we make our way to the underground parking garage. I see her falter. I reach for her and ask, are you okay? No, she says, looking down, concentrating on each unsteady step. We pause for a moment. She takes my arm, presses up against me. It's not far, I say. We are almost there.

And I think how glad I am to be here. Right now. Walking with her on my arm, pressing up against me. Here where it all began for us, so many years ago.

Teresa of Avila (1515–1582), reformer of the Carmelite order in Spain, once said that "one's suffering should be as incense offered before God." I've never cared for the smell of incense and never quite understood why God seems to have such a thing for it. Why do Catholics use it during Mass? Is this another reason Protestants exist today? Is it to make the place smell a certain way, or is it just to encourage some of us to cough at the mere scent of it?

In reality, of course, it is an expression of prayer, and it is in fact very scriptural, very Roman Catholic, and very Judeo-Christian. There is a recipe for incense in Exodus 30: 34–36, and incense is associated with divinity and reserved for God (Ex: 30: 37–38).

> *"For from the rising of the sun to its setting my name will be great among the nations, and in every place incense will be offered to my name, and a pure offering. For my name will be great among the nations," says the Lord of hosts.* ~ Malachi 1:11

I get all that. I still don't like it, any more than I like the suffering being foisted upon the love of my life! So Lord, this is my prayer; an offering of suffering as the incense of worship and praise to God. If it must be, then let it be a pure offering, the scent of which reaches your own heart that knows suffering. And also the heart of someone whose faith may be wavering in their present affliction, who feels discarded and abandoned in their own great testing time.

Be the One. The One who cares. The One on whom we can all lean. The One who sees us stumble but will not let us fall. Help us to discover again the great power of prayer. May our relationship grow deeper and stronger with each unsteady step.

It's not far. We are almost there.

I will rejoice and be glad in your steadfast love, because you have seen my affliction. ~ Psalm 31:7

14

Questioning

The harvest season was over. It was time to find a place to live in Seattle and settle down to school, jobs, and the life ahead. Our University district upstairs apartment was tiny. The kitchen was so small that every corner could be reached from one spot in the middle. The eating area was a booth in the corner, the living room a hall between the kitchen and bedroom and the shared bathroom was out on the back porch. Lucky for all of us, the next door couple were quiet and clean.

Ward enrolled in Northwest College and we both found jobs. Ward was a typesetter at Sound Printing and I, a secretary at the Seattle Fire Department. I really hated the job, but I met a friend there. Barbara, and her husband Dick, a UW Forestry student, became our good friends. We ate many spaghetti dinners together in each other's homes the next two years.

Seattle was a new kind of environment for me. Oklahoma was a dry state – no legal alcohol sales permitted. The route to my new work place took me along a street in a revolting part of the city where drunks lay passed out on the sidewalk, sleeping it off in their vomit, including women. What a revelation of my new home!

Growing up during segregation in a segregated state I had seen prejudice but had never been on the receiving end. The fire chief believed I was Jewish from my looks; cause enough to not interview me. This was only after he had insisted his secretary telephone first to ask if I was black because of my name on the application. Dixie was just too doubtful for him.

Six months was all I could take until another job opportunity came my way. At Minneapolis Honeywell, my boss was a womanizer who had trouble keeping his secretaries. I was no exception. Sexual harassment in the work place would cost him his job today; but then the workplace was a man's domain.

I eventually settled into a job that was a good fit and paid well at Carter Oil in downtown Seattle. I was the manager's secretary and all was going well until I discovered I was pregnant. Morning sickness and my boss's long, green cigars were not good companions. His wife had just delivered a new baby and he recognized my symptoms. The cigars disappeared and all went well until unexpected symptoms at five months made bedrest necessary.

Soon after Ward's graduation, our 8 pound, 3 ounce Michele Lenea (pronounced Lenā) arrived. It was 23 July 1958. A precious bundle had dropped into our lives and it was love at first sight. Every experience was new. I was on a steep learning curve when it came to infant care. The nurse taught me how to put a diaper on, how to bathe and feed her and how to hold her. This was just the beginning of a lifelong adventure with the daughter of our dreams. She is a wondrous love gift from God.

With college behind us and seminary ahead, we moved to Portland, Oregon, when Michele was five weeks old, to be in time for Ward to start classes. I had a job waiting for me at the Carter Oil Portland office. However, my post birth body was not cooperating. Luella flew down to help us, but upon her arrival realized the seriousness of our situation. The next day the three of us, Luella, Michele and I flew to Wenatchee and I went straight to the hospital. Luella and Michele went home to Coulee City. Ras stayed with me. What was God doing? Weren't we following his plan? Seminary had been our plan since before our wedding.

Several weeks later, Michele and I rejoined Ward, the seminary student. We hired another student's wife to take care of Michele and I returned to work, driving fifteen miles each way to my job, crying all the way. Those were bleak days for both of us. Ward was questioning our circumstances, his call to military chaplaincy, and I was questioning everything about my existence. We both wanted to be in God's will, but we weren't sure what that was. Neither of us were quitters, but that's exactly what we did. Ward quit seminary, I quit my job, and we became evangelists. ~ DLT diary, 2015

15

The "What if" Question

Recently Ward has asked repeatedly the "what-if?" questions. What if we had stayed in seminary? How would our lives have been different? What if we had stayed in Springfield where we first began? We were following what we believed to be God leading, even though we were both scared and unsure about the direction we were going. We were like blind people holding onto each other on a very narrow path.

We moved all our earthly belongings to a tiny rented house in Coulee City and for the next year and half we were evangelists. Ward studied every day and preached every night. We stayed in other people's homes, ate what they offered, and took what they could pay us. During the summer Ward worked in the harvests and I cooked for a harvest crew, while Michele stayed in the safety of her play pen. When summer was over, we moved our things into the attic at Nadeen and Earl's and when not in services somewhere, we lived with them as lingering house guests. Robin and Michele, a year younger than her cousin, grew up as good friends and remain so today. ~ DLT diary, 2015

It is not easy to think back now on our post-seminary days. With no money and only one meeting scheduled, we set out to serve

God in the only way open to us. We drive to Marblemount, Washington, a small town in the northwestern part of the state, at this time situated literally at the end of SR 20. The pastor is a passing acquaintance who has invited us for a two-week revival series. Thus the end of the road is the place we are to begin. It's all we have going for us. Someday I need to talk to God about his sense of humor.

These are days in which itinerant evangelists hold revival meetings as community outreaches. I have seven sermons in my pocket when we begin. The meetings go on every night and twice on Sundays. This would be sixteen sermons in case you've not been counting. Dixie and I sing a couple of songs each night and I preach. During the daytimes, Dixie watches out for our baby girl and I pray and study, putting more messages together.

We have no clue really as to what we are doing. Neither of us have any clergy or formal church experience ourselves, or in our families, other than what we observed growing up. The folk here are kind, good-hearted mountain people, who for the most part hunt and fish and work in the forests or in agriculture. They are evenly split politically, and the religious majority are the "nones," meaning those never seen in or interested in church.

But something begins to happen in the little church at the end of the road that is far beyond our doing on a human level. In spite of our naiveté, God goes to work. Word spreads around town and in small neighboring communities that there is a young preacher they should go hear at the local church. We are told later that even customers in the area's bars and taverns are talking it up and many leave their drinks to come listen to this young stranger preach God's Word. When an invitation to come forward and receive Christ is given, people drop on their knees to repent of sin and begin a new life in Christ. Dixie and I are amazed and excited. It is all new and wonderful. At the same time, I am dying a little every day, having to come up with something new to preach the next night.

Toward the end of the second week the pastor stands and, without discussing it with me first, asks the good folk filling the church by now how many would like to go on for a third week of meetings. The response is overwhelming. The die is cast! Eight more sermons! And I am back on my knees praying and studying and hoping I can make it to the end. It was great, really, and I am still grateful to the good folk in Marblemount for loving us and giving us an opportunity to launch our public ministry there.

Not every place we go is as successful. There are times when I wonder if anything I say is making a difference. I remember preaching in one small town over Easter weekend when the pastor of the church actually goes somewhere else that Sunday and leaves me with his little flock. I want to go wherever he went because his flock wasn't so much. Rain pours down day and night and mud is everywhere. I can't really blame people for staying home. I wouldn't go out if I didn't have to. There are nights when all I have to preach to are the pastor and his wife, the lady in whose home we are staying, Dixie, our baby daughter and me. These are tough and humbling days.

We are at the mercy of other people's generosity, living in the homes of friends and of total strangers, eating their food and following their schedules. Dixie never complains, but I know we are not built to sustain this kind of life.

Eastern Washington. It is cold and foggy, very dreary weather. Winter is here for certain. We've been at this for almost a year now. God continues *to provide miraculously for our needs. Saturday, when we left sis's home, we possessed a little over one dollar. Before we arrived in Kittitas to begin our next meetings, God had given us $40 more. Surely his hand must be upon our lives for some special purpose. ~ WT diary, December 1959*

It is getting much harder for Dixie to travel. While grit keeps her going, her nerves are near to giving way. We believe God is directing us out of the evangelistic field, but do not know where or what he would have us do. Earlier in the year we receive a one hundred percent vote from a congregation in South Dakota to be their new pastor. As much as the idea of settling down is appealing, we don't feel right in accepting. So we take a pass and continue on for almost another entire year. As it turns out, that church gave us the only one hundred percent vote we ever received.

Therefore I tell you, do not be anxious about your life, what you will eat or what you will drink, nor about your body, what you will put on. Is not life more than food, and the body more than clothing? Look at the birds of the air: they neither sow nor reap nor gather into barns, and yet your heavenly Father feeds them. Are you not of more value than they? And which of you by being anxious can add a single hour to his span of life?

And why are you anxious about clothing? Consider the lilies of the field, how they grow: they neither toil nor spin, yet I tell you, even Solomon in all his glory was not arrayed like one of these. But if God so clothes the grass of the field, which today is alive and tomorrow is thrown into the oven, will he not much more clothe you, O you of little faith?

Therefore do not be anxious, saying, "What shall we eat?" or "What shall we drink?" or "What shall we wear?" For the Gentiles seek after all these things, and your heavenly Father knows that you need them all. But seek first the kingdom of God and his righteousness, and all these things will be added to you.

Therefore do not be anxious about tomorrow, for tomorrow will be anxious for itself. Sufficient for the day is its own trouble. ~ Matthew 6:25–34

༄

The Scripture that sustained and informed me during those months was Matthew 6. Our first pay was an offering given to us just as it was collected, in cash. I recall pouring it out on the bed and counting how much we had earned for the week. It totaled $28.00. That needed to stretch for gas in the car, baby food, and any other baby essentials. I waited for Ward to leave the room to cry. It still amazes us how all our essential needs were met during that stressful time. God was teaching us to look to Him as our Provider. A truth that is etched in our hearts.

We were always housed and fed in the homes of others during those eighteen months of our evangelistic ministry. Michele learned to crawl and walk in the varied homes of others; some clean, others not so much. Looking back through time's rear view mirror, I'm sure I offended many homemakers by scrubbing their floors before letting Michele's knees or feet touch down. ~ DLT diary, 2015

༄

We talk about what might be next. It seems to be one of two things—either back to Western Evangelical Seminary to finish the training we started over a year ago, or to some pastorate that has yet to open up. We pray God will do what he has promised, namely, open doors where there are no doors. And then one Monday in December the Lord impresses upon both of us at different times in the day what he would have us do. When we come together to talk about it, we are agreed. God is preparing us to begin a new phase of ministry. We are going to be pastors and it will be soon. We just don't know where or when. But soon.

We begin to pray for God to not only prepare our hearts to meet the challenge of pastoral ministry, but to prepare those we are to going to serve to receive us with open hearts. If only God will allow us to reach at least one entire community with the gospel message, what more could we ask?

We conclude a fourth week of meetings in Medical Lake, Washington, on a high note. It seems God has done a good work in the hearts of the people here. Then early in 1960, two specific opportunities come simultaneously during this season of new beginnings.

First, the pastor in a well-established congregation in Spokane invites me to be his associate pastor, with an emphasis on working among the youth. At the same time, a small congregation situated in the farthest west incorporated community in America's lower forty-eight states invites us to present as candidates for pastor.

The city is bigger and the salary better in Spokane. The other community is much smaller and remote, sixty miles in one direction to Port Angeles, and more than a hundred miles in the other direction to Hoquiam/Aberdeen. When asked later why we chose one over the other, the bottom line? I knew I needed more experience as a preacher and pastor. Together, we felt the Lord leading in that direction and so we chose one "what if" over the other.

Nothing is ever easy. The February tryout weekend is insane. Saturday evening, we celebrate my cousin's wedding. I sing, I think it was four songs during the ceremony. After the wedding, we drive for hours through a mountain snowstorm, arriving in Seattle at 2:30 in the morning. We sleep for a couple of hours in a cheap motel.

Leaving the room at 5:30, we arrive at the Edmonds/Kingston dock, just as the ferry is pulling away, forcing us to double back into Seattle to catch the Seattle/Winslow ferry. Next it is the Hood Canal Ferry, followed by driving around Lake Crescent a couple of hours later. Michele becomes carsick, throwing up all over herself, her mother and the car seat. By the time we get to Forks we are an hour late and smell terrible. I preach three times that day. We return home on Monday.

Miracle of miracles, on 29 February, Earl Hamilton, secretary of the board, calls from Forks to tell us the church has voted us in as their new pastor. We are elated.

16

The Restless Years

Michele was eighteen months old when the call came from Forks, Washington, inviting us to consider serving the local church as pastor. The scrutiny was intense. Ward was a gifted speaker, Michele was a charming toddler and I was a big question mark.

It was 1960. Jackie Kennedy had influenced the fashion world with her pillbox hats and sophisticated style. Having learned to sew my own clothes out of necessity from weight loss during the evangelistic months, I tried to conform to the Jackie Kennedy "look." This did not impress the women of this isolated logging community. One woman said later: "I wasn't going to vote for you, but you looked okay when you came without your hat to the evening service. That's when I decided to vote FOR you."

The scrutiny didn't lessen much as the years stretched to almost five and half. Make-up, skirt lengths, child discipline, housekeeping, serving others, all were evaluated. It felt like I ended up in the minus column most of the time. ~ DLT diary, 2015

While a pastor in Forks, I learn to hunt and fish. Well, sort of, because that is what you do if you are going to be a real Olympic Peninsula man, living in Forks and the beautiful surrounding rainforests. I thought I liked to fish until I discover how seasick one can get in small boats on the Pacific Ocean. I shoot my first deer and kill two more with my car on U.S. Highway 101, the road running through our town.

No one plays golf or tennis in Forks. In a locale where it rains 144 inches each year, these kinds of sports are not a high priority. There is a community softball team and I pitch for them in pick-up games. I am involved in community affairs and with the city council. The congregation grows and we build a new auditorium for worship, with more classrooms beneath. The Congregational Church is periodically without a pastor and I fill in with their weddings and funerals whenever needed.

We love the kids and spend lots of time with them. Actually, we aren't that much older than the teenagers in our church. I celebrated my twenty-third birthday a few days before beginning our ministry here. Much of our time is involved in working with the children and young people of our church and community. I also speak at youth rallies and retreats throughout the western part of the state and we assist in Fort Flagler children and youth camps where our young people attend each summer. It is good fun since several pastor couples living on the Peninsula are also involved, the result being camaraderie for this isolated couple.

In 1960, I sell my first article to Pulpit magazine. At 10 cents a word, who could help but take writing seriously.

The following year, I join other pastor/youth leaders, driving round trip to Springfield, Missouri, and a National Youth Directors Conference. It is my first taste of a ministry that will one day be a full-time role for me.

On 27 April 1961, I am formally ordained into Christian ministry. It is a thrilling and moving experience. After more than two years of active ministry involvement, I listen attentively as

RJ Carlson, the district superintendent, preaches at Stone Church in Yakima, Washington. His text is from John 15:16, "I have chosen you and ordained you..."

As the presbytery move down the line of candidates for ordination, I feel a growing awareness of Christ's presence. Kneeling when my name is called, I give my Bible to the superintendent. I am shaking with emotion as dear old Brother Gray, one of the earliest district superintendents and a pastor for many years in Tacoma, lays his hands on me and prays. A public confirmation of God's calling. An experience I shall never forget.

A cherished gift arrived in our family during our time in Forks. Stephen Wesley was born on 25 August 1961. It was exciting for the congregation to have a baby in the parsonage. Everyone adored Michele who had charmed her way into the hearts of most. Grandfathers carried candy in their pockets to dole out to her every Sunday. She knew exactly who they were.

Stephen was a happy child who was both verbal and outgoing. We always had people who were willing to babysit for us when duty called, as it did frequently. The teenagers in the church became a focus for our time and energy. We drove them countless miles in an old school bus to camps and youth rallies as well as on trips to the beach. Some of our teen babysitters then, grandmothers now, still keep in touch.

These were struggle years for me in almost every way. I felt inadequate for the role as "pastor's wife." Having never lived in a small town, I did not understand the ways and priorities of the congregation. The weather was also daunting for this Oklahoma dry-land girl. The rainfall each year left thick mildew on windowsills and walls behind pictures and in closets. I was miserable.

Ward's priorities and energies were expended on "the church." I was mentally, emotionally and spiritually slugging through 144 inches of pure mud. ~ DLT diary, 2015

⁓

These are not easy years, a time in which we learn in real life the truth of Pierre Teilhard de Chardin's words, *"My self is given to me far more than it is formed by me."* These are restless years. A season of growing spiritually, in life experience, and in the development of pastoral skills, gifts and wisdom. We are so young, but most people are good and patient with us. We grow together.

However, it is an especially difficult season for Dixie, given her background. Here she is the brunt of criticism that is pretty much a weekly experience. Being a woman who is often a prime target of conversation among women of the church is hard. It is not the life she signed up for.

One woman in particular makes it her mission to come to our home before 9 o'clock every Monday morning, staying until noon to recite what she has allegedly overheard in conversations among women on the previous Sunday. Your skirts are too short. Others agree. Too much makeup. This is not the big city, you know. You are too lenient with your children. You'll learn. You are too this or too that. I knew you'd want to know. I don't want my girls to turn out like you.

Being young and inexperienced, Dixie takes it on the chin, but after the woman is gone she often weeps alone. Finally, one day I step up (something I should have done long before) and tell the woman where she can take her weekly critiques. She leaves crying and I feel good for having caused her tears. For a while.

It's not long before I recognize the mistake I've made. I had done what needed to be done all right, but in anger, not in tough love. And so I call and make an appointment to apologize. I can still see her standing there in her home, with husband and her several children gathered around her so as not to miss anything, while I apologize for having lashed out in anger. It is a lesson in humility that has served me well. Obviously, I have not forgotten it these many years later.

There are times of crises to get through as a church family. I shepherd church families during the trauma of President Kennedy's assassination. We celebrate births. We mourn over deaths. My first wedding is conducted in a home on the Lapush Indian reservation.

I become immersed in my first building program as we expand the classrooms and erect a new sanctuary. I do all the electrical conduit, the wiring, heat relay systems, lighting, everything electrical, with the oversight of a local electrician. Since I've never done anything like this before, it is nothing short of an act of God.

I work at preparing sermons and bible studies, conducting weddings and funerals, doing visitation. With me being so consumed by the church in this way, I'm guilty of neglecting my wife and children. Finally overcome by what life is giving her, Dixie reaches her limit, packs her bag and the children into our car and leaves.

But where can she go? Oklahoma by herself with two small children is out of the question. Options are few. She eventually arrives across state at her in-laws' home. My mother is smart enough to know there is a problem and wise enough not to ask for details.

The next morning, she simply says, "Dixie, if you want to go to the church and pray, I will watch the children." And so she does. The next day is the same. And the next, until two weeks have passed. It is a time of deep soul searching, of looking for her Father.

Her father has disappointed, abused and abandoned her. Her mother's personal pain and fears, her bitter disappointments, has made life grim for her on most levels. Dixie wonders, was she the reason for their brokenness? Now it's happening all over again. The father of her children is doing basically the same thing, abandoning her for the church. For God of all things! How does one stand up to that? She has tried everything she knows to be of worth and valued just for who she is. But all she feels is failure. Her dreams are dashed. Nothing works. She is at the bottom.

The heavenly Father is her final solution. There is nothing else.

The days pass slowly. I continue my work responsibilities, but my mind and heart are not in the daily tasks. I, too, am praying, searching my heart, feeling torn between the calling of God and my love of wife and children. I am racked with feelings of remorse and failure, caught in a web of my own making, excuses unraveling, guilt increasing, unsure of my next moves. It seems both God and my wife need and expect more from me than I am able to deliver. Will she be coming back? Is this the beginning of the end? What will it be like when she returns? How did I ever let things get so messed up? It's all my fault, isn't it?

When she returns home, Dixie has changed. Both her countenance and attitude is different. We talk our way through tears. Now it is my turn to change. The relationship we once treasured more than anything has become frayed with the cares of life. My priorities are out of whack.

Slowly, hearts that are wounded and fragile begin to mend and be strengthened by the repositioning of priorities, by making God, not just the church, our center; putting our life together truly and forever in his hands. Is it all well and wonderful after this? I would like to say, yes, but the truth is, no, not always. Like most married couples, especially I believe, those of us in ministry, we have other challenges to work through. Other times when priorities are again misplaced.

Successful marriages are not easy. They do not just happen. But we continue to learn as we go, to pray and work as equal partners, to listen, to talk, to forgive, and most of all to love regardless. The end result is an *extra*ordinary life together; life filled with love and many moments of sheer pleasure and delight in each other, resulting in an *extra*ordinary marriage.

The skills development I experience in teaching a weeknight Bible study, preaching twice each Sunday, and engaging in a building project from start to finish, molds and shapes me. Nonetheless it remains a hard season for Dixie as she comes to terms with the life she is in and the sacrifices that are hers to make as a pastor's wife. And a lesson for me as I wrestle with priorities and purpose in life and ministry.

We speak often of the mission field during these years. We are invited by several missionaries to consider the lands and people they serve, specifically Thailand, Indonesia, and Guatemala. In each situation we open our hearts to God. We even discuss becoming Wycliffe missionaries. But there remains a hesitancy, not with regard to the physical difficulties that might ensue, but as to whether or not this is truly the direction our lives should take. We endeavor to be of one mind on the big decisions and so we cool natural enthusiasms of the moment in order to be clear about next steps.

After more than five years of doing our best to serve this church and its surrounding community, I am elected by pastors and church delegates from across Washington and northern

Idaho to be the next denominational district youth and men's ministries director. Back home in Forks, we are treated to a special farewell luncheon by community leaders, say a fond farewell to our church family, and soon we are on our way.

⌢

This next move takes us to the suburban city of Kirkland, Washington, east of Lake Washington, near Seattle. At the time, this is the headquarters city for the Northwest District of the Assemblies of God and the new campus of Northwest College (now University), my alma mater. For the next four years, I am in youth ministry, while serving concurrently as district camping coordinator, Men's Ministries director, Royal Ranger (scouting) director, and whatever other assignment is given me in the absence of formal leadership by anyone else.

It is an exciting time doing what we love, working with young people. One of the major events each year is the Northwest Youth Choir program. Young singers and musicians audition from churches across Washington and Northern Idaho. As many as one hundred fifty selected youth gather in Seattle over the Christmas holidays to work with recording artist, Bud Tutmarc, in creating a long-play record album. When the album is cut, these same young people make it available to family and friends in their churches and communities to help pay their way on one of two three-week concert tours in the following summers.

The larger groups are divided into two smaller traveling choirs ranging anywhere from 45–75 in number. Concerts take place across America, including Alaska and Hawaii, in churches and public auditoriums, denominational conferences and national parks, military installations including Fort Riley, Kansas, and the Air Force Academy Chapel. Dixie and I are on the road with these young people for six weeks every summer. It is an incredible experience for everyone. Many of these youth go on in vocational ministry or as professional Christian business leaders.

Then, one dark and stormy night while returning from having preached in Olympia, Washington, I am involved in a serious auto accident that totals my Volkswagen and leaves me in the hospital with major surgery being performed on my face and right eye. It is one of those wake up calls reminding me that, once again, I am doing too much, going too fast, trying too hard.

A few months after this, I receive an invitation to consider becoming the AG National College Youth Director, a role that would necessitate a move back to the headquarters city of Springfield, Missouri, where for a few short weeks we had begun our married life together.

At the same time, I am invited to become Director of Public Relations for Northwest University. And another "what if" decision is made. I take the post at NU with the proviso that I can resume my graduate education at nearby Seattle Pacific University's School of Religion.

Dixie often declares this seven-year period, during which we make our home in Kirkland, as the best time in our lives. Once both the children are in school, she takes a position as administrative assistant to the NWAG District Secretary/Treasurer. The income helps make ends meet in our growing family and we purchase our first home. She eventually takes time out to be a full time mom, then later on, works part time as an assistant in the University bookstore. She does well emotionally and physically. The people pressure she had experienced in pastoral work is gone. She feels rested and alive and accepted. And she loves the new friends she makes with other youth workers and college faculty.

The one downside is that I travel so much in order to do the work. I am gone on most weekends and for weeks on end during summers in choir tours, youth camps and retreat events. She travels with me, joining three other couples who serve as adult chaperones on youth choir tours, and goes with me as I lead the Northwest University choir and orchestra on a musical ministry tour into Scandinavia. On many of these trips we take our son, Stephen, who loves traveling with the young people. Michele is much more interested in staying with Gramma and Grandpa Tanneberg and her cousins, while Mom and Dad are away.

Still, it is for me a restless season. With my studies at SPU nearing an end, I want to move out of promotional activities with the college. I love the people with whom I work. I just don't love the work.

17

Success and Sadness

Don't tell anyone you are starting a new church.
Just do it inside your head and in your heart.
~ Bill Yeager, former senior pastor
First Baptist Church (CrossPoint), Modesto CA

When a call comes from a small church in Dublin, California, asking me to bring my family to the Bay Area to serve as pastor, I am unsure. This is not part of our dream for the future. I'm not interested in taking on another church, one even smaller than our first. But after prayerful consideration, in the autumn of 1971, we begin what will eventually be twenty-three years of pastoral ministry in that community.

During the first three years it appears as though we are failing, faster and with greater certainty than anything I've ever done before. I am sure I've made a huge mistake. After seven months, only seventeen of the forty-five people who voted for us to come still remain. I am depressed. Dixie is hanging in. The children are struggling in their new schools. Outside of the few who make up the church, we are strangers in a foreign land. In the Northwest, we had a sterling reputation with lots of future upside. Here we have a struggling church with a Christian elementary school in its second year. We have people being transferred by their companies or simply leaving because we have no formal youth ministry. We have difficulty meeting the basic budget.

It's at this point the church board decides we should meet together early on Tuesdays to pray about the situation. I don't want to pray. I want to go back home to the Northwest where life was a whole lot easier. But how do you tell your deacon board you don't want to pray? And so we gather. The first Tuesday there are two others with me. The second Tuesday there is one other and me. The third Tuesday, a dreary foggy morning, there is just me.

Frustrated and angry, I pour out my heart to God. And since no one else is around, I tell it like I think it is. I dump a huge weight off my shoulders and onto God's. I say things to God that remain between only the two of us to this day. It isn't a pretty picture. Finally, after a long period of complaining and dumping, I stop, breathing heavily and exhausted. It is silent for a long time as I remain there on my knees, face buried in the front pew of the auditorium.

I cannot say I hear an audible voice. But I can say I hear the voice of God as clear as though someone is right beside me, speaking. And the conversation goes like this:

"Are you done yet?"

"What?"

"Are you done yet. Is this the best you've got? Is there anything else you'd like to say to me?"

"Well... no... no, I think I've pretty well summed it up."

"Then let me ask you a question."

"Okay."

"Who are you trying to impress?"

"What?"

"Who are you trying to impress?"

I had to stop and think about this for a long moment.

"Well, I guess it isn't the people who asked me to come here in the first place. Most of them are already gone. There are a few hangers on, but look for yourself. I'm failing, and I don't know what to do. Can I just go now?"

"No. Listen. You are not going anywhere. This is what you are to do. I want you to open your heart to whoever comes through that door (I remember looking up at the main entrance door leading into the sanctuary). It doesn't matter who they are or what their religious background is, or if they even have one. I want you to be open to everyone."

"But what if they don't believe in our church doctrines? What if they disagree with some of the things we hold to be tenets of the faith?"

"It doesn't matter. Just do it. Keep an open mind and an open heart toward everyone and let the Bible be your guide. You preach the Word. I'll do the rest."

I cannot adequately express how profound a moment this is for me. I return home to tell Dixie what has just happened. I think she is grateful. If this really is God, at least he knows we are here. She had not wanted to come to California in the first place. But if he really is with us, well, let's give it our best shot.

Things do not change overnight, but it is different. I am different! God has spoken to my heart in such a clear way. Then one day a pastor I have known for just a few minutes gives me another word of wisdom. He is the senior pastor of First Baptist Church of Modesto, California. We are at a conference and he and I are talking about my situation in Dublin when he says to me, "Why don't you just start a new church?"

I say, "Are you serious? I can't even keep the one going I have now."

"No, that's not what I mean," he responds with a chuckle. "Don't tell anyone you are starting a new church. Just do it inside your head and in your heart. Begin building the congregation you believe God wants you to grow. New people will join with you in your new church. Others already there will do one of two things. They will either drift away, which will happen sooner or later anyway. Or they will see how exciting things are in your new church and become a vital part of it with you."

It sounded a lot like what I had heard on a cold and foggy Tuesday morning while kneeling in the chapel. And so I did. And soon we did.

The years at Valley Christian Center are a wonderful time of spiritual and numerical growth. The church soon outgrows the Little Chapel, and for seven years we rent auditorium space in the Dublin High School. We also rent space in various buildings nearby for our children's ministries and office space for our growing ministry team. More classroom space for our Christian school, by this time preschool through grade 8, also needs to be rented.

One day, as we drive along the Interstate north toward Walnut Creek, I glance at Dixie in the passenger seat. She is looking out over the rooftops of houses on the right side of the freeway and her lips are moving, but no words are coming.

"What are you doing?" I ask.

"I'm praying that God will somehow let us bring the gospel of Jesus into everyone of these homes."

"Wow," I said, "that's a great big prayer."

Eventually we seek and receive licensed access to a public television channel that covers the five-city area we serve. Her prayer is answered in an amazing way. We are actually invited into every home that has a television set, broadcasting the Good News twenty-four hours a day, every day of the year.

○

We have many grand times in our family as the church continues its new upward spiral.

Like the infamous bicycle trip.

It all starts while joking with Mom about taking a bicycle vacation as a family. We can go down scenic Highway 1. We'll have a great time together. After much teasing, since we are certain she will never do it, one day she says, "Okay, I'm in!" The kids and I are stunned, especially me. But the gauntlet has been thrown down and once that happens in our family there is no turning back.

5 Dixie went fishing once - the only fish she ever caught - 115 lbs!

What's the first thing we have to do? Get in shape? No, the first thing we have to do is buy some bicycles. Only Stephen has a bicycle and it will never stand up to this kind of trip. The rest of us haven't been on bicycles in years. At first we decide to pedal as far as San Simeon, the highlight being a visit to Hearst's Castle. That will be educational, right? Then we can pedal back.

I'm not saying who came up with the next idea, but someone, while checking out a Coastal map says, "Look, we're half way down the coast at San Simeon. If we just keep on pedaling, we can go all the way to Mexico! We can visit the zoo and Sea World in San Diego and when we are done, we can take the train back. Just look at the map. Going south it's downhill all the way."

And that's how it begins.

When my Rotary Club hears about it they decide to raise money for a project, posting so much per mile, thinking we will not get any further than Santa Cruz. It becomes a front-page story in the daily newspaper and results in a lifelong spiritual friendship with the editor who writes the piece.

Dixie and I train every Monday for six weeks. On our final outing we do forty-five miles on a Class-A-rated bicycle route. Breathless upon our arrival back home, we look at one another and ask, "Are we really going to do this?"

But early the next summer Monday morning, our executive pastor drives us to Half Moon Bay, just south of San Francisco, drops us off with our bicycles and our packs, waves goodbye and drives away. And here we are. All alone. Looking down the highway at a first day trek of sixty miles to Santa Cruz.

I give my best words of family wisdom to all within earshot; to my beloved wife who cannot believe she has allowed this to happen to her, as well as to our two eager children, Michele, age 16, and Stephen, who turns 13 on the trip. "Okay everyone. This is going to be great fun. Michele, you take the lead. Stephen, you're next. Then Mom. I'll bring up the rear. That way if anyone gets hit by a car, I will be the first to go. Okay? Oh, and one more thing. We are not going to have a cross word from anyone. Agreed? No yelling, no fighting, only positivity. All right? Everybody happy? Okay."

And off we go.

Before we have gone two miles, Stephen is busy touching Michele's rear tire with his front tire. Michele is yelling at him to stop it. Stephen is laughing and still touching. Soon they are both off their bikes and in the ditch. Michele is ready to destroy her brother and Stephen can't stop laughing. I am alongside, yelling at them both. And Mom sits astride her bicycle with an I-told-you-so-smirk that finally has us all in stitches!

The sixty miles that day takes an extra ninety minutes over my estimated time of arrival. Stephen and I jump into the motel pool while the girls shower. We are sore in places no one ever told us existed. I hire a cab to take us to a nice restaurant. No sense suggesting we could ride there on our bicycles. Not if I want to sleep inside tonight.

The next day we are on our bicycles again, albeit almost too sore to sit, off on the next leg of our journey, this time to Carmel. Fifteen days and way too many funny stories later we have pedaled 726 miles all the way to and through Greater Los Angeles and San Diego until we arrive at the Mexico border. We ride home on the train.

In spite of the logistic dilemmas caused by the growth in numbers, God continues to bless our work. Then comes the acquisition of

49-acres overlooking the Tri-Valley area of Dublin, Pleasanton, Livermore, San Ramon and Danville. There follows a complicated property development and several building programs, and the opening of Valley Christian High School.

In responding to an appeal for spiritual leadership and training made by the growing number of Valley Christian Center women, Dixie is asked by the church board to consider leaving a job she loves as office manager at TJKM Engineering, to become pastor to women and minister of adult Christian education. It is a huge decision for her. She enumerates all the natural reasons why she should not accept, her reluctance wrapped in great feelings of inadequacy and humility.

Still, she is urged to think about what she could do if she would reconsider. It is only after becoming certain in her heart, and with the affirmation of the congregation, that she agrees to accept this very important transition on her sacred journey. In the final word, it is not a call by the church board that elicits her yes. It is the call from her Father.

These years, however, also have a dark side. My dad is the first to leave us. I miss him greatly. He was always such a solid and loving man, greatly respected in the community, a real leader. I often find myself measuring my own life by his, wondering if he will approve of my making this decision or that. He became a follower of Jesus at age seventy-five, just three years before his passing.

We visit my parents during Dad's final days in his battle with cancer. I ask if he would like to go out to the farm again and he says he would. I help him into the car and we make our last trip together. We drive the eleven miles to the farm and park in the dirt driveway. I turn off the motor and watch while he gazes at the old house we had once lived in, the work shed with its tools and farm implements scattered about. Then he points to the two fuel tanks mounted on a wooden platform, about a hundred feet away. "Would you mind turning off that valve?" he asks. "Someone left it on and it's leaking fuel."

I look to where he is pointing and cannot see anything out of the ordinary. But I learned long ago to do what Dad tells me and, sure enough, it is exactly as he says. I twist the handle to off, still not sure how he saw it.

I drive the car a little way into a nearby field. He opens the door and gathers two or three heads of wheat, rolling them in his hands, as farmers have done for centuries, to tell the ripeness of the grain. I have seen him do this so often, it causes me to smile. "Not quite ready yet," he says. "Maybe two or three weeks unless it warms up some."

We drive on a few miles further out into the country to a location he wants to see for reasons still unknown to me, and then he is okay, ready to go home.

The next day, we drive with Mom and Dad to Wenatchee, from where Dixie and I will leave for California. I get out of the car, lean back in, and give Dad a long hug.

"I love you, son," he says, a tear in his eyes.

"I love you, too, Dad."

And that's it. A farmer and his son say goodbye. A few days later he is gone. I make a mental note of the fact that it is the first time I can ever remember him saying those words to me.

"I love you, son."

But never for an instant in my entire life did I doubt it. He was old school. His parents came to America from the old country of Denmark. If you show love no one needs to wonder. Still, I treasure the memory of hearing the words that expressed what I have felt all of my life.

Six years later, it is my mother. She has sold the farm and moved to Wenatchee. She visits us in California two or three times each year and we love having her with us. During these times she takes over household duties, including meals. I bring her to staff meetings with me and she and Dixie go shopping in San Francisco to get her wardrobe changes. We are all so good for each other, but especially Mom and Dixie. They each mentor the other in different ways, and have for as many years as they have been family. And now she is gone.

Eighteen days after my mother, and two thousand miles away, it is Dixie's mother. A massive heart attack. Now both have been suddenly taken from us. On our way home from the funeral in Tulsa we talk about our church family. What must they be thinking? Every time we turn around of late it seems something bad is happening. But it isn't over yet.

Not long after, our children, always a bright light in our lives, are the next to suffer pain. Satan knows how to attack at our greatest vulnerability. For us it is our children. Our grandson, Kristian Andrew, is born prematurely, weighing only two pounds and living a mere thirteen days. His mother is with him, holding his tiny hand, every day. Hundreds gather with us outdoors at the cemetery in saying this latest goodbye. It is also a hard season for our son as his young marriage ends in divorce.

It is difficult when bad things happen to you.

Harder when it happens to those you love.

This is one of our darkest seasons as one loss piles upon another. All within ninety days. We know our children are hurt, angry, heartbroken. Tearing away in relationships of their own, and from us as well.

The following summer of 1985, Dixie and I fly to Europe on our first sabbatical. For ten weeks we wander through the cities and countrysides of western Europe, as well as several days in Russian-controlled East Germany. It takes considerable time, but we are finally able to break through the emotional trauma of our lives and feel once more that things are going to be okay.

We return to our work in Dublin and for the next ten years continue serving as senior pastor and pastor to women and adult Christian education, respectively, at Valley Christian Center. We conduct marriage enrichment seminars in our church and throughout the Western states. There will be more growth, more challenges, more staff and family difficulties, a 49-acre property acquisition and raw land development, several building programs, more stress. Eventually, Dixie retires from her staff role, continuing to train and mentor her successor.

She and I take long walks early each morning during which times the conversation often turns to the future. Our children are at the center of our thoughts. They are both struggling. We are absorbed with grieving over their losses and ours. Life is not a yellow brick road. Not anymore. Not for them or for us.

There follow periods of parent/child estrangement. The close relationships we had nurtured through a lifetime seem to have vanished. We have no one to talk to but each other and the counselor who tries to help with insights as to what is happening in our lives. Dixie sees the toll life and ministry is taking. What used to be exciting and fun isn't anymore. And so on our long morning walks the conversation shifts to what life may be like for us after Valley Christian Center.

One morning I see Dixie reading her Bible and ask what portion she is in. She looks up with sadness in her eyes and says, "Job." I nod and say, "Me, too." I have grown to believe one understands Job best when read at a feeling level instead of a theological level. You have to *feel* Job to understand Job.

And so, in the summer of 1994, I make my way to Turkey for three weeks to research the novel, *Pursuit,* that I am currently writing. Before leaving, I meet with the church board and submit to them my formal letter of resignation, allowing for a four-month interval of time until I step away from my leadership role. Dixie and a group of travelers from our church meet me in Athens. We continue on together, leading an educational tour through the Greek Isles and Israel.

On the week following our return, thoroughly spent and emotionally exhausted, I resign my leadership role as senior pastor. The following year we move to Palm Desert, California.

18

Full Circle

The breath of God, the Holy Spirit, breathes "life" into my being. Lord, I'm grateful for your very breath that gives me life. It's like the continual breathing of your Spirit into my needy life. Breathe on me breath of life. Fill all my being with you! The gentle breeze that moves through the branches of the trees outside my window reminds me to breathe in the life-giving breath of God. ~ DLT, June 2014

We think we will be here forever. After months of searching places where we might go to live following our lifetime in Dublin, we settle into our desert home and begin making new friends. We love our new home. It is the first time we've ever chosen to live anywhere without it being related to our work. We are like bottles bobbing on the water, pressure free. Our daughter and granddaughter, Katy, also live nearby.

Our sojourn in the desert is at first recovery time, emotional, physical, and spiritual. We need to renew our lives following the years in which we have given our best effort and complete energy to the people and the development of the church and Christian schools, counseling center, and television work. Too

6 Mom and Michele were never far apart.

much perhaps. And so we turn to repairing our family and our own lives as well.

This period in our sacred journey is a time to help Michele and Katy restore relationship with one another and with us. I spend many 100+ degree days in the afternoon sun watching our granddaughter become the slugger on her softball team. Her batting average makes her one of the best in the valley, boys or girls. Game times are followed with a stop at Carl's Jr., refilling her depleted energy with a cheeseburger and coke, and then a swim in the pool until Mom gets off work. Building relationships. Providing a safety net that spells family for a young teenager caught up in a dysfunctional world not of her own choosing.

Dixie is the real key in this time of renewal and restoration. Stephen has remarried and is living in Savannah, Georgia. Their relationship with us is made more difficult by distance. Michele is closer geographically and this affords time for her and Mom to walk and talk on picturesque sidewalks and golf course pathways. It is an essential time for Mom to be the mom, to come alongside our daughter who had been hurt on so many different levels.

In 1997, I finish a book with a writing partner who lives in Oklahoma City. We are together in San Diego for one day to address the necessary final edits and other required changes. I return home and the following day, feel a bit under the weather. Nevertheless, our friends, John and Betty, drive us to the Palm Springs airport and say goodbye.

We board a plane bound for Boston where we plan to launch a New England exploration for a large home needing a lot of work (that would be son Stephen) with an ultimate goal of opening a commercial bed and breakfast (that would be daughter Michele) for tourists and others who want a weekend getaway. One that would also be suitable for pastors and spouses needing a place to rest and renew during the weekdays. It seems like a noble idea and a way to involve our whole family in a project together.

However, when we land in Denver, I am removed from the plane by EMTs, placed in an ambulance and am unconscious before we get away from the airport. I am rushed to Denver University Hospital, arriving with a temperature over 105 degrees. When I regain consciousness, I am on an ER cool bed while medical staff try their best to lower my temperature.

Meanwhile, Dixie is left alone at the airport to recover our luggage and find a taxi into the city. The eventual diagnosis is E-coli bacteria throughout my entire system. That night I continue to worsen and am transferred to ICU, where I remain for the next seven days. A late night surgery is performed, but to no avail. After all that can be done appears to have been done, doctors encourage Dixie to call the children to come, if they want to see their father alive one last time.

Every doctor and nurse in the hospital who knows how to pray is praying for me. Friends back home, our former church family, people everywhere who know us, pray. As a last resort, I agree to receive an experimental drug not yet on the market. For seven days, Dixie and friends from our former church who live in Denver, stay at my side. Then suddenly, on Day 7, after doctors say there is nothing more they can do, the fever breaks. Three days later and twenty pounds lighter, I am helped onto an airplane and return to Palm Desert and home.

While recovering at home, Dixie comes into the bedroom with coffee and toast. Smiling she leans down, brushing her cheek against mine and says sweetly, "So, what do you think we've learned from all this?" It is a question for which she is famous around the family dinner table after times of stress or on special holidays.

To which I reply, "There is only one thing I know for certain. I don't think we're supposed to go to Boston!" And we don't.

The opportunity to "come full circle" begins with a suggestion in the summer of 1998 to consider joining a pastoral staff in the locale in which we had lived before coming to California.

Initially I say no. I have never been part of anyone else's church staff and am not interested in starting now. But months later, after much prayer and several interview visits, we agree to leave our home in the desert and return to the Northwest. We have been away for twenty-eight years.

It is hard for me to believe, but I am now a member of the pastoral staff of Westminster Chapel of Bellevue, Washington, a nondenominational church in which I have never attended a worship service or heard the pastor preach, until the one in which Dixie and I are introduced.

My initial assignment is to lead in pastoral care. Eventually I am asked to serve as the church's first executive pastor. We have been here about a year when Dixie is asked to fill in the women's ministry department until a new leader can be selected. It is not long until a recognition of her calling and capable leadership is recognized. She continues filling in for six more years as Westminster's minister to women. Once again we are both extremely busy.

Our home today is located in what I call the urban rugged cities of Seattle/Bellevue, surrounded as they are by the Olympic and Cascade mountain ranges, and separated by a large body of water known as Lake Washington. We live on the Eastside, in downtown Bellevue. The driving distance around the lake shortened for commuters by two engineering marvels, the I-90 and SR 520 floating bridges.

It is Wednesday when we leave our Bellevue apartment and "give to Caesar what belongs to Caesar," passing through the all-electronic Good to Go! toll area. At the same time, we "give to

God what belongs to God," by indulging in scenes of deep blue water and green trees, pleasure boats and endless traffic. We gaze at the beauty of snow-capped Mount Rainier, tall and majestic in the distance, and for a few brief minutes do a floating bridge version of "walking on the water" before entering downtown Seattle.

The afternoon is taken up with Dixie prepping for and accepting another CT scan with IV contrast, as doctors continue to update their patient's status. We are informed that the "automated exposure control and statistical iterative reconstruction techniques substantially lowered patient radiation dose." This is meant to be reassuring? Actually, it's okay. It's the least of our concerns right now. The outcome is what is important to us. Another blood draw follows to ensure white cell counts are responding to last week's booster shots.

On Thursday, we meet with the always pleasant, always thorough, always late, Dr. Gabriela Chiorean. The CT scan report states the patient is "status post Whipple without evidence for local recurrence." Dr. Chiorean explains that the liver lesions seen previously are no longer visualized, indicating they were indeed infections that have responded to treatment. They are not cancer. There is, however, a new area of hyper-enhancement noted in a different location in the liver. They are not sure what this new discovery might suggest, but another round of antibiotics is prescribed. Short-term follow-up imaging to exclude subtle metastasis is also recommended. Bottom line on this day, no new pulmonary nodule can be seen and there is no evidence of new distant metastatic disease. Another victory? One is never quite sure.

Following our time with Dr. Chiorean, we go to F5, where Dixie is readied for her third chemo infusion of *Gemcitabine*. To help offset the nausea side-effects Dixie has been experiencing, an anti-nausea drug is given before the infusion. And an additional prescription to take home. At last we arrive home at 5:30, where we are welcomed by Margaret, a dear friend who has been patiently waiting in the visitors' area with a homemade berry pie no less. A pleasant intermission in a not so perfect day.

Next week, Dixie has drawn a bye week, as the Seattle Seahawks would call it. In sports it's a week when the team doesn't have a game scheduled and can give bruised and banged up bodies a rest. She needs this big time for her own body, still recovering from surgery and the effects of chemotherapy. It is a hard time but we are grateful for what we are learning.

19

Farewell for Awhile

It is always harder to be left behind than to be the one to go…
~ Brock Thoene, Shiloh Autumn

⌒

Sunday 11 May. In 2008 I accepted the position of president/executive director of CASA 50+ Network, a ministry targeting pastors and lay leaders of church ministries for people in life's second half, one in which I have been involved as a guest speaker, editor and writer since 1998.

Now, six years later, Dixie and I are about to be separated once more by thousands of miles of land and seas. One of the projects we developed over the past year is happening right now. *"A Journey with the Apostles: Exploring Turkey & Greece,"* is an inspirational and educational program that follows the ministries of Paul and John, both saints and part of our spiritual heritage in the truest sense. Today we say goodbye at SeaTac International as I join others gathering at airports in Seattle, San Francisco and Dallas, ready for their journeys into the modern/ancient world of Christianity's earliest beginnings.

I leave with mixed emotions huddled in the corners of my heart. It is good to do this on several levels, yet bittersweet, for this is a journey Dixie and I planned to make together. She has been looking forward to it and I miss her already, even before our plane has left the ground. She remains behind with many friends surrounding her in my absence, good medical care, and she has our daughter, Michele.

While Stephen was with us for a week before returning to Hong Kong, he and Michele had opportunity to spend quality time together. Geographic distance is always an issue where he is concerned. For a while, emotional distance broke down lines of communication as well. Intentional effort on their parts and ours have restored these bonds. Now, among the many things brothers/sisters share with each other, they have their "where are our parents tonight" conversations, replacing the "where are our children" conversations of an era gone by. Our children's parents have always been hard for them to keep track of.

Stephen and family have lived in distant places all their married lives. Michele has somehow managed to stay geographically close to us throughout. Having one of our children nearby has been a gift to us. She and Dixie enjoy a mother-daughter closeness, having developed a deep and healthy bond that has survived and thrived through the years, in times both good and bad.

Dixie and I discussed the timing of this particular travel event. While I had canceled a teaching assignment in Russia in March, along with other responsibilities, our long-standing commitment to so many on this journey into Turkey and Greece was one we agreed we must honor. In a way, this is also mine and Mark's gift to Michele and her mom. Two weeks for them to live and laugh and play with just each other. Making memories. Mark decides to go with me rather than camp out at home alone.

I'm thinking this is a good thing as the plane lifts off and banks to the north and east. At least it is my rationalization. Still, I miss her already.

I was really lonesome today. As a matter of fact, I still am. It seems like every day it gets a little harder. Not harder to wait for you, but harder to keep my mind off you until I get so lonesome I am miserable. However, I can truthfully say that I would rather be lonesome and miserable waiting for you than not to have you at all. At least I know you will be here sooner or later. Sooner I hope. I was thinking the other day how completely happy and contented I am. I even feel closer to God. Maybe it's because we've both prayed so earnestly for God's perfect will that he has given me the very best there is in you. ~ DLT letter, June 25 1955

Letters seem to be such a poor substitute for you, but I am really proud of you, and I'm glad you're doing what God wants you to do. You mentioned in one of your letters there would probably be lots of times when we would be separated from each other. The more I thought about that, the more I realize it's true, but Ward, the reward will be so great. Maybe not here on earth, but when we get to heaven. I want to have "sheaves" to lay at the Master's feet and hear him tell us, "Well done." Even with all the separation and things that might come our way, I would rather spend my life with you in the work of God than anything else I can think of. ~ DLT letter, 30 June 1955

These are more of those days we imagined would come, in long ago letters during our courtship. Even in the first year of our courtship, we were apart more than we were together. To my younger readers, I cannot over emphasize counting the cost ahead of commitment to a lifetime with the person with whom you've fallen hopelessly in love. I know, hormones rage, the moon is full, and romance is in the air as it should be. I get all that.

But for all the reasons why you are certain you will live happily ever after, there are also reasons why you will not. Examine those reasons honestly and carefully ahead of time as best you can. For us, one of our costs has been the many times of separation. Sometimes two or three days. Sometimes two or three weeks. A part of our commitment to serving our Lord and those he loves. Each separation comes with its own price. Some higher than others.

Friday 16 May. We are driving through rugged south-central Anatolia, 5500 feet above sea level, on our way down to seaside Antalya, where we will spend two nights. It has been a hard week for Dixie as side-effects of chemotherapy are in play. We talk together every day via FaceTime. (Technology definitely has a good side.) But I see in her eyes she is suffering. It hurts my heart.

Everyone here keeps her in their prayers each day. I urge her to check in with SCCA to apprise them of what she is experiencing. On Thursday night she looks better, but we both know there is more to come. Two travelers, Lorilee and Cindy, both cancer survivors, send Dixie advice about what to do should there be hair loss. It is one of her ongoing practical concerns.

At a roadside restaurant high in the Taurus Mountains, our journey family celebrates birthdays for two in our group, replete with cakes and songs and laughter. We even sing the birthday song in Turkish. The yin and yang of life. Two days ago we were 400 meters (1300 feet) above ground in a hot air balloon, and 60 feet below the earth in a cave labyrinth carved out by the hands of generations, beginning with the Hittites and continuing to the earliest Christians. All in the same day. Joy and happiness. Pain and suffering. Life. We must be careful not to seek only good times and curse the bad. Both are the ingredients from which a rich and complete life is made. Jesus taught us this by his word and in his example.

I remind myself of this important truth as Dixie resumes her chemotherapy schedule at SCCA; a second round of *Gemcitabine* infusions that will happen each week for three more weeks. Every Thursday. Our prayer is for victory over this Enemy Cancer. We ask for wisdom and great care from doctors and caregivers. Strength and health for body and soul. Understanding and patience as we dig our way through life's labyrinth. Joy and happiness. Pain and suffering. All in the same day.

For you are our glory and joy. ~1 Thessalonians 2:20

More days and nights come and go. Soon after our arrival in Athens, Mark manages a text contact with Michele. He reports that she and Mom have just arrived home and are preparing something to eat. I check the time difference in my mind. It is past 8:30 PDT. Why so long a day for them? No word on this. The connection has been interrupted. Attempts to reconnect do not work. We've had long hours before at SCCA, but this late? Is something wrong? Separated by so much land and water and sky, I can only wonder. And pray. Technology has failed me. Mark reassures me that all must be well or they would be reaching out through our predetermined emergency chain of contacts. Still...

Saturday 24 May 7:30 AM (9:30 PM Friday PDT). Days ago in Istanbul, one of our travelers placed in my hand a rock on which is inscribed, *For he will order his angels to protect you in all you do ~ Psalm 91:11.* And so it has been.

Two weeks have passed. We are on our way home, flying somewhere between Athens and Frankfurt. Everyone is safely on board. No serious illnesses. Two successful, inspiring and educational weeks behind us, trekking through modern Turkey, the Aegean Isles of Patmos, Rhodes, Crete, Santorini and, finally, Corinth and Athens, unpacking the biblical world of early Christianity. I am pleased that everyone is returning home with happy hearts.

I, too, am looking forward to home, to reuniting with Dixie and our daughter, Michele. It has been three days since seeing or talking with either of them. Internet connections are too poor for FaceTime in the islands, and almost always onboard ship. Hotel Internet in Athens was no better.

I listen to the voices and laughter of our travelers gathered in the aisle around me, sharing news of their respective journeys with new friends, a group from Texas having spent the last four days in Athens. Swapping stories of guides and coach drivers, sounds and smells, hotels and scenic byways, all the things that enrich the traveler's soul. Memories soon to be shared with family and friends at home are being tested and refined with strangers whose only real affinity is that of having recently returned from their own fields of adventure. It is all so natural, so necessary to do. Yet my own thoughts take me to a distant place, one that draws closer with each passing hour as we fly from east to west with the sun.

We are homeward bound.

The pilot informs that we will soon be landing in Frankfurt, where we will transfer to our next flight. An attendant tells us, upon arrival we should hurry to ensure making our connection, noting since we are Americans we may have to pass through two security check points instead of one. It seems Americans have become high maintenance in today's world of travel. We say goodbye to Elizabeth, who is flying directly to Dallas. The rest of us prepare for the remaining eleven-hour flight to Seattle.

Saturday 24 May 2:05 PDT. I send a text to Dixie, "Hummer landed." We arrive almost a half hour late, disembark, and with hundreds of other citizens and guests of our great nation, patiently make our way through customs and passport control, while being welcomed by smiling uniformed agents into the United States of America. We wish our Californians well as they hurry off to be among the last to board their connecting flight to San Francisco and just like that, for the first time in two weeks, Mark and I are alone! We text the girls again as we slowly make our way to the arrivals area.

In a short while, both Dixie and Michele greet us curbside and on the twenty-minute drive from SeaTac International Airport to our home, I hear the good news. While the treatment on Thursday had taken considerably longer, the results were worth the effort. New anti-nausea drugs were included with this chemotherapy and Dixie has had no recurring upsets since.

Michele has been the consummate caregiver. Dixie is eating small bites of anything she wishes every two hours (Michele arranged an automatic timer to sound off as a reminder), plus larger bits at mealtimes. All in all, a very positive step forward in the wellness process. The only new 'shadow' is a first notification from our medical insurance that some treatments already received will not be covered. "If we wish to appeal, etc..." And so it begins. Still, this is not enough to overshadow the progress, the renewed light in her eyes, the smile on her face as I gather her into my arms.

Welcome home!

20

Any Port in a Storm

Autumn is the most beautiful time of the year, when all the trees change to reds, golds, amber and orange. All favorite colors, with the depth of greens of all shades. What beauty!

God spoke all that beauty into being with words. Jesus spoke healing and the beauty of life into a 12-year-old girl, calmed a roaring sea, painted word pictures for people to understand. "He said" is a common phrase in the Gospels that mimics God the Father's voice throughout all of Scripture.

God still speaks through sights and sounds. The apostle Paul prayed for the Ephesians that the "eyes of their heart may be enlightened" to hear him speak and understand.

May my heart see and hear you with clarity and understanding. Thank you for the anticipation of all that I will yet experience. "No eye has seen no ear has heard, no mind has conceived what God has prepared for those who love him." May my eyes and heart reflect that joy! ~ DLT diary, September 2008

Tuesday 27 May. We meet again at SCCA with doctors from Infectious Diseases. The two liver spots having been treated with antibiotics are gone, but a new spot in a new location is now visible. They are unsure as to what this may represent, but will continue a regimen of antibiotics and schedule another CT-scan with dye, re-examining the liver, abdomen and lungs.

We are led to another room and our next appointment. A "New Port Teach" with everybody's favorite nurse, Deb Leslie (whom I tag as an SCCA equivalent of the career Master Sergeant). Loud, passionate, professional and caring, possessing what Israelis sometimes refer to as sabra spirit, tough and prickly on the outside, warm and mushy on the inside. She brings us up on what to expect regarding the new port insertion planned for the next day.

Wednesday. Following a blood draw, Dixie is prepped for what is slated to be "a minor surgical procedure that will not require general anesthesia." We meet the team that will do the deed. Eventually, I am politely excused to my home away from home in the waiting area and told it will be "one or two hours and someone will come looking for me." And so the process begins. It is being done because of the myriad blood draws and medications that have overwhelmed her veins abilities to cope.

In surgery, the port is placed just beneath her skin, the end of the catheter inserted into a large vein with the catheter tip placed near the heart. The port is located in her upper chest area just below the collarbone. Once the port is placed under her skin, it's ready to deliver medication into the bloodstream.

A special needle can be inserted through the flexible cover of her port, which connects to a catheter. She feels a mild pricking sensation during needle insertion and is given a tube of anesthetic cream to numb her skin an hour before each time her port is used in order to reduce discomfort. She never uses it. The port provides a method for collecting blood samples and may also deliver contrast media for CT scans.

Her port is designed to deliver medications and chemotherapy through the chosen large vein directly into her heart. This allows the medication to be diluted more quickly than if it were given in peripheral veins in her arms or hands. Also, by delivering chemotherapy directly into her heart, it will not further break down the peripheral veins, which already seem to roll up and run for cover whenever another needle is pointed in their direction.

Thursday. Early in the week, medications have held nausea at bay. Not today. This morning, vomiting returns with a vengeance, leaving her weak and thoroughly exhausted in the fight to regain control. The day continues its downhill roll when at 1:30 we arrive at SCCA for a blood draw, only to find the lab technicians will not draw from her port until it has been in place for at least twenty-four hours. During the patient checkup with Lisa Vanderhoef, PA-C, Dixie decides she is not up to taking the scheduled chemotherapy. Lisa checks with nurse Deb and they agree. Come back tomorrow. We drive home and Dixie goes straight to bed.

Friday. After resting through the night, we return for her initial port draw. It is a success. On we go to F5, where the new port is used again, first for a 72-hour anti-nausea medication, followed by the rescheduled *Gemcitabine* infusion. By 5 o'clock we are home again. It's been a busy week. Good days. Bad days. But all are days in which our Lord is never far away.

I've heard it said when the minister grows older, he learns to content himself more and does not expect so much from people. He learns to live with his disappointments. Can this be God's plan for us? Is there no more than this to expect from ministry? God help us all if this be true! I cannot reconcile myself to such a fate. Prove yourself and fulfill your promises in us. Use wherever and however you choose – but use us in a fruitful ministry, not one that is barren! ~ WT diary, November 1963

Last summer, we had the joy of celebrating 50 years of Valley Christian Center's existence in Dublin, California, the church we served for twenty-three of those years. This weekend, Westminster Chapel of Bellevue, Washington, where I served as care pastor and executive pastor and Dixie as minister to women, is celebrating its 50th anniversary. Once more we are filled with joy for what God has done on our respective sacred journeys.

And on this, one of their busiest of afternoons, we receive a lovely e-note from Pastor Gary, giving thanks for our having come to serve for a season as part of the Westminster staff, and for our mutual friendship. His warm note concludes by saying, "Celebrations are important. I felt like celebrating the two of you today and wanted you to know."

Relationships among colleagues in ministry are, I believe, divinely meant to bind us together. Such was the case with Paul, Barnabas, Timothy, young Mark and Peter. There are lists of others whose names are recorded in the Bible. Sadly, even the chosen Twelve discovered, as have we through the years, that such divinely appointed relationships do not always come to full fruition. But when they do it is very special, even transformational, leaving us forever changed for the better; more like Jesus, at having faithfully served together those whom Jesus loves.

21

Always a Bride

My thoughts today turn to being your bride. What does it mean to "be the bride of Christ?" After I had made the commitment to be Ward's bride, I set about planning a wedding... a party really. What I would wear, whom to invite, what to serve, how to decorate... all the important stuff.

7 The wedding - L-R Wanda, Dixie, Ward, Clyde

Ward, however, set about planning where and how we would live out our lives...plus, he made every effort to be with me as much and as often as possible. And in the "between times" he reminded me of his love through letters. All his efforts pointed toward the day we would be "together" for our lifetime.

If I had spent my preparation time and effort focused on spending a life of "singleness" and putting roots down where I was instead of preparing to go to live with him, I am sure he would have wondered about my commitment to become his bride.

How much of my time and efforts and preparation are focused on my comfort and life lived here, instead of preparing for when I shall come to live in the place you are building, in preparation for when we will be united in "marriage"... the bride of Christ?

Lord, lift my head so I can focus more on eternal things. Help me to keep perspective on this temporal life as it is just that... temporary... until I go to be with you.

In the meantime, help my "preparations for the wedding" be like planning the party that it is: invitations, serving, decor, and my clothing in righteousness and garments of praise. ~ DLT diary, June 1996

The evening is hot and muggy. I watch nervously as Dixie comes toward me, looking amazing, absolutely stunning in the bridal dress she has especially chosen for tonight; while I and the guys with whom I have sung and lived and traveled throughout much of America for the past two years, the guys directly responsible for our being introduced to each other in the beginning, now stand as a band of brothers looking on with me as I reach for her hand.

It is 2 June.

We sit at a table for two, gazing out at boats slipping across the water. A ship is passing as the sun prepares for its exit, bowing in silent elegance to the city across the harbor. It is Monday evening, not Saturday. The city is Seattle, not Tulsa. And the year 2014, not 1956. It is surreal. I look into her eyes. She returns the gaze with a smile that says she knows. I reach for her hand and utter a brief prayer of thanks as God and we together... in the same moment... are remembering.

How many times have we done this, since that first night? The night that I reached for her hand and we pledged our love to God and one another, "for richer, for poorer, in sickness and in health, 'til death do us part, so help us God." A cherished moment, then and now, as the three of us continue the sacred journey we began together, fifty-eight years ago. And I wonder... is this our last time?

Her hand is different tonight; warmer then, thinner now, and cooler from the chemo treatments she has endured these last weeks. And yet it's the same. This same hand held our children, while with the other she fed them their meals. This same hand held thousands of other hands through the years, as with an infectious smile and a warm hug she offered words of hope and encouragement and the promise of better days ahead.

8 Dixie wears her wedding dress on her 50th anniversary.

22

Why Do You Think You're Here?

Whoever reflects earnestly on the meaning of life is on the verge of an act of faith. ~ Paul Tillich

⌒

Thursday 5 June. Her day begins with an eight o'clock appointment at UWMC Radiology / Oncology Department, where she undergoes the latest CT reevaluation scan with dye. The liver still has small spots, but the doctors seem not too concerned. The spots do not look like cancer. The lungs appear to be stable, but one spot in this area is slightly larger than before (from 2mm to 4mm). Still too small to be of great concern unless it should grow to a full centimeter. They will keep a watch on this as well. Even the littlest of things are important now.

"Why do you think you're here?" Those are the words from the radiation oncologist. I give an explanation as to what I understand; then he asks what further questions do I have. My questions have to do with longevity and quality of life. He answers by reciting survival percentages, with and without radiation. Favorable percentages FOR the treatment prescribed push me in that direction. ~ DLT diary, 2015

Discussion continues regarding the purpose and plans for the radiation treatments that are about to become a vital part Dixie's wellness recovery regimen. The radiation treatment is being designed to pinpoint the precise location where the tumor had been, in order to lower the risk of cancer cells returning. This particular ampulla of vater carcinoma is very rare and aggressive and can return to the original site, while spreading to other areas at the same time. The combination of chemo and radiation therapy lowers that risk. She is told of studies showing the two treatments together having lowered risk of return on average from 40–50% to 10–15%.

Of course there are side effects to radiation therapy, as with chemotherapy. Localized aggressive treatment at the target area may cause damage to the surrounding tissue, like a scar from a cut on your hand. There is a small risk that the resulting scar tissue might require surgical removal. There may be additional nausea, needing to be managed with anti-nausea drugs similar to those with chemotherapy. Most certainly there will be added fatigue. The cumulative effect of radiation will build over the first three weeks, with fatigue and nausea becoming even more of a problem during the final three weeks of the regimen.

In the afternoon, at SCCA, Dr. Chiorean tells us the blood work of May 30 looks very good. The earlier schedule, after consultation with Dr. Kim, the attending radiologist, is being changed. No more chemo infusions for now. Her body will likely not stand up to it. Instead, she will take the chemo pill, *Xeloda*. Two in the morning and one at night, Monday throughout Friday, while undergoing radiation.

She is assured *Xeloda* is easier on the body, but can still cause mouth sores, nausea and / or diarrhea. Also the skin on palms and feet may become swollen and sore. While it is unlikely, she may also feel a tightness or burning in her chest. If any of these things happen, she is to stop taking *Xeloda* and call Dr. Chiorean. She is told any negative effects are reversible.

Dixie is to begin taking vitamin B6 (100mg) three times per day. Vitamin D (5000mg) once per day, along with the *Xeloda* and an antacid on the morning of radiation. This will help minimize the effects of radiation on the stomach. *Ondansetron* the morning of radiation will also help with nausea. It all sounds a lot like an advertisement for a drug on the evening news, during which all the predicted unwanted side effects take longer to tell about than do the reasons why you should take the medicine in the first place.

Next a visit with the Nutritionist and ideas designed to help regain weight. Dixie weighs in at 100 pounds, a 20 percent loss since this ordeal began. Use three-tablespoon equivalents of olive oil per day. Put it in smoothies along with rice protein powder from the health food store, vegetable juices, soups. Keep juices in the refrigerator. Drink less water and more juices, 60oz of fluid a day. Try *Kombucha*, a lightly effervescent fermented drink of sweetened black or green tea used as a functional food. For taste use a slow cooker for richer tasting food. Cook with chicken thighs for more fat. Trader Joe's has simmering sauces that will give flavor. In other words, do everything you can to regain some of the lost body weight. Really?

Later that night, Dixie keeps warm under a blanket in the library while writing in her notebook:

The lingering question still reverberates through my mind: "Why do you think you're here?" Only now the question has to do with my physical presence on earth and my present age. I am closer to the next "0" birthday than to the last. I've been engaged in ministry for all my adult life. My children are launched. I've enjoyed grandchildren, and even a great-grandchild. Do I still have a purpose? Why do I think I am here?

I am unable to answer that question as yet. Answering the oncologist was direct and on target. I was there to learn about the ramifications of radiation and what to expect, to learn about side effects and prolonged life. Answering a life question does not, in the immediate, seem so direct. And yet, isn't it much the same? If I am asking that question of God or he is asking it of me, what would my answer be?

"Why do you think you're here?"

Peter couldn't face the life "facts" that Jesus gave him about his future, so he diverted the direction of their conversation by asking about the life "facts" of John. Paul faced his life "facts" directly: "For to me, living is Christ and dying is gain" ~ Philippians 1:21.

I eagerly expect and hope that I will in no way be ashamed but will have sufficient courage so that now, as always, Christ will be exalted in my body whether in life or in death. For to me, living is Christ and dying is gain. If I am to go on living in the body, this will mean fruitful labor for me.

Fruitful labor. Does God look at percentages as the oncologist would? I think not. God looks for obedience and what it will do in and for the life of the individual.

Why do I think I am here at this time, in this condition, for whatever the length of time remaining on earth? What is of greater importance to life than to be obedient to God's will? To fulfill his purposes in and through me. This is why I am here. ~ DLT diary, June 2014

Friday. We cross the SR 520 bridge and return to UWMC. At 1:30, the Nurse Teach goes over the radiation procedure once more. There is the formal signing of a legal agreement giving permission to all that will be done and assuring the powers that be of all the things we will not do should anything go wrong. This is followed at 2 o'clock by yet another CT scan with dye and simulation, as the computer continues what it had begun the day before in making a high tech model of the target area on and in her body.

The radiation schedule is established, pushed out a few days because she has had the CT scan with contrast two days running. The contrast dye needs a chance to make its way through the kidneys. Too much all at once. The first radiation day will be Monday, 16 June, at 12:30, followed by treatments each morning at 8:30, Monday through Friday, for six weeks, ending 25 July.

23

Where Help Comes From

Lord, you know what's in my heart and you know what's in my way. Help me to fully surrender the first and fully conquer the other.

~ DLT diary, August 1990

As America's favorite author, storyteller, humorist, and radio talk show host, Garrison Keillor might say, "It's been a quiet week in Lake Wobegon." And a pretty good week, too, judging by recent week standards in our lives.

I take care of several appointments during the week, completely blowing one I had especially looked forward to, by getting too involved in some much needed catch up work. I've since been granted a second chance by this long-suffering friend; it seems more than the usual amount of grace is needed in my life these days. Is this something you notice in your life too?

Of course no week would be complete without the obligatory trip across Lake Washington to UWMC, or, as was the case this Thursday, a visit to the good folk at SCCA. All this week there have been no chemotherapy sessions, a big reason why it has been a "pretty good week." But this is about to change. So the trip to SCCA for a pharmacy teach with Dr Roy Mark is the last preparation event before the radiation / chemo combo gets underway on Monday.

The drug *Gemcitabine* is being replaced with *Capecitabine*, a type of chemotherapy that is used to treat many different cancers, including breast, colon and rectal cancers. *Capecitabine* interferes with the growth of cancer cells. And it is an oral medicine available in 150mg or 500mg tablets, Dixie's being the latter. The good doctor apologizes for the co-pay before he tells us the amount (always the harbinger of bad tidings when this happens). We are taught how and when to take the tablets, what to do if a dose is missed and, of course, the ever-present possible side effects.

The palms of your hands and soles of your feet may tingle, become red, numb, painful, or swollen. Your skin may become dry or itchy. If blisters, severe pain or ulcers occur, you may not be able to do your daily routine. Avoid tight fitting shoes, clean your hands and feet with lukewarm water; avoid hot water, and take Vitamin B6 to help mitigate this side effect.

There are other side effects including diarrhea, nausea, vomiting, and decreased blood counts (lowered platelet, red and white blood cells). Sores can occur on the tongue, the sides of the mouth or in the throat. Such sores and bleeding gums can lead to infection. One's skin may sunburn easily (welcome to summer). And fatigue. With the combination of daily radiation and chemotherapy (weekends excepted), increased fatigue is guaranteed between now and 25 July. There is a list of medicines to take, one after another, until one actually offsets the side effects if and when they come. We are assured these are the most common side effects, but there are others. We don't ask.

After July, two rounds of additional chemotherapy by infusion are anticipated, concluding sometime in September. If nothing untoward arises between now and then, seven months of healing and wellness will have come and gone. For Dixie and me, for our family, and for thousands of precious friends who have been our prayer partners through it all, a new day will dawn. Once again, our days will become weeks, and weeks will turn into months as health and strength is regained.

It is daunting. At times almost overwhelming. All the more reason we live one day at a time for now, with a huge dependence on prayer partners in the US and Canada and around the world. There are days when my prayers don't seem to make it past the ceiling. On those days, I just step outside. I like it outdoors, where it feels there is nothing at all between God and me. I get it that the Father is everywhere present, and the Holy Spirit resides in all his potential in the life of every Christ follower, the One true and living God; not just outside in the great outdoors, but in our homes and in our hearts. It isn't about his inadequacy that I'm concerned. It is about mine.

And on the days when I do step outside and look to the hills and mountains, the forests and the sky surrounding and watching over our city, there is an amazing eternality about it all. Suddenly it is hard for me to imagine how anyone could miss it. I know if you were standing here with me right now, you would see it, too. And when I ask, "From where does my help come, Lord?" I am certain in that moment I feel him smiling. He knows I know. But like a father to his son, he says it anyway, gently reminding me, "My help comes from the LORD, who made heaven and earth" (Psalm 121:2).

Today as I feast on the awesome beauty around us, the snow-capped heights, the green and various other colors of hills and flowers, I'm aware of your majesty and beauty. And my response can only be "YES." "YEA GOD." Thank you for the opportunity and the eyes to behold it.

When I think of your majesty, I sometimes wonder how to approach you. Do I barge into your presence as a child would an earthly father? Or do I approach you as an adult child would their father, with honor and dignity and respect?

Jesus taught us to "hallow your name" as we pray. Do "barging" and "hallow" belong together? Probably not, especially since I am an adult child... or should be by now.

So, how do I reconcile Your Majesty, hallow your name and still be comfortable with "Abba Father?" Are there seasons of appropriateness for both, or are they both appropriate at all times?

My desire is to give you honor and glorify your very name as holy, and still approach you as comfortably as a child would their father. Perhaps that's the answer. I can say, "YEA GOD" when I see your majesty and still see you with my soul when I understand our relationship is like a loving Father with an insecure child.

Thank you Almighty Father, Abba Father...Daddy! ~ DLT diary, February 1996

With deep faith come deep longings.

24

Left Alone

...So the woman was left all alone... ~ Ruth 1:5

This phrase is from the amazing love story of mother-in-law, Ruth, and daughter-in-law, Naomi, in the Bible. A beautiful story beginning with pathos and tragedy, ending as with all great love stories in triumph and blessing. But in the middle, lies a story dark with cruel hardship and sadness. Trapped in life's out of control circumstances, Naomi finds herself too far in to turn back, yet not far enough in to see the light at the end of her difficulty.

The middle. It always seems to be the hardest, doesn't it?

It was in March that Dixie and I first met in consultation with several doctors, one of whom was Dr. Edward Kim, the radiation oncologist, who reviewed her medical tests and completed a physical examination. Dr. Kim discussed with us the potential benefits and risks of radiation therapy, answering any questions we could think of at the time. A radiation oncology nurse was also assigned, educating and guiding us through the treatment process. And now, weeks later, after a major Whipple surgery, rounds of chemotherapy, a liver biopsy, pills and shots, hospital rooms and doctor's visits, we have arrived.

In the middle.

Monday. To be effective, her radiation treatment must be aimed precisely at the same target each and every time it is given. With this in mind, Dixie has been measured and marked with colored, semi-permanent ink and small skin tattoos, to help the team aim the treatment safely and exactly at the target area. A plastic mold of her head and shoulders has been designed to help her remain immobilized, in the same exact position during each treatment.

Special computers are used in planning where and how the radiation will be delivered. Shields have been made, some are in the machine, all put into position before each of her treatments to shape the radiation and keep the rays from hitting healthy tissue. This preparation process is time consuming and has taken several days to complete.

Her visit involving the treatment machine today is a Verification Simulation final test run. The procedure ensures the plan that has been customized for her treatment lines up correctly on her body and covers the abdominal area. No treatment is given. Today is just a rehearsal. The real action begins tomorrow and continues every day thereafter, excluding weekends, for six weeks. She is told to plan at least 30 minutes for each appointment.

Tuesday. We arrive at UWMC shortly before 8 o'clock in the morning, check our car with the valet, a first for us, but part of the service offered to all daily patients. Elevator down to F1. Check in. The receptionist hands Dixie a buzzer. At 8:35 it goes off. I watch as she disappears down the hallway. I'm not permitted to go with her. In half an hour she returns and, without a word, we walk to the elevator. I understand this much as I look into her face. It has not been a pleasant experience.

Finally, I break the silence. "How was it?"

"Scary," is her one-word answer, as she stares straight ahead. Nothing more for now. We drive home, allowing the silence to linger between us. This will not be a good time for conversation. The facts and feelings will come later, in bits and pieces, over the next couple of days.

Meanwhile, the CASA Network board of directors have flown in this week. And I am their leader. They will be here until Thursday noon concentrating on ministry plans, challenges and opportunities for present and future ministry to and through those in the second half of life. Our daughter is working. Our son is in Hong Kong. Other family members are scattered. Life goes on as usual for everyone around her, while she battles for life itself.

...So the woman was left all alone...

Wednesday. A friend, Nancy, drives Dixie to UWMC while I host my early morning C3 Forum of business leaders and retirees, moving on to a day with the CASA board. The topic centers on leadership transition as I have already informed the board that I will no longer be able to continue in this role. Meanwhile, Dixie is adjusting to the new normal.

When undergoing External Beam Radiation Therapy treatment, each session is supposedly painless, like having an X-ray taken. In Dixie's treatment, radiation is directed to the abdominal area from a machine located outside of her body, called a linear accelerator. These x-rays can destroy cancer cells and with careful treatment allow the surrounding normal tissues to avoid being radiated.

Each treatment takes 15–30 minutes. Much of this time is spent spelling out her full name, letter by letter, together with her birth date, positioning to ensure accuracy for the treatment, and the remaining time for actual treatment delivery. To deliver the treatment, the therapist goes outside the actual treatment room and works the linear accelerator from a designated control area. The therapist closely monitors her via a camera and intercom system, while Dixie is by herself in the room. No one else. Just more time to do battle with depressing fears and loneliness.

Thursday. This morning is the final day of CASA board meetings. Niece Robin comes to be Dixie's driver. One or more directions may be used for her treatment delivery and the beam may be on for anywhere from ten seconds to several minutes for each field. Today's radiation therapy is followed by a visit with the resident radiation oncologist and nurse who are assigned to follow Dixie's progress, evaluate whether she is having any negative side effects, recommend treatments for those side effects and address any concerns she may have.

The darkness she felt earlier in the week is gradually lifting. Back home, she prepares to join CASA board members and some of their spouses who have traveled here with them. They have been looking forward to seeing their friend. We have a Mexican dinner at Tapatios in nearby Factoria, and later welcome them into our home for dessert. She is greeted warmly by all these who are also her friends and prayer partners. At the conclusion of an evening full of shared laughter and life stories, our friends gather around us to offer heartfelt prayers and words of encouragement. Faith, hope and love. These three. And the greatest is love.

If you've never read the Old Testament story of Ruth and Naomi, you should. If you have, it's worth a do over. Like all great love stories, there is a happy ending. Naomi's daughter-in-law,

Ruth, marries Boaz and gives birth to a son whom they name Obed. Naomi is a grandmother, a dream she had thought might never come true! Years later her grandson, Obed, becomes the father of David, who is chosen to be King of Israel. And in the generational lineage from Naomi's grandson, we eventually find another whom we all know, a man named Joseph, whose wife is Mary... virgin mother of Jesus, Son of God.

Have you experienced it? Fear? Loneliness? Hopelessness? Loss? The battle is not merely physical or emotional is it? It is spiritual, too. "You will not fear the terror of the night, nor the arrow that flies by day" (Psalm 91:5). "For God gave us a spirit not of fear but of power and love and self-control" (2 Timothy 1:7). Followers of Jesus know this. He's been there, done that for each one of us. Experienced it all and more. He gets it. He understands.

On the eve of his most fearful and loneliest of nights, Jesus gathers his closest friends on earth around him and says, "Look, the hour is coming...it has come...when you will be scattered, each to his own home...and will leave me alone. Yet I am not alone, for the Father is with me" (John 16:32).

Better than her husband. Better than her children. Better than the best of her friends anywhere on earth. In a lonely room, a scary place where only Dixie can be...*Abba Father...Daddy* is with her. She is not alone after all. He never left her side!

...So the woman was left alone...but not all alone.

"YEA GOD!"

25

Satisfied ... Not Settling

I'm often not really satisfied with a purchase or a hairstyle after a time because I have just "settled" for something. Most times the purchase has been on sale and I've settled for something that doesn't quite fit or fit in. Or a hairstyle that may be the latest, but not the best for me. Settling... not really satisfied.

I shudder to think how often I have blamed God for my dissatisfaction. It hit me today, those were choices I made. I didn't really even consult God. However, the times I have consulted him, then waited until he directs me, I have found great satisfaction for a long time. I am astounded that it has taken me so long to understand the concept... that truly God is enough!

Lord, I repent of settling for mediocre, a life "on sale," instead of living the life you offer that is so deeply satisfying. It's not always an easy life, without pain and difficulties, but you satisfy all the deep longings of my being.

God is enough.

He is my

>*provision*
>
>>*he knows my needs*
>
>*protection*
>
>>*he knows my fears*

presence

he knows my desires

He supplies sometimes in adequate amounts, sometimes an abundant amount. However, he is always enough.

When I feel he is absent, what does he want to teach me about my needs, fears, desires? How do I usually respond to him? How does God desire for me to respond?

The history of my experiences with God tells me in very many ways that truly he is enough.

He continually teaches me to trust him in all things. When I forget to trust or choose not to trust... he waits for me. I am learning.

Thank you Father, for being trustworthy. ~ DLT diary, January 2008

One does not soon forget a week in the wilderness.

In years past, Dixie and I have traveled the same Sinai wilderness region that Moses recalls in Deuteronomy, near the end of his earthly journey, when he says, "The LORD our God spoke to us at Horeb and said, 'You have stayed in the area of this mountain long enough. Get up now, resume your journey' Then we left Horeb and passed through all that immense, forbidding wilderness that you saw on the way to the Amorite hill country as the LORD our God had commanded us to do, finally arriving at Kadesh Barnea" (Deuteronomy 1:6, 7, 19).

Not much has changed there in the passing centuries from Moses' day until now. It is still a "forbidding wilderness."

Soon after, Moses sent twelve men on to spy out the Promised Land in order to determine what lay ahead for them. Their KB (Kadesh Barnea) experience, once filled with purpose and possibilities, became instead a scene of fearfulness and failure. Ten returned with frightening tales of giants and overwhelming odds. Two brought back tasty fruit from the land and, trusting God, urged them on. But the majority won out. And what was it they won? Forty years in the wilderness. Zero Promised Land!

The fruits of promise, suggesting hope and love and better days ahead, came to us this week from unexpected quarters. Encouraging comments from friends on Facebook and CaringBridge. A surprise card in the mail. Flowers from Mike, Mary and son William, good friends in South Carolina, sent just because "you were on our hearts this week." Irene's link to Joni's song, "Alone Yet Not Alone." I purchased it and placed on Dixie's iPad.

Jeanne, who brought a tasty meal. A lovely visit from three nieces, Candy, Tami, Robin, and sister-in-law, Patsy, as well as from our daughter, Michele, and another from granddaughter, Katy. And of course the little dude, our 2-1/2-year-old great-grandson, Corbin, was happy to be picked up at the daycare center and romp with Papa in the park near our home; then burn off some remaining energy with GG, who never fails to find berries and cheese in the refrigerator to recharge his always-on batteries.

All this and the completion of week 2 at UWMC radiation.

Thursday. With the UWMC radiology team, Dr. Edward Kim, and at SCCA with Dr. Gabriella Chiorean, we listen as they reaffirm Dixie's blood tests being good and that she is responding well to treatment at this time.

And perhaps best of all, each day this week, while alone undergoing radiation treatment, Dixie tells of finding great comfort in whispering silently to herself verses of Scripture as the Holy Spirit brings them to mind, though now she doesn't recall exactly what they were or where they are to be found. Fruits of promise given in Dixie's own KB experience, consumed in the very moment in which they are needed.

The real difference between the two spies—Joshua and Caleb—and the ten other guys is *perspective*. Joshua and Caleb looked back at who their God had been for them, remembering their triumph over Pharaoh and recent deliverance from slavery in Egypt. Based on how far their experience of trusting in God had brought them, they looked ahead to who and what their God would be in the face of new challenge and great opportunity. The result was a true perspective. For the two spies, theirs was the God of the impossible. The ten didn't see God; they just saw the impossible. They could not get over their human inability to accomplish what lay ahead. The giants in the land were too big. Their God was too small.

The failure of the Israelites at KB is the central theme of Psalm 95. This Psalm begins with a call to worship, and ends with a warning; a warning not to be like the Israelites at KB (and wherever else they did more than their fair share of complaining). Praise is the preventative cure for complaining. It focuses on God and urges us to do likewise. It looks back upon the greatness of God and what he has done. It inspires faith and obedience. Our Lord's gift of salvation at Calvary becomes the central point in our worship each time we approach the Lord's Table (Eucharist).

All of us will experience some kind of KB experience at least once in our lives. A moment turning an otherwise ordinary day into the one where God allows a challenge to confront us that looks impossible. One requiring a ton of faith and obedience? Not necessarily. Maybe a mustard seed size faith will do

(Matthew 17:20). Either we trust in God's promises and power, obedient always to his will, or we are overcome by doubts and fears, remaining forever in a wilderness of defeat.

Dixie and I choose to go with the *two* and not the *ten*. The majority may rule, but their results are not always promising. We choose to walk by faith and encourage you to do likewise. That way when your KB comes along, and it will, you will be ready to meet the challenge, trusting God for the miracle, while at the same time obedient always to his will, finding strength, comfort and ultimate victory in him.

His plan is for us to develop, as apprentices to Jesus, to the point where we can take our place in the ongoing creativity of the universe. God is grooming us for leadership. He's watching to see how we demonstrate our faithfulness. He does that through his apprenticeship program, one that prepares us for heaven. Christ is not simply preparing a place for us; he is preparing us for that place. ~ Randy Alcorn, Heaven

26

Seeing with the Eyes of God

I am thinking much recently about a biblical worldview. What does the world look like through God's eyes? I believe we can know that to some degree from searching God's Word. How do I view the world? How should I view it? How do I and how should I view myself in that world? Most importantly, how do I live in the world as it crowds out God and his followers?

I have a voice, but I often don't feel heard. How do I modulate my voice so others will listen? I also believe I have some knowledge but often

9 Dixie teaching Women's Bible Study

feel too vulnerable to speak out, especially in places of uncertainty. Teach me, Lord to see as you see; to hear you clearly so I can speak out with certainty. Open your Word to me and give me understanding and wisdom.

"*Those who know your name put their trust in you, for you, O LORD have not forsaken those who seek you*" *(Psalm 9:1).* ~ DLT diary, November 2012

Saturday 05 July. *Interdependent* on Independence Day.

Some years ago, Dixie and I had occasion to be in Paris on 14 July, Bastille Day. The French Independence Day is so called because it commemorates the storming of the Bastille, a famous prison, during the French Revolution in 1789.

Later, we made our way to Switzerland in time to celebrate, on 01 August, their Swiss National Day, a date since 1891, serving as a reminder of the founding of the Swiss Confederation of 1291, an historic alliance that would become the core around which, over centuries, the nation of Switzerland was constructed and formed their independence.

One year in June, we were swept up in a Jerusalem Day celebration in Israel, a national holiday commemorating the reunification of Jerusalem and the establishment of Israeli control over the Old City, in the aftermath of the June 1967 Six-Day War, and regaining access to the Western Wall.

We've been privileged with opportunities such as these and are grateful, taking nothing for granted. Such celebrations are different when viewed as foreigners, outside our native land, so to speak.

Here in our homeland, after the vote to declare American independence from the British Crown was done by the

Second Continental Congress on 2 July, a final Declaration of Independence was prepared, debated and approved on 4 July.

The day before, John Adams wrote to his wife, Abigail, saying, "The second day of July, 1776, will be the most memorable epoch in the history of America. I am apt to believe that it will be celebrated by succeeding generations as the great anniversary festival. It ought to be commemorated as the day of deliverance, by solemn acts of devotion to God Almighty. It ought to be solemnized with pomp and parade, with shows, games, sports, guns, bells, bonfires, and illuminations, from one end of this continent to the other, from this time forward forever more."[6]

Well, John missed it by a couple of days, but he had the right idea. Americans, Swiss, the French, whomever and wherever, we all celebrate more or less the same way when we are truly "free and independent." We do so with our respective cultural brands of "pomp and parade, shows, games, sports, guns, bells, bonfires, and illuminations...from this time forward forever more."

Yesterday, Dixie and I celebrated the USA's Independence Day with our own, very low-key touch. A short walk around City Park, kitty corner across from our home, where about sixty thousand of our closest friends gather on this day each year. Chili and hot dogs, an all-American touch made multi-cultural with German sauerkraut, French onion dip, Louisiana Tabasco-spicy catsup and strawberry/rhubarb dessert topped off with all-American vanilla ice cream. At 10 o'clock, to the musical sounds of a live band, the City of Bellevue's fireworks (made in China?) are shot off across the street from our apartment, so close we can hear and feel the impact from each blast. It's about as American as it gets!

---

[6] ~ an excerpt from *The Great Republic by the Master Historians, Vol II*, edited by Hubert H. Bancroft.

But it also says something about our independence. The truth is, we are never truly "free and independent." Not from others and most assuredly not from God. We depend on each other, our ethnicities and cultures, skills and talents, knowledge and life experiences. We were designed by our Creator to be *interdependent*.

Dixie and I have, in recent times, experienced more of the feeling of being interdependent with each other, with family, with friends and neighbors, with doctors and nurses and technicians, with people we know intimately and with perfect strangers. And, above all, with the Lord God Almighty.

This week marks the halfway point in Dixie's radiation therapy. No small accomplishment. That she has thus far done so well in this aggressive treatment, we attribute to the faithful and supportive prayers being offered by so many on her behalf. Our doctors and their cohorts are wonderful and amazing in what they do, but they themselves understand they are only part of the health delivery program, not the whole.

While Jesus walked on earth, "he had healed many, so that all who were afflicted with diseases pressed toward him in order to touch him" (Mark 3:10). Our faith is centered in what the divine nature of a compassionate God and scientifically proven medicine can accomplish as mutually legitimate parts of mankind's health restorative process. This is where we live each day.

⁓

My life is no longer than my hand. My whole lifetime is but a moment to you. Proud man! Frail as breath! A shadow! All his busy rushing ends in nothing. He heaps up riches for someone else to spend. And so, Lord, my only hope is in you. Hear my prayer, O

Lord; listen to my cry! Don't sit back, unmindful of my tears. For I am your guest. I am a traveler passing through the earth, as all my fathers were. ~ Psalm 39:5–7, 12 (TLB)

༄

The terms "foreigner," "guest" and "traveler" were for those who were not native inhabitants in the Promised Land. The Israelites were to consider themselves as foreigners and temporary residents in Yahweh's land. And so are we as well. Interdependent. Inquirers. Travelers. Guests on this earth, in this life. God has been gracious beyond Dixie's and my dreams in the life he has given us to share together. Best of all we enjoy having touched, in small but important ways, many others whom God loves desperately.

༄

27

Against the Wind

Disappointment. What do I do with a lifetime of disappointment? Disappointment with the family of my youth, with the family of my womb, with the family of my intercession and labor. It's too big for me to handle anymore. My despair, Lord, I give to you. Help me to see that my life has meant something positive to you and to others. I long to see that relationships I've given so much of myself to have been worthwhile, that I've made a difference for the good. Help me Lord, not to drown in this wave of disappointment.

Lift my head; help me to see you. Help my "spiritual eyes" to focus on you so that my "emotional eyes" can see, too. Help the broken places in my heart to be closed and reinforced so that I can love those that disappoint. Teach me how to think about them so that my actions are done with integrity and congruence. Show me the way to see them so I don't lose hope.

And the vacuum, where disappointment has dwelled, please fill with your joy, so that I won't let it come back in. Today, Lord, in the face of the things that have caused me to be jarred, give me a smile, a gentle touch, and an encouraging word; let there be no rancor and give me the courage to love without expectations. Your strength will be needed every moment. Thank you for the moments. ~ DLT diary, May 1991

Have you ever had that terrible sinking feeling? You realize you've made a bad judgment call. An irredeemable mistake? Suddenly all of life seems like one big disappointment. Of course you have. We all have. You will find days of disappointment in every person's calendar, often unmarked, but poignant nonetheless. More than we wish to admit to. And if you find yourself to be the cause of someone's disappointment, well, that is disappointing, too.

The apostle Peter introduces a great story, with young Mark recording the retelling of a night he lived like that. A night he and his companions were in a fishing boat, straining at the oars, rowing against the wind, when Jesus suddenly appeared out of the darkness, walking on the water! (Mark 6:45–52). I'll bet Peter told this story at least a hundred times after it happened. But the fact is, he leaves out the best part, perhaps out of modesty or maybe embarrassment, leaving it to his friend and colleague, Matthew, to tell us "the rest of the story."

> *And in the fourth watch of the night he came to them, walking on the sea. But when the disciples saw him walking on the sea, they were terrified, and said, "It is a ghost!" and they cried out in fear. But immediately Jesus spoke to them, saying, "Take heart; it is I. Do not be afraid." And Peter answered him, "Lord, if it is you, command me to come to you on the water." He said, "Come." So Peter got out of the boat and walked on the water and came to Jesus. But when he saw the wind, he was afraid, and beginning to sink he cried out, "Lord, save me." Jesus immediately reached out his hand and took hold of him, saying to him, "O you of little faith, why did you doubt?" ~ Matthew 14:25–31*

Can't you see Jesus smiling at Peter in this gentle rebuke? Like a father who reassuringly takes the hand of his young child who is just learning to walk?

And when they got into the boat, the wind ceased. And those in the boat worshiped him, saying, "Truly you are the Son of God." ~ Matthew 14:25–33

Dixie and I were deep into our eighth journey in Israel, together with a group of friends, when we visited the Sea of Galilee Boat, also known as the Jesus Boat, housed in the Yigal Alon Museum in Kibbutz Ginosar. It is an ancient fishing boat from the 1st century CE (the time of Jesus), discovered in 1986.

The boat's remains are 27 feet (8.27 meters) long, 7.5 feet (2.3 meters) wide, with a maximum preserved height of 4.3 feet (1.3 meters). It was discovered by two brothers, Moshe and Yuval Lufan, local fishermen from the nearby kibbutz, who were also amateur archaeologists. They had always dreamed of one day discovering an ancient boat in the Sea of Galilee, where they and generations of their family had fished. In 1986, it happened. During a season of great drought that had reduced the lake to new water-levels, they stumbled across the remains of a boat buried in the mud along the northwest shore.

Upon report of their discovery, Israeli authorities sent a team of archaeologists to investigate. Recognizing the historical importance to Jews and Christians alike, a secret archaeological dig followed. Rumors spread the boat was full of gold and the dig had to be guarded night and day. Excavating the boat from the mud without damaging it, extracting it before the water rose again, required working together as experts along with numerous volunteers, an effort lasting 12 days and nights. Following its release from the muddy bottom of the sea, the boat was submerged in a chemical bath for 7 years, for purposes of preservation, before being put on public display.

Made primarily of cedar planks joined together by pegged mortise and tenon joints and nails, it has a flat bottom, that allowed fishing close to shore. This boat is made of ten different wood types, suggesting it may have undergone repeated fixes. It has been dated to 40 BC (plus or minus 80 years) based on radiocarbon dating; and 50 BC to AD 50, based on pottery (including a cooking pot and lamp) and nails found in the boat, as well as hull construction techniques. It had been row-able, and had a mast allowing its fishermen to sail the boat as well.

The Sea of Galilee Boat is historically valuable as a visible example of the type of boat used in the 1st century for both fishing and transportation across the lake. It is the same sort of boat used by Jesus and his disciples, several of whom were fishermen. Boats like this played a large role in Jesus' life and ministry and are mentioned fifty times in the Gospels.

It is likely to have been this kind of boat Peter and his friends were in that fateful night. A night that was perhaps not the worst they had known, but very hard nonetheless; a night when exhaustion was setting in as they rowed against the wind.

⌒

It has been a week of nights like this for Dixie. Not the worst that she has ever known, but hard nonetheless, nights spent rowing against the wind, often leaving her fatigued, drained, and still a long way from shore.

Friday marks the end of her fourth week of chemo / radiation. Each day brings a now familiar journey over the SR 520 floating bridge, arriving at 8:15am at the UWMC, handing car keys to the parking valet, walking to the Pacific elevators, down to Floor 1, checking in at the radiation center, waiting until her handheld buzzer sounds, at which time she goes to the Unit, while I remain in the waiting area.

She follows the same precise procedure under the watchful eyes of technicians who know her well by now and call her name like old friends. Upon the treatment's completion for the day, we exit the same way we entered, find our car, and drive the longer route across the I-90 floating bridge, to lend some variety to the routine, arriving home by 9:30, where she begins the rest of her day.

This not-so-routine treatment is taking its expected toll on Dixie's energy, leaving her physically and mentally depleted. A bit of ironing, preparing (or repairing) the evening meal, some of which has been dropped off by friends. A special night out on Wednesday to enjoy our neighbors and a gourmet-prepared meal in their home. Thursday is guy's night out, as the women shed themselves of their menfolk. Four of us guys head straight for Safeco Field, and for me, a mental break filled with junk food and Mariners baseball.

An ordinary week. Rowing against the wind. Not the worst of weeks. Not the best either. Moments during long Northwest summer nights, somehow made longer this year. In the darkest times, with the winds of circumstance pressing against her, I watch her straining ... rowing ... wanting to take the oars away from her ... desperately wishing it were me instead ... yet knowing in my heart that much of this dark crossing is hers alone to make ... and with that sinking feeling settling in, I am reminded again of Peter's story.

I imagine Jesus reaching out to catch me, saying, "You of little faith, why do you doubt? I have both of you in my hands.

I know exactly where you are, what you are facing...I've been here before, remember? These elements are beyond your control...don't waste your energy worrying about them...trust me."

And then he is in the boat with us...and the winds cease...and there follows a magnificent peace that is beyond understanding...as amazing as it once must have been on a dark night in a little boat on the Sea of Galilee. And those in the boat worshiped him, saying, "Truly you are the Son of God."

I know for some of you, my imaginings may appear to be little more than a crutch of desperation to lean on in difficult times, like wishing upon a star. I get that. And I'm not the least offended if you happen to feel that way. But it is this kind of imagining that makes me think Peter may have told his famous Jesus Boat story to young Mark in Jerusalem, right after Paul refused to take him on his second missionary journey, due largely to the way Mark had failed the team and turned back while on their first.

It would be Peter's style, I think, to encourage this young man who felt the invisible weight of failure carried by so many of us, to forgive himself and try again. After all, Peter understood failure. And shame. And forgiveness. He had experienced it all, but he sought and found true forgiveness and tried again.

It is for these same reasons, I offer up my simple imaginings for any who care to read and ponder. Perhaps, like Peter or Mark, it is time to forgive yourself. And in the same breath, to accept the forgiveness of Jesus. To acknowledge him in your heart of hearts for who he truly is. Wherever you are on the sea of your life, "may the Lord of peace himself give you peace at all times in every way. The Lord be with you all" (2 Thessalonians 3:16).

28

Lifting Weary Hands

Lord, with a heavy heart, I bring my cares to you to cast them at your feet so that I may walk away free of the burden. Thank you for the privilege of walking in your freedom.

Give me the strength to give grace to others when grace is needed. Help me to give "tough love" when that is needed and help me to know which is appropriate.

Lord, as I teach your Word, please help me teach with knowledge, wisdom and in the power of your Spirit. Give me favor with these people so they can receive what you have to give them through me... so they can make a difference for you in their world. Give me understanding so that I can lead them with a sure step. All for your glory. Amen. ~ DLT diary, November 1990

You may remember this Old Testament Bible story. It's one of my favorites. It is the day Amalek attacks Israel in Rephidim. Moses takes with him two of his best buddies and stands on a hill overlooking the scene, holding up the sacred staff representing God's presence and power. As long as he can hold the staff heavenward, the battle goes in Israel's favor. When he becomes weary, the enemy prevails. Back and forth it goes until finally, "When the hands of Moses became heavy, they took a stone and put it under him, and Aaron and Hur held up his hands, one on one side and one on the other, and so his hands were steady until the sun went down" (Exodus 17:12).

The battle was won that day, in part at least, through the faith and faithfulness of two men who humbly held up the weary hands of Moses until it was over. Aaron and Hur. You gotta love those guys!

⁓

Friday marks the end of radiation/chemo combo Week 5. Dixie's weight is holding steady and that is important. This next week will bring the greatest fatigue factor into play, so maintaining body weight and physical stamina is vital to her wellbeing.

Five more treatments.

There is a gong hanging in the waiting area. As each patient completes their final treatment, they hit the gong on their way out. Everyone in the room claps and cheers, offering sincere congratulations, while silently counting their own days, knowing their turn is coming. It can't come soon enough. It is just a brief moment. A cheery moment. A moment when we all hold up a stranger's hands and cheer them on in victory.

One week to go.

And then a month for her body to heal and become stronger. A month to clear the battlefield of hundreds of thousands of dead Enemy Cancer cells and to replenish the good ones, killed along with the bad in this war against cancer. A month to think good thoughts. To be reminded just how far she has come. Much of her success we attribute to the prayers of the many saints in our lives.

Prayer, a mystery to some, is like breathing for others. Something we may not have done before the Master of souls came into our lives. Something seeming so natural ever since. There are thousands around the world these weeks past who have been Aaron and Hur to us. Partners in prayer. Would that people everywhere might find such supportive power and peace.

Instead, all too often Evil delivers death to innocents in the skies. Bitterness and hatred light the night scene on borders around the world. Tragedy seems close to us all, and yet so far away. Anger and lust for power. Selfishness and pride. Cain and Abel.

Where do we go to navigate our journeys in times that are not always smooth, places where our footing becomes unsure? The truth is the answer is not to be found in where one goes, but rather in *how* one goes. All battles are not fought in ancient Hebraic texts, or half a world away. Some are fought right here, as near as your next breath or mine, and won with this strange weapon called prayer. Faith mixed with love ... stirred by a patient hope ... lived out in a spirit of humility.

Andrew Murray, a late 19th-early 20th century South African writer, teacher, and Christian pastor in the Dutch Reformed tradition, wrote, "Humility is perfect quietness of heart. It is to expect nothing, to wonder at nothing that is done to me, to feel nothing done against me. It is to be at rest when nobody praises me, and when I am blamed or despised. It is to have a blessed home in the Lord, where I can go in and shut the door, and kneel to my Father in secret, and am at peace as in a deep sea of calmness, when all around and above is trouble"[7]

Dixie and I are being served by so many humble, caring people right now, living out the essence of that Scripture passage.

---

[7] *Humility by Andrew Murray. fig-books.com 2012.*

Every ethnic and religious background. Doctors, residents, nurses, interns, cleaning staffs, parking attendants, the list goes on. A favorite of mine is an African American Buddhist male nurse who never stops smiling and always has a good word for us. Friends at church, neighbors, colleagues near and far. I'll say what I think Moses said to Aaron and Hur on their way back at the end of the day. "Thanks, guys, we couldn't have won this battle without you!"

Do nothing from selfish ambition or conceit, but in humility, count others more significant than yourselves. ~ *Philippians 2:3*

29

Ring That Bell!

> *David ordered the heads of the Levites to assign their relatives to sing in the choir, accompanied by a well-equipped marching band, and fill the air with joyful sound (as the Ark of the Lord's Covenant was carried into Jerusalem).* ~ 1 Chronicles 15:16 MSG

Friday 25 July. If it is good enough for God, King David and the children of Israel, we think it should be more than good enough for us. So we declare this week now ending, a week of celebration. On Wednesday, Dixie serves a tasty dinner for seven. Yes, that's what I said...seven! Celebrating our daughter, Michele's birthday.

A good portion of the day following is spent in tasks now all too familiar. A blood draw, a pharmacy visit for new prescriptions, meetings with Drs. Gabriella Chiorean at SCCA and Edward Kim at the UWMC, and finally, topped off by radiation treatment #29.

And now TGIF. It is Friday morning.

Tranquility. The peace that comes when energies are in harmony, relationships are in balance.

The words of the wise heard in quiet, are better than the shouting of a ruler among fools. ~ *Ecclesiastes 9:17*

The final day of radiation treatments. Though Dixie is having some not uncommon feelings of nausea this morning, there is as well a kind of peaceful anticipation. The first treatment day seems long ago now...that scary day! For the last six weeks this has been our way of life. A familiar, though not always looked forward to, routine. But that is all about to change. It's Friday. Day 30. Last day. Gong Day!

Wisdom. Knowledge, intuition and experience combine to guide us in thought and deed.

(My goal is) that their hearts may be encouraged, being knit together in love, to reach all the riches of full assurance of understanding and the knowledge of God's mystery, which is Christ, in whom are hidden all the treasures of wisdom and knowledge. ~ *Colossians 2:2*

Michele comes with us to celebrate her mom, the tenacity that keeps her going, the courage that turns a frightful synergy chamber into a holy place, the example she is to us all. How did she make it this far? Each morning as that thick door closes tightly behind her, leaving her alone with her thoughts, she begins reciting verses of Scripture, sends arrow prayers heavenward, gives thanks for her doctors and handlers, her family and, of course, her prayer partners. And each day her heart would fill with incredible peace and joy.

We watch again this morning as she disappears down the hallway for the final time.

Then at 9:00, she reappears, entering the waiting room with a huge smile.

Treatment finished!

⌒

Love. An inspired form of giving, love breathes life into the heart and brings grace to the soul.

So now faith, hope, and love abide, these three; but the greatest of these is love. ~ 1 Corinthians 13:13

All at once something spontaneous and wonderful happens! Something we'd not witnessed before in the last six weeks. As Dixie takes the mallet to hit the gong, technicians, attendants, office staff, doctors and nurses come out of their offices and work stations to watch and join us in applauding! There are smiles and hugs and laughter and many thank-yous all around as for a moment...gratitude reigns...filling a room often so seriously quiet with great joy, like the kind that comes at the end of a well-run race!

And at this same hour in Texas, Missy is ringing her treasured grandmother's bell in celebration of this milestone. *Grace*

10 Dixie rings the bell.

and peace! Marty and Joyce and Sheri and Nancy and Earl and Tawny and Connie and Mary Lou and Diana and many others ring doorbells and alarm clocks and bang on kitchen pots in California. *Joy!* Glenn and Charles and Sylvia and Deann celebrate in Washington. *Hope!* A bell rings out in a California preschool classroom as forty-five 4 and 5 year olds do a victory lap around their classroom. These children do not know her, but her gifts of inspiration and love, encouragement and sacrifice, helped build the very classroom in which they are marching. *Love!*

11 The radiation team joins in celebration

Many more are there, too, across the US and Canada and around the world, praying and ringing and celebrating with us.

∽

Courage. Not the absence of fear or despair but the strength to conquer them.

Be strong and courageous. Do not fear or be in dread of them, for it is the Lord your God who goes with you. He will not leave you or forsake you. ~ Deuteronomy 31:6

The stunning diagnosis. Pancreatic cancer! A new reality. Overlake Hospital. Seattle Cancer Care Alliance. University of Washington Medical Center. In and out since early February.

Major Whipple surgery. Chemotherapy infusions. The dreaded series of radiation/chemotherapy treatments. All completed. Behind us now!

Peace. To bring peace to the Earth, strive to make your own life peaceful.

> *May mercy, peace, and love be multiplied to you. ~ Jude 1:2*
> *Peace I leave with you; my peace I give to you. Not as the world gives do I give to you. Let not your hearts be troubled, neither let them be afraid. ~ John 14:27*

In this hour of completion, friends and strangers join in, both near at hand and far away to hail the victory won! A happy crowd fills the heavens with sounds of triumph and thanksgiving. Personally, I think King David may be watching, pointing to his friends, saying, "See there? See what's happening? It's still all good!" On this Friday, between 9 and 10 in the morning PDT, Dixie grasps the mallet in her hand and with a huge smile rings the gong, celebrating her own major mission accomplished!

Happiness. To be content and filled with joy.

> *Your words were found, and I ate them, and your words became to me a joy and the delight of my heart, for I am called by your name, O Lord, God of hosts. ~ Jeremiah 15:16*

Preparing to leave the hospital, we share hugs and contact information as we say goodbye to Brad and Kathy. Brad began radiation treatment for an inoperable brain tumor at Dixie's halfway treatment point, giving us time in the ensuing days to get acquainted with these dear people. We wish each other well, but the look in their eyes says it all. They've a very difficult road still ahead, and weeks of radiation yet to go. We assure them of our prayers.

And now a month off for Dixie. Weeks to be given over to whatever she wants to do, laced with lots of rest and renewal, to help rebuild an emotional and physical system that is completely exhausted.

(The six key words in the text above, Tranquillity, Wisdom, Love, Courage, Peace, Happiness, are from a traditional Tibetan prayer. The verse quotes are from the Christian Bible.)

12 Michele with step granddaughters: Karen,
Amy, Jody, Becky and Dixie

13 Our son, Stephen, Nancy and Jesse

14 Our granddaughter, Jessica

15 Our daughter, Michele, and Mark

16 (L-R) Our Granddaughter, Katy, Finnigan, Geoff, and Corbin

30

Selah

Prayer is a marvelous experience. Not only does it bring my own thoughts and feelings into focus; it also helps me clarify them. Is that because you, Lord, give me insight, helping me see "inside" something and then enabling me to see the "broader picture" by giving me perspective? Is the understanding that follows given by you or is it already inside us? Does the act of praying reveal to us what we already know, or do you give us "new" revelation? Whatever the answer is, the fact remains... we begin to understand life when we pray. Thank you, Lord, for prayer. ~ DLT diary, March 1996

The week following Dixie's final radiation treatment, we go to visit my sister in Wenatchee, a two and one-half hour drive east from our home, over the Cascade Mountains. She has been ill for some time. We pray and say our goodbyes. We know her end of life is nearing. We just don't know how near. Early the following morning, her daughter, Robin, calls to tell us, "Mom is with Jesus." We had had the opportunity to say, "goodbye for a while," to a sister (in-law) who means so much to us in so many ways.

Newly married and completely broke, she and Earl took us in for the duration while I worked in the surrounding harvests to earn transition money enough to move to Seattle for my junior year at Northwest University. She had helped Dixie learn the nuances of being a wife and mother through conversations and observation. We shared a summer together as a new part of our extended family. We remain forever grateful.

There follows another trip to attend Nadeen's memorial service, and a third to be with the family for her interment. These have been precious times of closeness with our extended family, but physically challenging for Dixie. Throughout August, the build back of strength and energy following radiation, for which we had hoped, seems illusive. We will soon understand why.

Monday 25 August. We return to UWMC for a follow-up visit with Dr. Kim and his team. Two days later we are at SCCA to consult with Dr. Chiorean, and to take Dixie's first blood draw and CT scan since beginning radiation. The scan results are good, with the exception of one new spot showing in the liver. This will be watched carefully to determine what it represents. However, we are handed a big new challenge, one we had hoped to avoid, something known as *Clostridium difficile infection,* or *"C. diff."*

When a person takes antibiotics, good germs that protect against infection are destroyed for several months. During this time, patients more easily get sick from *C. diff* picked up on contaminated surfaces or spread innocently from a health care provider's hands. This is why everyone keeps washing hands in hospitals. Those most at risk are the patients, especially older adults, who require prolonged use of antibiotics and medical care. Of course, Dixie qualifies on all the above.

C. diff spores are transferred to patients mainly via the hands of healthcare personnel who have touched a contaminated surface or item. In spite of every precaution it seems stuff happens. The symptoms include loss of appetite, nausea, and abdominal pain tenderness, all of which have been a part of Dixie's *difficile* (Fr., difficult or hard to deal with) these past weeks. Without being able to allow food to nourish properly, her body weight is maintaining, but not gaining. Her energy remains low.

The *C. diff* brings all resumption of chemotherapy treatments to an abrupt halt. She cannot continue treatment until the infection is under control. To do so will only exacerbate the problem. During the next several days, she takes *metronidazole*, an antibiotic that hopefully will prove corrective. One problem with antibiotics used to treat *C. diff* infection is that the infection returns in about 20 percent of patients. In a small number of these patients, the infection returns over and over and can be quite debilitating. We are praying for complete success with this treatment so she can resume the chemotherapy treatment.

Our perspective is positive, our attitude good, and our hope as it has always been, is in the Lord. *God is our refuge and strength, a very present help in trouble. Therefore, we will not fear though the earth gives way, though the mountains be moved into the heart of the sea, though its waters roar and foam, though the mountains tremble at its swelling. Selah.* ~ Psalm 46:1–3.

Isn't that a great thought? Our big deals are little deals to him. No problem at all for our great God. No fear at all for us. Frustration? Anxiety? Yes, but that's what *Selah* is all about. *Selah* is an expression occurring frequently in the Psalms, and it seems no one is quite sure what it means. It is thought to be a liturgical or musical directive, probably by the choral leader to raise the voice or perhaps the indication of a pause while singing the psalm. For me, this word has always been easy to translate. I never understood why Hebrew scholars keep scratching their heads over this one.

The word translates, *"Coffee break."* Of course it does. Pause, think about what you've just read; take a sip, sit back, give thanks, listen up...God is talking! At least this is the way I see it.

When we do this, something happens. Something divine. Strength overcomes weakness. Help makes trouble take a back seat. Fox News says, "the seas are roaring." CNN reports, "falling mountains." Bad news on all the networks. But the voices carrying bad news fade into silence outside the strong door of Our Refuge as we lean back, give thanks, and listen for his voice...in so doing we turn our attention to a different channel.

Can you hear it? Do you see it?

Listen up.

God is talking!

Selah.

31

Perspective

Never be afraid to trust an unknown future to a known God. ~
Corrie ten Boom

September. We are reminded once more of the 9/11/2001 attack on America. Thirteen years have come and gone since that terrible day in our nation's history. While speaking on the telephone with our son, Stephen, following the first tower attack that fateful morning, we watch in horror as the second plane disappears into the remaining tower in a devastating ball of fire. I say to him, "Life will never be the same after today, son." And it has not been.

The world continues to be rocked by the Evil One. Precious lives brutalized or murdered at the hands of those possessed by a wanton desire to kill and destroy. It is hard for we who believe every life is a sacred gift from God to fully understand. World leaders are in need of our prayers, as are those of our brothers and sisters who live in constant peril because of their faith. People of any religious faith appear to be targets these days, but it is a documented fact that committed followers of Jesus are the most persecuted people in the world right now.

Why do I begin this chapter this way? Because we all need perspective to maintain a balance in life. The sun is shining on a beautiful day in our Northwest corner of America. It is quiet and peaceful here. No religious police roaming our streets. No airplanes dropping bombs on our city. Our biggest concern may be traffic on the freeways as workers head home for the weekend or fans make their way to a baseball game tonight. Still, surrounded by much that is good, we live on the edge of an upside down world in which a mega human story with everlasting consequences is being lived out... however harrowing or challenging our own life journey may be.

Perspective. It's something that helps one avoid being overwhelmed by what we cannot control, while at the same time sorting all relevant data and gaining a realistic mental view of "how then shall we live?" We are more careful than ever about hand washing, if that were possible. Since last Friday, Dixie has been taking her metronidazole to reverse the C. diff infection. Who knew such a small thing as washing hands or sterilizing table space around one's plate would take on such importance?

Today, she undergoes a blood draw and an MRI to get a clearer read on things. Her blood work is okay, but the MRI reveals the spot in question from her earlier CT scan is still there. It has increased in size during the intervening time period. This is not the news for which we had hoped. It is actually the worst kind of news. It appears the original cancer cells may have metastasized after all, forming a secondary tumor in the liver.

We are to return to UWMC on Wednesday at 6:30 in the morning for more blood work and admitting procedures. There,

Dixie will undergo another liver biopsy. The procedure itself is about an hour, but she must remain for most of the day under observation, in similar fashion as her earlier procedure last April. It isn't the most pleasant way for one to spend the day. Dixie is weary. The hoped for "light at the end of the treatment tunnel" has eluded us for now. We need fresh perspective.

According to *Webster's Dictionary*, "*Perspective* is the art of drawing solid objects on a two-dimensional surface so as to get the correct view of their height, width, depth and position in relation to each other when viewed from a particular point. It is also a particular attitude toward something; a point of view; a true understanding of the relative importance of things; a sense of proportion."

They say the most important thing when flying is not the plane's *altitude*, but its *attitude*. Each airplane (or spacecraft) has an attitude indicator. This instrument informs the pilot of the orientation of the aircraft to the earth's horizon. If when coming down the nose is too far up, the landing will be hard and bumpy at best. If it remains pointed too far down, a disaster is in the offing.

Perspective. The way we view things is important. The place from which we view things is important. Just how high, wide and deep are the objects before us? Our present viewpoint is clear, though we can see only as far as today. Dixie's attitude is true, though life's wind shears and uncertain weather makes each day's landing more difficult. Our hope and strength is God, in whom we trust.

It's a battle out there, in whatever direction you want to point. It's a battle in here, too, where we live and move and have our being. We cannot tell for sure who will win the battles out there. We can be positive who will win the battles in here.

So we give thanks.

It's what you do when you can do nothing else. Let your attitude be healthy. Hold the flag of faith high. Take a victory lap. Remind yourself of the verse your mother marked in the Bible she gave you when you were just seventeen and headed off to a college two thousand miles away.

And I am sure of this, that he who began a good work in you will bring it to completion at the day of Christ Jesus. ~ Philippians 1:6

32

When Setbacks Come

Where is God? How does he act. Why doesn't he do something? Common questions my heart asks you, Lord. You have shown me yourself... you are here, all around me. Your presence fills the earth. You are never far away.

You have chosen to act through people. Yet without your presence moving to the inside of us, we are powerless to allow you to work through us. However, you never invade, you only come in by invitation.

Why don't you do something?

You won't because I won't. People fail to realize that we thwart your action by choosing to be ignorant or disobedient and even outright rebellious to your great acts of love and caring.

Where are you?

You are here in this room all around me.

How do you act?

You have chosen to act through me today.

Then why don't you do something?

You do... you are continuously drawing me to yourself, prompting me to good deeds, kind words, to loving even rebellious people.

Lord, help me today to allow people to "see" you through me. ~ DLT diary, September 1990

Wednesday 17 September. Dixie returns to UWMC, with Michele and me along for moral support. And to bring her coffee. We arrive early in the morning and are there most of the day for this biopsy. The first one in April proved to be negative. We are hopeful this will be the same. It is mid afternoon by the time we arrive home and settle in. Waiting for the results we know may take several days. Waiting is never fun.

Each day of waiting is a challenge for Dixie, with ongoing bouts of nausea and the lack of energy. Days are spent mostly reading, with naps interspersed.

Thursday 24 September. Dixie and I arrive at SCCA at one o'clock in the afternoon. Her first appointment involves a port blood draw. Shortly after 2 o'clock, Dr. Elizabeth, the oncologist filling in for Dr. Chiorean today, informs us our worst fears have come true. The results are positive. The original tumor has metastasized to the liver. One or more of the nodes, now removed, leading from the original tumor has already been a pathway for our Enemy Cancer to slip behind the battle lines to yet another organ. Until now, it has remained in hiding. No more. Now it is discovered.

It is a disappointing setback. Huge! Just when it looks as though the end is in sight, suddenly it is not. As if this is not enough bad news for the day, it is feared that the infection *C. diff* may have come back. More tests will confirm yes or no on this.

It is a recalculate moment. If you have a GPS in your car, you've surely experienced going past the intersection you were supposed to turn on. Once you go by, somehow it knows and a voice says, "Recalculate." Immediately a new plan is designed to get you back on track toward your destination. That's what Dr. Chiorean is now putting in motion. It's time for a heavy sigh.

⌒

At a point in which it seems things cannot be more depressing, two dear friends, Bob and Char Pagett, co-founders and president of Assist International, come to our city and take us to dinner at one of Dixie's favorite restaurants, having driven all the way from Bend, Oregon, just to be with us.

For four precious hours we push aside the devastating reports and the cares that threaten like dark rain clouds in order to share stories and pictures, catch up, laugh until tears come, remembering our nearly fifty years of sharing life and ministry, children the same ages, friends, victories and disappointments together. Cold dark nights on trains in foreign lands. Being threatened and robbed. Sloshing on wet carpets with live bugs in seedy hotels in post-revolution Bucharest, Romania. Water pouring through the roof onto my bed in the middle of the night in Jinja, Uganda. It all comes back to us now and we laugh at our adventures and close calls.

Twenty-five years before, we had added to our day jobs as pastors the beginning of what is now Assist International. Grimy nights in a borrowed Bay Area warehouse (everything was borrowed in those days), refurbishing and packing medical equipment and supplies we had earlier begged from hospitals and other sources. We recall our younger years, leading and speaking at youth camps and conferences, living in cabins and hotel rooms, traveling on buses, trains and planes, and the countless tennis matches we played, all shared over many years; gone but not forgotten. Grand experiences, tempered by mutual heartbreaks.

The loss of their sweet daughter. Our first grandson we hardly knew but cannot forget. Life and death. All part of the relationship we treasure and hold close to our hearts.

Encouraging moments of prayer together bring the evening to a close. As they prepare to leave, we put our arms around each other and shake our heads in amazement. It has been just what we need as we prepare for the week before us. And the week after that. What perfect timing. Friends have become more precious than ever at this turning in our sacred journey.

God attending to the smallest details of life.

33

Uncharted Territory

Strengthen me, Lord. I feel weak and inadequate and very tired. Thank you for your daily strength. ~ DLT diary, January 2013

Tuesday 30 September. At 8:45, Dixie and I are crossing over Lake Washington to SCCA. No blood draw today. Instead it is straight up to F5 and the Infusion Center. This will be Dixie's

17 The SR520 Lake Washington Floating Bridge

first chemo treatment since early this summer, before radiation; the pairing of *Gemcitabine* with *Cisplatin,* a powerful platinum based drug, will be the combination administered every other week for three months.

Chemotherapy is often given as a combination of drugs. Combinations may work better than single drugs because different drugs kill cancer cells in different ways. However, the potential side-effects are commensurate in strength, so we have to address them as well. These treatments will take the full day each time they are administered.

Dr. Chiorean will consult with Dr. Park as to a possible resection of the liver tumor at the end of chemotherapy. If that becomes the course of action, it will likely not take place until after Christmas. Sometimes in the midst of it all it is hard to keep one's prayer focus. This is one more reason the prayers and encouragement of others are so invaluable.

The eternal God is your dwelling place, and underneath are the everlasting arms.

~ Deuteronomy 33:27
(Dixie's special verse)

Kevin, a specially trained nurse, is overseeing today's treatment. Since it is a regimen that can easily damage the kidneys, a prerequisite as well as a post flushing out treatment must be done, adding another couple of hours to the already lengthy process.

An anti-nausea drug is also part of the chemo cocktail, designed to last three days. Altogether her treatment takes six hours.

C. diff infection has returned with a vengeance, plus another infection as well. Two different antibiotics are on tap this week for these. We return home with a half dozen new or refill prescriptions in hand. During her treatments, the prescription list is a living thing, constantly changing with whatever is happening in the moment.

The list of medications for this October include:

- **Anti-nausea and Vomiting Medications**
    - *Dexamethasone* (Decadron) 4 mg – one tablet by mouth 2 times a day for 3 days after chemo
    - *Ondansetron* (Zofran) 8 mg – one tablet by mouth every 4 to 6 hours as needed after 3 days from chemo
    - *Omeprazole* 20 mg – one capsule by mouth twice daily
    - *Prochlorperazine* (Compazine) 10 mg
    - *Lorazepam* (Ativan) 5 mg – one or two tablets by mouth every 4 to 6 hours as needed for nausea, vomiting and anxiety
- **Other prescribed medications**
    - *Creon* DR 24,000 units capsule – 2 capsules 3 times a day with meals. (pancreatic enzymes)
    - *Zolpidem* (Ambien) one tablet by mouth at bedtime as needed.
    - *Amox* TR-K CLV875–125MG Tab – one tablet twice a day for 2 days (prior to dentist visit)
- **OTC medications and vitamin supplements**
    - *Ranitidine Hcl* 150 mg (Zantac) one tablet by mouth 2 times a day

- *Docusate* Sodium Stool Softener – one to two softgels daily until first bowel movement, 1 softgel daily thereafter.
- *Senna* – (Sennosides) 8.6mg concentrate, natural vegetable laxative – two tablets once a day – maximum dosage 4 tablets twice a day.
- *Tylenol* Extra Strength as needed
- *B6* 100 mg – one tablet daily
- *D3* 5000 – one softgel daily

It is a dizzying array of medicines to keep up with. It's my job to administer these at home. There is no way for the patient to do this. Remembering with clarity is too much to expect. Different medicines at differing times of the day. Cancer treatments are hard stuff.

Wednesday. In the morning, my C3 Leaders Forum commences in our living room at 7:00. By 7:30, twelve men are present for a lively discussion that wraps up four months on pop-culture's effect on our personal lives and on today's society, led by retired history professor, Dr. LeRoy Johnson.

This evening, the dinner menu includes chicken soup, salad, and great chocolate chip cookies, left at our apartment door by a wonderful neighbor. We watch a pre-recorded program from the new television series, *Madam Secretary*.

Thursday. I teleconference with the CASA Network board this morning, while Dixie reads the Seattle Times. She then gives up more than an hour in conversation to a young, newly married woman who is searching and who has sought Dixie out for older adult connectivity. Most young people today seem to have an abundance of peer friends, but not enough seasoned adults who will take an interest in and reach out to them. Dixie is one of those seasoned adults who can't resist reaching out. When the young woman is gone, she has obviously expended all her energy. I just smile. This is Dixie being Dixie.

Friday. Pastor Gary visits with us today, always a special time, concluding with prayer and assurances that he and Jorie will walk with us in the days ahead. Marie, a member of our former pastorate in California makes a surprise telephone call to tell us of her love and appreciation. Susan and George, also from our VCC family, write an e-letter giving much encouragement, even as Susan is undergoing chemotherapy treatment herself. It has been years since we've seen some of these who write notes, send cards, email, or text to share their love and concern. I read each one aloud to Dixie. The incredible gift of friendship!

Rejoice in the Lord always; again I will say, rejoice. ~ *Philippians 4:4*

34

Midcourse Check

The Winter View.

The skies are gray today and the bare limbs of the trees are stark against the gray. It's a beautiful sight to see how carefully each branch is formed to hold the leaves of spring with all their beauty, while continuing to hold their own beauty now, stark as they are.

The "winter of life" can be and is beautiful, too. I am in my "winter" time and as stark as I feel at times, I know God is here. Life has slowed... and I am slower, but there is still life in my limbs.

Thank you, God, for your life in me. How very rich I am. ~ DLT diary, January 2008

Since the physical upset attached to Dixie's earlier rounds of chemotherapy in May and June was severe, we did not know what to expect following her first infusion with the pairing of *Gemcitabine* and *Cisplatin* chemotherapy drugs.

Gemcitabine, a relatively recent advance in pancreatic cancer care, is not reputed to be as debilitating as some other forms of chemotherapy. But it resulted in a great deal of nausea, physical upset and fatigue when used alone during her first infusion series.

We wonder what will be her body's response when doubled down with powerful, platinum-containing *Cisplatin?*

During the days following, we find out.

It is more of the same, but different, too. Tuesday through the following Tuesday are hard days. There is an inability to summon the drive and energy for even normal day-to-day activities. Hard for one used to being so active and energetic. Her digestive system regresses into similar patterns of upset and physical discomfort. The anti-nausea drug administered this time, together with chemotherapy makes a difference. There is nausea still, but this time there is no vomiting in response to the nausea.

After a week of days have come and gone, Wednesday is a turning point as the light in her eyes flickers and slowly returns.

Dixie, ever the consummate teacher/mentor, volunteering from the very beginning in Fred Hutch and UWMC cancer research projects, understands carcinoma of the ampulla of vater is rare, with comparatively little research being available. I mention at the time of diagnosis, "Wouldn't you know, you'd have your own designer illness?"

Early on, we discussed how to approach this with family and friends as well as those who look to us for spiritual guidance. As mentioned before, we are private people who have lived a very public life. It is not always easy. The first reaction to Dixie's diagnosis is to withdraw and become invisible. Let's just be sick now and tell people later after its all over. Ultimately, however, we agree we will not waste *our* cancer. This terrible illness is also part of our sacred journey. Others need to know. Is there a difference in the way followers of Jesus face suffering and death? If so, what is it? Or are we all the same?

We have no illusions. This terrible illness will eventually take Dixie's life. Then why go through the battle if there is no hope of winning? Why not just surrender?

We anticipate some will criticize her acceptance of medical treatment because of her age and the low chance of success. Still others may see it as a lack of faith and trust in the healing power of Jesus. Second-guessing another's actions is human nature. It is what we do. But after discussing it with family, Dixie makes her own conscious and prayerful decision on two levels.

One, her initial cancer diagnosis is Stage II, and doctors believe there is a reasonable chance it can be treated and stopped at its initial source without metastasis. If successful it will offer precious additional time, perhaps years to enjoy our two great-grandsons. And, of course, the rest of the family will enjoy her, too. This is of high value to her.

Secondly, if left untreated and short of a divine miracle, the median survival duration from the time of diagnosis until death is arguably the worst of any of the major cancers, about 3 1/2 months. American Cancer Society prognosis figures estimate the twelve-month all-stage survival for pancreatic cancer to be 20%, and the five-year rate at about 4%. Those who received the Whipple surgical procedure in one study (from an experienced Johns Hopkins team) were reported as having a 21% five-year survival rate, with a median survival of 15.5 months.

Once she qualifies for the Whipple and subsequent treatments, it appears to be the right choice. It promises the possibility of more time with those whom she dearly loves and who love her. Her willingness to help protect future generations from this disease that will inevitably take her life is in keeping with her character; as important to her as her own short-term comfort and wellbeing. Of course it is her choice. She must bear much of this alone; but in a very real way it is our family's choice as well. Once she says, yes, we are all in!

And so there follows:

Days as a teaching hospital patient, filled with waves of
- Uncertainty
- Anxiety
- Fear
- Loneliness
- Emotional overload

Weeks filled with
- Schedules
- Pharmacies
- Blood draws
- Scans
- MRIs
- Biopsies
- Chemotherapy treatments
- Radiation treatments
- Infections
- Antibiotics

Months filled with
- Hospitals
- Medical centers
- Surgeries
- Pain
- Nausea
- Weight loss
- Sickness
- Fatigue
- No appetite

Scores of doctors, resident physicians, interns, nurses, technicians, administrative staff, attendants

⌒

And yet:

There are things I've experienced more deeply than I would have, were it not for my Enemy Cancer. This is a different, perhaps even a more important victory.

A Trust more total than I've ever known.

Psalm 32:10…the Lord's faithfulness overwhelms the one who trusts in him (NET).

A Joy more full and all consuming.

Psalm 16:11 You lead me in the path of life; I experience absolute joy in your presence; you always give me sheer delight.

A Peace that brings such physical and emotional rest.

Psalm 4:8 I will lie down and sleep peacefully, for you, Lord, make me safe and secure.

A Hope making real all I have believed since becoming a follower of Jesus.

Psalm 119:74 Your loyal followers will be glad when they see me, for I find hope in your word. ~ DLT diary, 2015

⌒

There are Good Days—with short walks on a sunny, tree-lined street.

There are Bad Days—ending as they begin, physically spent, emotionally drained.

We've stood through the years with hundreds of others in the Valley of Shadows. Laid to rest family members. Made our way back from two near-death experiences of my own. We are meant to live with a divine sense of trust, joy, peace and purpose. Yet these are not won easily. Jesus teaches us this by his own example. Yes, this is a special time…a sacred journey through the shadows.

O Son of Mary,
how wonderful
Your friendliness to me!
How deep! How unchanging!
Help me pass it on.

Help me to find my happiness
in my acceptance
of what is Your purpose for me:
in friendly eyes; in work well done;

in quietness born of trust;
and, most of all,
in the awareness
of Your presence in my spirit.

Come, Lord Jesus, come as King.
Rule in our minds: come as peace.
Rule in our actions: come as power.
Rule in our days: come as joy.

Thy Kingdom come among us. Amen.
~ Unknown

35

My Journey Through the Valley of Shadows

(Dixie shares the power of Scripture on her sacred journey. This chapter includes some things already mentioned, and some new as well. In her own words, in a e-letter to her prayer partners, she opens her heart to God and to us in life's most difficult time):

Being a private person who lives a very public life is never easy. Acceptance of public visibility into all areas of my life as a minister's wife has been a great challenge for me, as it is for many pastor's wives. It is hard work to stretch and grow to meet the challenge. Ward has always been the consummate cheerleader for my every endeavor. For this I am so very grateful. He knows me well enough to understand I will come around. Eventually.

My "coming around" in this difficult season has brought me your messages of love and encouragement. These have been life-giving to me. They come in forms of cards, letters, flowers, phone calls, email and visits. Most of all, your prayers sustain me through the grim and difficult moments. Thank you for loving me so tenderly. I am blessed! Now, let me share a little of my journey and trust it will remind you of God's faithfulness.

I memorize Psalm 23 when I am nine years old. The world is at war, and since America is being drawn into it, every home is touched by its horrors. All the while, another war is being lived out, in many ways even more frightening to this young girl and much more personal, as it is being fought inside the walls of our home.

Life for this nine-year-old is scary; I am a target for the physical and emotional upheaval of angry parents. I feel lonely and unloved. Unwanted. While I don't fully understand the content of Psalm 23, I like it. Its words feel comfortable to me. They promise security to an otherwise insecure little girl. Now, looking back from the distance of seventy years, I realize it is a metaphor for my life.

"The LORD is my shepherd, I shall not want. He makes me lie down in green pastures. He leads me beside still waters. He restores my soul." I didn't know much about sheep, and still don't. I'm a city girl. I do know this much. They have no natural defenses and are prone to wandering off from the flock, unaware that danger can be lurking close

18 Dixie finds still waters.

by. Obviously, sheep need a shepherd, someone who cares enough to lead them to safe places for nourishment and rest.

In the Psalm, sheep are made to lie down in green pastures for their safety, comfort and nourishment, and for rest that restores their energy for the next stretch of territory they must cover to get to more green pasture. Sheep are afraid of running water. Their wool is heavy when it is wet and can easily pull them into the water, causing them to drown. Quiet water is safe for stepping into and drinking fully. I guess if I can trust the Shepherd to restore my soul in "green pastures and still waters," I can also trust him to "guide me in paths of righteousness for his name's sake."

I am a Christ-follower. I am His namesake—Christian. He guides me for the sake of his own name.

I often pray the verse in Psalm 25:4,5. "Make me to know your ways, O LORD, teach me your paths. Lead me in your truth and teach me."

I love my Shepherd for who he is! I love what he does for his flock. For all the unnamed fears and insecurities of this child-now-become-woman, the images of not being in want, of lying down in green pastures, of being refreshed by quiet waters all restoring to the soul, of being guided in righteous, though not always along easy paths for his name's sake; all these over my lifetime have become enriching and enlarging descriptors for my view of God.

In these recent months on my journey, as with David, the Psalmist of old, I am being led into the Valley of Shadows, where the pronoun for God is changing from "He" to "You."

For me, the Lord as Shepherd is a personal pronoun in this Valley. David could look to physical things like a rod and staff to comfort him. These were the things he knew. He drew from his own experiences with his sheep. A rod to kill any predators that might harm an innocent lamb. A staff with which he could rescue a sheep wandering from the fold.

Shadowy places can be scary and dark. This part of my life journey is all of that. Dark and scary. And lonely, too. Yet here in my Valley of Shadows, I have discovered what should have been obvious going in. Without light, there can be no shadows. Looking to the Light of my life has been my rod and staff that brings me comfort. The shadows are a reminder that my Light is always with me.

When we first heard the diagnosis "cancer," it was a surreal moment. I was numb. I had no other immediate emotion or reaction. I even asked the doctor how I should feel about this diagnosis. His response was a one-word question. "Nervous?"

I do not feel nervous. Instead, I seem to be wrapped in a cocoon of peace. That peace remains with me most days as I move along the pathway through shadows of surgery and chemotherapy and biopsies and scans. Jesus' words, "Peace I leave with you; my peace I give to you" take on new meaning for me. All the peace Jesus exhibited while here on earth, he gives to me now. His peace feels as warm and comforting as the blankets caring nurses wrap around me to keep me warm and comfortable.

But when the shadow of radiation looms over my pathway, it is not a shadow I merely bump into. It looms large and engulfs me. My radiation experience is a solitary, everyday procedure lasting six weeks. Technicians set me exactly in place. They place huge machines around and over me and then leave me alone in the room. They can see me on their screens, but I cannot see them. I am alone and terribly afraid. I can't move. The machines seem huge to me and make weird noises. It is cold. I am cold. I am wrapped with warm blankets, but much of me remains exposed for the radiation to do its work.

Then I remember the words of David in Psalm 56, "When I am afraid, I put my trust in you. In God, whose word I praise, in God I trust; I shall not be afraid." I begin to praise God for all the attributes that come to mind: his love, kindness, strength, his knowledge of suffering, his ability to heal, his comfort. Before long an unexplainable, sustained joy explodes in my inner being. Radiation's fearful shadow melts away in the pure Light of Jesus. Radiation is never scary for me after that day.

August is to be a month of respite from radiation and chemotherapy. We look forward to a trip to Victoria, a walk through the beautiful Butchart Gardens, and a regaining of normalcy. Sadly, it is not to be. My recovery is slow. Ward's sister, Nadeen, a special mentor in my life as a young bride, has struggled with health issues for a number of years and now, in August, she dies. I want to use every ounce of stamina for several trips to Wenatchee. We are able to say our "goodbyes" the day before her passing. The following trips for her memorial service, then again for her interment, take what remaining energy I have to expend.

Chemo infusions scheduled for the end of August are delayed because tests intimate the possibility that the original carcinoma ampulla of vater has metastasized to the liver. CT Scans, MRI and a liver biopsy further delay the resumption of infusions until the end of September.

I experience feelings of discouragement and disappointment at the slow pace of my healing, and over Nadeen's death. Depression shows its ugliness at times and I wonder, "What is the use?" Still another shadow in my valley. Then one morning during our devotional time, Ward reads from Revelation 21:23 "The City has no need of sun or moon to shine on it, for the glory of God gives it light." It is amazing how quickly my shadow of depression turns into hope! Hope for the place where Light casts no shadows. Just the anticipation of this City as my future dwelling continues to give me hope in this, my Valley of Shadows.

The confirming diagnosis of liver cancer, and the recommended regimen of treatment is another shadow I now must face. A new chemotherapy is paired with the one previously endured. This one is stronger and with brutal side effects. The infection known as C.Diff returns, this time with a vengeance; and if that isn't enough, a UTI infection declares itself present as well. Physically and emotionally depleted, I think to myself: "I cannot do this."

In that moment, my Light shows up again, dispelling the shadow this time with the promise of rest. Deuteronomy 33 is Moses' blessing to the tribes of Israel. I have taken this as my blessing as well: "The beloved of the Lord dwells in safety. The High God surrounds him all day long, and dwells between his shoulders." Again: "as your days, so shall your strength be." "The eternal God is your dwelling place, and underneath are the everlasting arms." Finally, Psalm 91 promises those "who dwell in the shelter of the Most High will abide in the shadow of the Almighty." How good is this?

I find myself asking God, as David did in Psalm 17, to "hide me in the shadow of your wings." He offers me "shelter" in the midst of shadows where I can rest. Rest, I must admit, is not my finest or easiest endeavor. When I lie down to rest, I feel the tense muscles attempting to untangle themselves, entering into a relaxed state, and my racing mind trying to cease the unnecessary "what-ifs." Resting might just be my most challenging shadow of all. It is proving to be the most dense so far.

Finally, I love the picture the Psalmist paints in Psalm 131. "But I have calmed and quieted my soul, like a weaned child with its mother, like a weaned child is my soul within me." The child no longer needs to grasp at mother's breast. She is content to just rest in loving arms. That is my goal.

Thank you dear friends, near and far, for all you have done to make my sacred journey that much more special. You are loved. I am hugging you all one by one! ~ Dixie in an e-letter and diary entry, October 2014

36

Road Trips

Yield, trust, obey. Absolute necessary attitude of my soul toward God. A response to who God is. Can I truly, wholeheartedly, believe that God is

19 Dixie waits for the plane at Budapest Ferenc Liszt International Airport

that aware of me? O Lord, help me in my struggle to believe. I will believe! I choose to yield…to have perfect confidence in you. ~ DLT diary, July 1990, St. Raphael, France

⌒

Saturday. I return to the familiar corridors of UWMC today, this time to visit with Tom and his wife, Judy. Tom is one of the guys who meet regularly each Wednesday morning in our home. Two weeks ago, he and Judy drove to their SoCal desert home for the winter months. A week later at Eisenhower Hospital, Tom is diagnosed with Acute Leukemia. They return immediately to Seattle and to UWMC and SCCA to prepare for chemotherapy treatment in the same renowned research and treatment centers in which we have been served for the last nine months. Cancer is a dreadful disease for anyone to negotiate. So I go to say, "Hi," to my friends, to pray with them, and share the love of Jesus.

Monday. Dixie continues fighting off the residual side effects of her third chemotherapy treatment in this series, while preparing for a much looked forward to trip out of town.

Tuesday. *On the road again.* She is feeling better this morning as we leave our home, stop for coffee at Starbucks, then drive onto I-405, heading south through heavy rains toward Oregon and beautiful Cannon Beach. Dixie loves road trips. It doesn't really matter where, if by car. And if we are flying to someplace in the world we've not been to before, so much the better. She is all in. A combination of ministry and curiosity have taken us to all but one of the USA's fifty states, and over fifty different countries and cultures, some several times. But, with the exception of my sister's passing, this is her first time away from the Seattle area since January. About four hours and fifteen minutes from start to finish. As we make our way south, I recall how it was about the same drive time as this, each way between Springfield, Missouri, and Tulsa, Oklahoma. Years ago. We were so in love. It's a wonder I didn't kill myself.

During the school year on Fridays I would drive to Tulsa, then back to Springfield on Saturday late and go with the guys to wherever. Our quartet had weekend concerts and Sunday morning services as far away in the opposite direction as St Louis or Indianapolis. Always we were back in time to sing live on ABC radio's *Revivaltime* broadcast every Sunday night. My mother, in our small eastern Washington farming town, never missed tuning in. Mothers are like that. (If she had known what kind of schedule I was keeping, she would have had a heart attack.) And I was sure that in Tulsa, the beautiful young woman who would forever be the love of my life was listening for our song as well.

In June, soon after my sophomore college year, we married.

Late in the afternoon, this same young woman and I check into Ocean Lodge, a beautiful birthday gift for Dixie from the guys who meet in our home on Wednesdays. Minutes later, we step out of our beachfront room onto a sandy shoreline that stretches past Haystack Rock, disappearing into a bank of low hanging clouds in the distance. It feels like November warm, and we are arm-in-arm together, ready to celebrate a special occasion, to live a special birthday moment, wrapped in lifetimes of memories.

Wednesday. We take short walks on the beach, rest in between, and read. Stroll through the small vacation village, with its plethora of quaint shops and restaurants, then back to our room to rest again. Her energy vanishes all at once, then after an hour or two, she is ready to go again. We investigate. We talk. We eat at places others have told us about. All good.

On this evening we sit near the fireplace in a house converted into a tiny restaurant, the only customers at this early hour. I watch as she eats well, and it tastes good to her. This is an answer from a caring God, who, I am sure, has arranged this holy adventure through a divine network of thoughtful friends. Sacred moments with just the two of us. We have Oregon friends with whom we do enjoy visiting; just not this time. At last we say goodbye to our server, Wendy, and walk carefully in the darkness across the gravel parking area to our car. Another car rolls to a stop beside us as Dixie is getting in. "We'll take your place," he calls out.

"Enjoy," I reply back to the driver, while closing her door. "It is very good."

Thursday. It's early, but we hear it for the first time. This is it. At last. The flip side of why we have come to this place in November. Gray black clouds. Waves piling high onto the beach. It's the storm! Winds rage against the walls of our corner room, driving rain against the glass, spilling downward in sheets of water, washing onto the deck and away to the rocks below. Glorious. *This* is what we came to see and hear and feel!

A visible reminder of the lives we are living. Not just us, but all of us. Days sunny and bright, with clear skies of blessing and joys that words are inadequate to describe. We speak of such times gladly with those surrounding us. Lifting our own spirits in the telling. Hoping it is the same for others as well. But storms we keep close, hiding them away, unwilling to show our fear of the winds that trouble us, the waves that break against us, overwhelming us. Believing that others should see only the sunshine in our lives and not our deepest dark nights of the soul.

Then he got into the boat and his disciples followed him. Suddenly a furious storm came up on the lake, so that the waves swept over the boat. But Jesus was sleeping. The disciples went and woke him, saying, "Lord, save us! We're going to drown!" ~ Matthew 8:23–27

Perhaps we are more like these disciples than we think. Not sure why we got into the boat in the first place. Knowing we should have read the storm signs before it was too late to turn back. Helpless and fearful and not sure God even cares. After all, he is sleeping, isn't he? While we are all about to drown? God may seem to be sleeping...but lest we forget, he *is* in the boat with us. Right? You have learned this, too? The storm beats down on us. The wind, the rain, the waves are pounding. And we are sheltered! This old boat is built for days and nights like this.

Friday. Time to leave this place of awesome magic, its sights and sounds and fresh smells of the sea. "I will remember this," she says wistfully at dinner on the night of her birthday. My feelings are too near the surface to chance real words in response. Memories kept secret. Quiet thoughts. Stories. Dreams of a future where chemotherapy is forgotten. Fresh ideas. How then shall we live once this storm has passed? Christ's second half of life callings. What will we ever do to top this glorious evening? Will there be another like this? Ever? Finishing well. "Yes," I say at last. "I will remember this, too."

And God saw that it was good. And there was evening and there was morning. ... ~ Genesis 1:12b-13a

...and it is our last day here.

The sun is shining on the waves. The winds are silent now as we walk in the early morning light along the shore. It's all good. We are on the road again. Heading home.

Dixie loves road trips!

37

The Bad Week

If I forget,
Yet God remembers! If these hands of mine
Cease from their clinging, yet the hands divine
Hold me so firmly that I cannot fall;
And if sometimes I am too tired to call
For Him to help me, then He reads the prayer
Unspoken in my heart, and lifts my care.
~ from God, Thou Art Love, Robert Browning

It is reality check time again this week. On Monday, we spend the day at SCCA, beginning with a blood draw, followed by an appointment with Dr. Chiorean. Then on to F5 and the infusion center for the rest of the day.

Dixie's blood work looks good this week, with the exception of white cell counts. Two weeks ago, it was over 6000. Today, only 1600. Since the count is low, in addition to the *Gemcitabine / Cisplatin* chemo cocktail, another steroid, and a 72-hour anti-nausea medication, before and after IVs to protect the kidneys, she is given a white cell booster shot in the tummy.

I serve as the gopher, bringing a turkey sandwich, a bag of chips and a cookie for lunch and, later on, a decent cup of coffee. These things are all found on F2 at the Red Brick Café. It isn't gourmet dining, but adequate, all things considered. This particular SCCA building, tucked into a hillside near the Mercer Street exit off I-5, with mesmerizing views across Lake Union, is a red brick building, one of several red brick buildings constituting one of the world's leading cancer institutes, the Fred Hutchinson Cancer Research Center.

Fred "Hutch" Hutchinson was born in 1919. While still in his teen years, he was becoming a well-known baseball pitcher, winning his nineteenth game on his 19th birthday. He played for Seattle in the Pacific Coast League, and then for eleven years with the Detroit Tigers. As a manager, he led Cincinnati to the World Series. At age 44, he was diagnosed with lung cancer and died a year later.

His brother, Bill, a Seattle surgeon, wanted to establish a living memorial to Fred: the Fred Hutchinson Cancer Research Center is the result. The Hutchinson Center is a world leader in research on the prevention, diagnosis and treatment of cancer, HIV/AIDS and other life-threatening diseases.

We feel fortunate to live only a 20-minute drive from the Center. Some come long distances, from far-flung points around the globe to be treated here. All the while, whatever illnesses we are up against, we know it is important to keep perspective: doctors treat ~ Jesus heals.

This week is the bad week. The one always following the treatment described above, filled with days of weakness and an almost total lack of energy. Rest is the only real answer while her body fights back against the Enemy Cancer. She sleeps off and on through the day. Still she remains in good spirits. Next Friday, more scans will be taken and we will know better how things are going.

∾

Living the life I was designed to live.

Why would I ever think of disregarding the commands and laws of God, which reveal to me the way he desires me to live, and believe God would give me the life I desire? He designed me in a way to bring him pleasure, but I am designed to also bring his good pleasure to me. That is my deepest desire… to live as I am designed!

~ *to glorify God*
~ *to drink deeply from his source*
~ *to live joyfully, lovingly, richly*
~ *to bring pleasure to him*
~ *DLT diary, March 2012*

∾

38

The Thousand-Year Day

The primary discipline of prayer is waiting. Waiting requires patience and perseverance. ~ WT

Mark Buchanan in *Your God Is Too Safe* calls this "the holy habit—living out the conviction that the Lord is not slow in keeping his promise, as some understand slowness. What we expect may take almost forever—a thousand years, anyhow—can happen in a day. More often, what we wish would happen in a day may take a thousand years. The holy habit is getting used to the reality that with the Lord one is like the other."[8]

On Dixie's sacred journey, a day like today can become a week, a month, a year, all rolled into one. We prepare for our scheduled visit with Oncology, and another normal Destroy-the-Enemy-Cancer infusion day. Books, iPad, Dixie's new birthday Kindle (replacing the old one she has literally worn out from reading) are in the carry bag. We cross the SR 520 bridge on our way to SCCA. Once there, the usual blood draw on F1, then to F4 and an appointment with Dr. Chiorean's young colleague,

---

[8] *Mark Buchanan, Your God is Too Safe, Multnomah Books, 2001.*

Dr. Lisa Vanderhoef. We know already that Dr. Chiorean is on hospital call at UWMC this week.

Lisa goes over the blood test results. All good. After a few minutes she begins discussing the CT scan results from last Friday. These, she says, are not so good. While the size of lymph nodes in question have decreased and no other organs show positive, the tumor on the liver has doubled in size since testing two months ago and the lungs show increased cancer cell activity. In other words, *the chemo treatment is not working!*

Lisa pauses and asks if there are questions. Seriously? Of course there are. What is a reasonable prognosis? She admits this is a question beyond her professional skills to answer. She recommends meeting soon with Charlie or Pam who work with Palliative Care to talk about future goals and plans. We sense Lisa is not used to this kind of duty as she sits in for Dr. Chiorean. She is doing her best. It just doesn't meet the need. We feel empathy for her. We have been here often for others during our lifetimes. And now it is us.

A day like a thousand years...thinking along that scale is hard to get my arms around. But one that *feels* like a thousand years? I get that. When one asks for answers, assuming there is enough faith (does anyone know how much is enough?), we should get the answer we are hoping for, right? Not necessarily. Factor a thousand years into the equation, and it is another thing, isn't it? God is not obligated to dispense answers like dollars in a candy machine.

Yes, the primary discipline of prayer *is* waiting. It does require patience and perseverance.

It is, however, intended to encourage and strengthen, not to distress and leave us hanging.

Three times the apostle Paul asked for a physical problem in his body to be resolved. He wanted it to be taken away. The

Lord's response was, "My grace is sufficient for you, for my power is made perfect in weakness...For the sake of Christ, then, I am content with weaknesses, insults, hardships, persecutions, and calamities. For when I am weak, then I am strong" (2 Corinthians 12:9,10).

Today Dixie mentions a new thought has come to her regarding Romans 12:1, "I appeal to you therefore, brothers, by the mercies of God, to present your bodies as a living sacrifice, holy and acceptable to God, which is your spiritual worship...that by testing you may discern what is the will of God, what is good and acceptable and perfect." She says this is what she is doing.

I remind her that this is something we've done throughout much of our lifetimes. To which she replies with Psalm 31:15, "But this is different. This is what I am doing today. I'm presenting my physical body to the Lord. I'm not going to feel sorry for myself. I am going to live as I would if I did not know my life may be shortened. I choose to live in the fullness of joy and with purpose until my life is done. There is only One who truly knows my end date. It is he of whom David writes this affirming word, 'My times are in your hand.'"

I mentioned this to our primary care doctor earlier today. Dr. Bankson was the first to suspect the root cause of Dixie's illness last February. (How many doctors have we become acquainted with since then?) She smiles and shakes her head. "She is one courageous lady!" I agree.

We will continue to do as our doctors recommend. After Thanksgiving, Dixie will resume infusion treatment with yet another form of chemotherapy called *FOLFOX*. This chemotherapy regimen is designed and used in patients with advanced, metastatic colorectal cancer. It consists of the drugs: *Folinic acid*

(*Leucovorin*), *Fluorouracil (5-FU)*, and *Oxaliplatin (Eloxatin)*. Strange new words to us.

Wednesday 26 November. Tonight Dixie and I are sitting in a borrowed and thoroughly beautiful island home, looking out onto the Puget Sound. Members of our family who live here in the Northwest will be joining us for Thanksgiving Day. Granddaughter, Katy, and husband, Geoff, will open the envelope telling us the gender of our newest great-grandchild, due in March. We are hoping for a girl or a boy. Either will be just fine! New life. We are excited.

She leans into me, her eyes fixed on some distant point. I look to where she is looking. Is she thinking what I am thinking? Like many older couples, our thoughts often run together after all these years. I don't want to go there, but I cannot help but wonder... could this be our last one? Our last Thanksgiving together? I keep looking... to where she is looking... but I cannot see that far.

God is good. We are good.

I love you, O Lord, my strength. The Lord is my rock and my fortress and my deliverer, my God, my rock, in whom I take refuge, my shield, and the horn of my salvation, my stronghold. ~ Psalm 18:1,2

Happy Thanksgiving!

39

Doctors Treat ... Jesus Heals

Kenya Africa's Tenwek Hospital is a Christian medical community. Their motto, "We Treat—Jesus Heals," is Tenwek's guiding belief and the hope that is offered to each patient.

⌒

We treat.

First Thursday 4 December. The day gets under way at 5 o'clock at Starbucks. Today Michele and I talk about our recent family Thanksgiving celebration; four generations enjoying one another in a beautiful Northwest island home. We experience sun, rain, snow and a powerful windstorm, all within four days, a picture of our today lives, painted by God's hand from nature's palette.

And we talk about her brother, Stephen, Nancy and Jesse. They are flying home from Hong Kong on the 19th and will be with us until early the 24th, when they go on to celebrate Christmas with Nancy's side of the family in Tennessee. Her parents are retired missionaries. Our granddaughter, Jessica, will fly in from Denver to be with us as well. We are excited to see them again. Especially all at the same time. A rare treat for us.

The *FOLFOX* treatment scenario is new. The doctor describes it to us as like "bringing in the Marines." It is designed for a heavy jolt that hopefully decreases, or at least holds at status quo the liver tumor that doubled in size during the last two months of chemotherapy. At the same time, it should arrest whatever else may be happening in her lungs, where some spots yet too small to biopsy are showing an increase in size. We pray for minimum side effects and maximum punch on the liver tumor and lung activity. This chemotherapy is a bag full of heavy duty stuff!

Fluorouracil (F-5) is a chemotherapy drug used to treat a variety of cancers. *Oxaliplatin* is a chemotherapy agent used to treat cancers of the colon, as well as other types of cancers. *Leucovorin* is used to "rescue" normal (non-cancerous) cells and increase the anti-cancer effects of Fluorouracil. Whoa, the Marines really have landed!

After all is done, an ambulatory infusion pump is attached to Dixie's port to maintain the chemotherapy infusion process after we are home. She will carry this with her at all times, even to bed. The infusion of the drugs will continue non-stop until 4:30pm, Saturday, when we return to SCCA and the pump is disconnected. We are shown how to operate the pump and how to handle accidental chemotherapy spills or tubing leaks. We've even been given an action plan in case of an emergency or natural disaster while attached to the pump. It sounds like an all-or-nothing Normandy-style invasion. The Marines are fighting back. We are grateful, but anxious at the same time.

Nurse Deb is assigned to Dixie for this infusion. She brings another nurse in to meet her. She says the nurses all are talking about how Dixie is the "youngest woman," given her actual age, they have ever known. Deb asks questions. How long have you been married? Really? That long with the right person must be wonderful. It hasn't always been smooth and easy, Deb, but yes, we made it through the hard times and today it is the best! Children? Grandchildren? *Great-grandchildren!* Are you serious? I listen quietly to their conversation. The nurse smiles at last and says to Dixie, "You have a rich life!"

We've been with SCCA doctors, nurses and techs since early this afternoon. We have two or three more hours before we get out of here and head home. Long day, but it's true. We have indeed a very rich life. Not simply in things, but in what really matters. Through good times and bad.

⌒

Jesus heals.

Our 'rich life' is made richer still as we wend our way on this long journey through the Valley of Shadows, a journey we know will end before we want it to. When one surrenders his/her life to the Lord, it means we go where he wants, for as long as he wants, do whatever he wants, and wait patiently when we are done for his next call. The Captain of our souls is our true north. This is how we choose to live.

⌒

And he said to them, "Follow me, and I will make you fishers of men." ~Matthew 4:19

⌒

40

Merry Christmas!

"... And you shall call his name JESUS." You were uniquely named by your Father, and sent with a mission to fulfill... "for he shall save his people from their sins." Your very name was a reminder to everyone who spoke to you that you were a wonderful gift to them; but somehow, even in your short life as a man, that truth was lost.

No wonder in our modern day, names are lost; their meanings forgotten, overlooked or ignored. The **Cheers** television series was popular because at Cheers, "Everybody knows your name." The lovers in the movie, *Children of a Lesser God*, were hurting because he just wanted his deaf and speech-impaired lover to say his name. How hungry people are today to "make a name for themselves," or simply to be called by their name.

Thank you, Father, for knowing my name. You have written it in your Book of Life, because Jesus fulfilled his purpose. He fulfilled the meaning of his name.

On this day I can say the name "Jesus" and understand "Savior!"

~ *DLT diary, Christmas 1995*

For eleven days, the *FOLFOX* infusion trio, *Fluorouracil* (F-5), *Oxaliplatin,* and *Leucovorin,* have been at work, searching out

Enemy Cancer cells and destroying them wherever they can be found. However, as with precise bombing or rocket fire tactics designed to take out enemy killers, innocent cells going about their normal life-serving duties are also destroyed. Tagged as collateral damage, it is the calculated cost of this never-ending deadly warfare.

Regretfully, Wednesday is a bad day. She is dressed and standing at the door, ready to attend a C3 Leaders Forum Christmas dinner, when she looks up at me and says quietly, "I'm sorry. I just can't do it." I help her back upstairs and into bed. Once I am sure she is comfortable, since I am the group leader, I attend the dinner alone.

Friday is better. She visits the annual Christmas party in our condo community, where residents who truly love her and are glad to see her, surround her. She enjoys the evening, eventually leaving early, savoring the human touches and sounds of warm goodbyes, then returning to our apartment, fatigued from giving out so much of her depleted energy reserve, but exhilarated from feeding off the friendships of good neighbors.

Life changes on a daily, sometimes hourly basis for us now. Going forward in the weeks, months and years ahead, we choose to give to our time together as much love and attention as is possible to do. It has been fifteen months since beginning a medical search for an elusive "something is wrong" problem; ten months since the dreadful diagnosis launching surgery, radiation and now, her third round of chemotherapy, which we expect to continue at least until the end of January. She remains as active as strength will allow, with weakness and fatigue increasing each day. Late in January, fresh scans are to be taken and we will know whether or not this chemo round is working and to what extent.

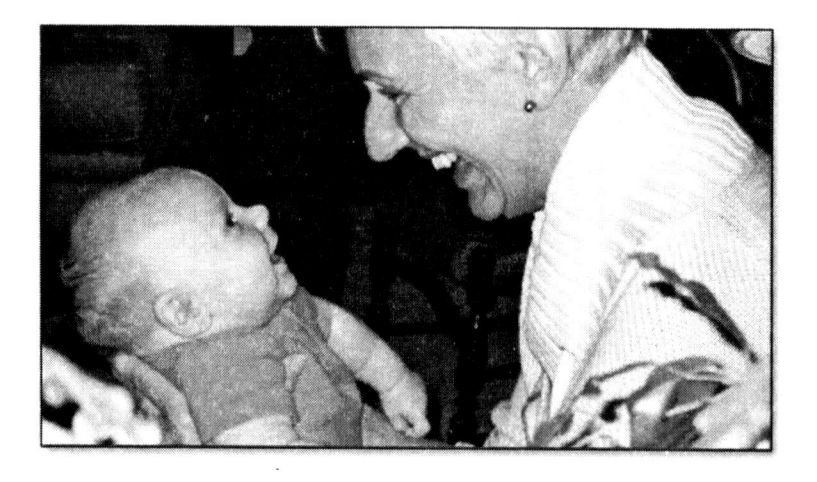

20 GG and great-grandson, Corbin

We are grateful for thousands of prayers directed to the ear of God, as well as the best medical resources we could hope for; we are also realists, understanding we are a very small part of our Lord's grand scheme. Whatever is ahead, his will in all areas of our lives remains the main thing. We are not anxious. We are at peace in our Lord's promises. He is forever trustworthy and we are trusting in him. We are confident he hears our prayers. No question.

God is our refuge and strength, a very present help in trouble. ~ *Psalm 46:1*

Christmas! For much of our married life, we've lived at significant distances from our parents, siblings, children and extended family members. Special holidays like Easter, Thanksgiving and Christmas have not been celebrated with all these primary family members present, but with the cherished people we love and serve in our congregations and elsewhere throughout the world, who continue to be our family in Christ. This is also a reality for many of our colleagues and their families with similar callings and responsibilities as ours. If it's true in your church this year, it is a gift. Enjoy your pastors or priests; tell them how much they are loved and be blessed in so doing.

This year for us will be different, with our children, grandchildren, great-grandson (with #2 on the way), together on the weekend before Christmas, a rarity since we live so geographically spread apart ~ providing us with many looked forward to delightful moments. Those from far away will arrive on Friday to link up with our Northwest family.

Merry Christmas!

41

The Greatest Small Gift

In the beginning was the Word, and the Word was with God, and the Word was God. ~ John 1:1

Behold, the virgin shall conceive and bear a son, and they shall call his name Immanuel (which means, God with us). ~ Matthew 1:23

And she gave birth to her firstborn son and wrapped him in swaddling cloths and laid him in a manger, because there was no place for them in the inn. ~ Luke 2:7

And the Word became flesh and dwelt among us, and we have seen his glory, glory as of the only Son from the Father, full of grace and truth. ~ John 1:14

These four simple, yet incredibly profound verses describe the greatest small gift ever given to mankind. It is the reason Dixie and I celebrate this Christmas. It isn't simply that we believe God is great (he'd have to be to put this universe in motion, would he not?). Nor is it that he may possibly be out there somewhere looking with disinterest upon all he has created. It's because we believe he loves enough to be omnipresent among us all, to identify with what and with whom he has created, to offer up the greatest gift in a tiny, helpless person... *the gift of his presence.*

⁓

Thursday 18 December. Before Christmas week, we arrive at SCCA for a blood draw, followed by an appointment with Dr. Chiorean. Our long term patient / doctor relationship has by now morphed into more of a symbiotic association, a mutual interaction between different individuals linked together by a common problem.

As our appointment nears its end, I ask the question that has lingered in my mind, "Doctor, you have set up an appointment for us with Palliative Care. It feels as though you may be moving us from curative more toward comfort care. We need to know. Is this the direction in which you are thinking?"

"No, no, not at all," her reply comes quickly. "Often people hear palliative care and imagine the cancer or heart patient, or whatever the long term illness is being made comfortable in an end-of-life hospice type setting. Palliative care is quite different. It is an emerging new medical specialty in the last few years... and no, as good as hospice is, it's not the same.

"Palliative care doesn't serve only patients in the final stages. Instead, it focuses more broadly on improving life and providing comfort to people of all ages with serious chronic and life-threatening illnesses. In short, this new medical specialty aims to improve one's quality of life, however you define that for yourself. Your palliative care providers work with you to identify and carry out goals having to do with symptom relief, counseling, and spiritual comfort; in other words, whatever enhances your quality of life."

"Thank you," I reply. "That's helpful to hear. We've been at this so intently and for so long now, we are beginning to wonder when there will be a light at the end of this tunnel."

Dr. Chiorean continues, "This may help. I've also spoken with Dr. Park. He remains open to the possibility of liver surgery, providing we see sufficient improvement from this current chemotherapy series. But you can receive palliative care while at the same time pursuing other treatments for your illness. We are hopeful *FOLFOX* will help us turn the corner. If it does not, there are other possibilities to consider, including a clinical trial in which some good results have been reported."

I counter with, "Numerous other non-medical suggestions have been offered up by friends. Some report good results. What do you think?"

"Bring to our attention anything you want us to look at, please. Many of our modern medical treatments have their origins in plants and in nature's other curative elements. We will be happy to consider alternative treatments with you, in addition to what we normally work with, and will go over them with you carefully."

Later on, while undergoing the infusion treatment on F5 Bay 15, we discuss what we have heard from the doctor. After reflecting, we agree. It is not so much *"what"* was said as *"how"* she said it. It was her tone, her attitude that left us feeling more positive than we have been for awhile. Was it a sense of false hope being offered up, or a reaffirming belief that she and others at the clinic are doing their very best, studying, thinking ahead, consulting together interdisciplinary? We are not sure, but of this we are certain. She has given us the greatest small gift...*the gift of her presence.*

In truth, nothing has changed. We are still right where we were, in the Valley of Shadows. The home infusion pump continues to send chemo chemicals into Dixie's body as we head home. It will continue for forty-six more hours. Yet this long day ends with a deep awareness of *God's presence,* of having completed today's part of our sacred journey with One who knows the way.

Friday. It's ten o'clock, and I am at SEATAC, gathering up our son Stephen, Nancy and Jesse, who look tired and happy to be on the ground again, having just flown all the way from Hong Kong, via Tokyo. A half hour later, Jessica is in the car with us as well, having come the opposite direction, from Denver. And a half hour after that we are all home again, beginning an extended pre-Christmas family weekend, the first in eleven years for us all to be together at the same time. Each minute is precious as laughter blends with delightful flavors around the food bar. When asked if anyone wants to do anything special, everyone agrees. We are doing it. So we just hang out together. Like family.

Saturday. Everyone enjoys a tasty brunch prepared for us the day before by two of our good friends. Michele has taken a half day off from work to help oversee the kitchen. Neighbors place cards and small gifts at our door.

We leave the rest of the family to arrive at SCCA at 4:30 for home pump removal. The nursing staff is nearing the end of a long week. Conversation is light, humor is the balm. Within the hour we are "free at last." At least for another week. We head for home.

Mark, Katy, Geoff and Corbin have joined us. Michele is the soup chef, presenting us with family tradition main courses of clam chowder and tomato bisque soup, bread and olives. After dinner, presents are shared with those who must leave before Christmas Day, to be with other family members elsewhere. As is often the case, presents are most enjoyed by those newest to the family, happy to be here, too young to know why.

Jessica presents our three-year-old little dude, Corbin, with three small Jurassic-Park-style prehistoric animals. He proceeds to roar around family forest with them in true beast mode (it helps if you are a Seattle Seahawk fan) the rest of the evening. An endearing moment of innocent pleasure. No electric cords. No batteries. No flashing lights. Just three small hard mold toys and grateful thanks (twice I observe Corbin pause and say, "Thank you," to his gift giver before roaring on by).

Watching, I realize we can all learn something here. This wouldn't be near the fun if his gift had just mysteriously turned up...if there had been no giver to thank...or if the little dude had to roar about the forest all alone. It turns out the real present is not the Jurassic-Park-style toy figures after all. The real present is *presence*. Presence of the giver. Presence of others with whom to share the gift. Presence makes one happy. Period.

Jesus declared, "I thank you, Father, Lord of heaven and earth, that you have hidden these things from the wise and understanding and revealed them to little children." ~ Matthew 11:25

Sunday. Jessica returns to Denver this afternoon. The rest of us come together again in the evening for dinner. And while there are not many die-hard sports fans in our family (where did I go wrong?) the Seahawks do manage to make Seattle proud once more.

Wednesday 24 December. A Tuesday evening dinner at a favorite Mexican restaurant is followed a few hours later by an early 3:00 am Christmas Eve drop off at SeaTac International. Stephen, Nancy and Jesse are on their way to Memphis and from there to Brownsville. They will visit Nancy's mom and dad, four sisters and their families, all from the eastern US, before flying back to Hong Kong on the 30th.

Yes, the distances keeping us apart are indeed wide... but for this one week, we all agree. It's a small world after all.

∽

We ought not to be weary of doing little things for the love of God, who regards not the greatness of the work, but the love with which it is performed. ~ Brother Lawrence, *The Practice of the Presence of God*

∽

The greatest small gift ever given mankind we celebrate on Christmas Day...Jesus' presence mingled with ours...with those we love in our human family...and in the family of God.

∽

42

When Rights Are Not Always Right

Darkness cannot drive out darkness: only light can do that.
Hate cannot drive out hate: only love can do that.
~ Martin Luther King Jr., A Testament of Hope:
The Essential Writings and Speeches

♾

This is Dixie's bad week again, five days since Monday; for Dixie a day of appointments and chemo infusion. The bad days usually last well into the following week now, before she begins to feel what we call her "new normal." Our far away family members are all safe at home after being with us for Christmas. It is quieter here, so for a few brief moments, we look at a wound on the world that, like a cancer of evil, is infecting the human spirit of us all. A wound that will not easily heal.

"*Suis-je* Charlie?"

"Happy New Year," seems like an inappropriate cliché, uttered by gushing greeters at a mass funeral when one considers this week's tragedy in Paris. Our new 2015 year begins with a sad and sobering reminder: we are indeed at war, though some on the world's leadership stage appear to feel it is not really war if the word "war" is not spoken. It is not a conflict driven by a desperate need for food, or for a coveted patch of land, or even the result of misguided politics. It is a random fanaticism, fueled by confused religious and insular ideologies, goaded by a consuming hatred, often silent and unseen until striking with chaotic and deadly force. As is the case this week in January in Paris (additional terrorist attacks take place in Paris in November 2015). Sadly, by the time you read this, there will have been more terrorist acts and innocent victims elsewhere over which we must grieve.

To the French today, whose ancestors many decades ago were the first to befriend America's dream of being "one nation, under God, with liberty and justice for all," we add our friendship, hopes and prayers to those of others being offered up in your behalf around the world.

When rights are not always right.

Truth be told, I am not Charlie Hebdo and I do not endorse what his editorial colleagues were selling or how they were selling it. There are times when the media acts like the neighborhood bully, arbitrarily exercising the right to push others around and beat up on them just because he can; because he is bigger or has a weapon, or because they are simply incapable of defending themselves for whatever reason.

In social media cartooning, there is a fine line between free speech and aggressive provocative mockery of politics, religion or race. When it comes to religious satire, be it Christian, Judaism, or Islam, I personally believe Charlie crossed the line too many times, far too often abusing the right to free speech and freedom of press for shock value. Actually, it isn't just Charlie; it happens to Christians every day in the conversations we hear, the books we read and the movies we see. When have you ever watched a movie and heard Mohammed's name spoken as a curse word?

Is it possible to abuse one's right to be right? The answer is yes. Perhaps at one time or another, we've all been guilty. Parents have the right to expect their child to obey, but not the right to beat them until they do. Having said this, no sane human being can ever justify the retaliatory Islamic act of murder in the name of Allah that the world witnessed this week in Paris, killing seventeen innocents in addition to the three terrorists taken out by the police.

In rhetoric and ethics there is the phrase, "two wrongs don't make a right." It's a proverb used to rebuke wrongful conduct in response to another's transgression. So let me trample on this old phrase by saying, "Three wrongs do not make a right either." It is wrong for us to sit back in judgment and say, "Charlie asked for it." It is wrong to heave a sigh in relief, "Glad it wasn't me." And it is wrong to waste the lessons evil teaches by simply hoping the odds are in favor of it never happening to us.

What should we do?

It is hard, if not impossible, to give a single sentence, complete, all-encompassing answer to this question. Perhaps we could start by praying for forgiveness for our own lack of charity and our thoughtlessness. Honestly, has it been a while since you have loved your enemies?

You have heard that it was said, "You shall love your neighbor and hate your enemy." But I say to you, Love your enemies and pray for those who persecute you, so that you may be sons of your Father who is in heaven. For he makes his sun rise on the evil and on the good, and sends rain on the just and on the unjust. For if you love those who love you, what reward do you have? Do not even the tax collectors do the same? And if you greet only your brothers, what more are you doing than others? Do not even the Gentiles do the same? You therefore must be perfect, as your heavenly Father is perfect. ~ Jesus in Matthew 5:43–48

We can pray the wounds felt by our French brothers and sisters in the human family (as well as our faith family) will send us all back to the God who "so loved the world, that he gave his only son..." (John 3:16).

And we can pray for wisdom to manifest itself among our nation's leaders, many of whom profess to be men and women of faith (in the 114th Congress—Christian 91.8%; Jewish 5.2%; Other 1.4%, None 1.7%).

Dixie and I live day by day through this trying season in our lives. We are glad we can do it together. If there were a magic potion or a single pill that healed and restored one to health, Dixie would take it. If there were a prayer that guaranteed Dixie's return to perfect health, we would utter it a thousand times. The same is true of this world in which we remain very much a part.

The fact is, there are no winner-take-all, easy answers here. Not in the world's problems. Not in France's pain. Not in mistreating a defenseless child. Not in Dixie's suffering with cancer. Healing, whether the wounds of the world or the suffering of the human body, begins with minds that are open to God's Word and hearts that will trust in him. It's that simple, really. This is my personal view. I do not speak for my neighbors, my church or for anyone else. I speak freely and openly, just for me. It's what I get to do in America. Exercising my right to free speech and hopefully make my point without denigrating others.

You keep him in perfect peace whose mind is stayed on you, because he trusts in you. ~ Isaiah 26:3

May our Lord keep us all in his peace.

43

It's Not Over 'til It's Over

Count it all joy, my brothers, when you meet trials of various kinds, for you know that the testing of your faith produces steadfastness.
~ James 1:2,3

Life for Seattle football's 12th-MAN crowd doesn't get any more exciting than this last weekend. It goes like this: fifty-seven minutes of complete frustration while the Seahawks drive body parts up against a great Green Bay's Packers football team, plus an eternity of sheer pandemonium packed into a half dozen game closing minutes. The result? A trip for the Seahawks to Arizona and the Super Bowl!

Some ticket holders leave the game early, having given up on their team's chances. Outside in the parking lots, they hear the roar of the crowd and rush back. But the rule is, once you leave through the gates, you cannot return. There is no coming back for them. So they can only watch television screens through the barred gates or listen on the radio. And miss seeing firsthand the finale of quite possibly the most exciting game in Seahawk history.

The way GB plays these 57 game minutes, it appears the game is theirs. The pro analysts who figure these things say, given points behind, plus time left to play, equals a one in one hundred chance that Seattle can rally to win! I am being texted throughout the game by various Seahawk and Cheesehead friends scattered around the country (one whose son is a GB coach) and, let me just say, it isn't pretty. But at the end of regulation play (for those few of you who live on another planet) the game is tied, 22–22. A coin toss will decide which team gets the ball first. The visiting team gets to call heads or tails. Seattle wins the toss. All I can say is that moment (and really the entire game), while the coin is in the air, gives new meaning to "finishing well."

Forty-eight hours later, I am sitting in the quiet of SCCA's F5 34 treatment bay. We've been in the building since 9 o'clock. It is nearly noon. We should be home by 5 o'clock. Amy is our nurse today. Her voice is raspy, her throat sore. She's not sick, she says reassuringly. She and her husband have season tickets. They were at the game on Sunday. Yelling insanely. Part of the NFL's noisiest crowd.

Dixie is sleeping to the gentle beep-beep of the chemotherapy infusion equipment on the other side of her bed; unmindful of the murmur of voices in the hall beyond the curtained entrance. Her Kindle book lies open on her lap. She needs the rest. It will have been a long day for her before we are done. Tomorrow should be a feel good day, but by evening the chemo side effects will likely have kicked in.

Fluorouracil (F-5) plus *Oxaliplatin* to kill the Cancerous cells. *Leucovorin* to rescue normal (non-cancerous) cells and increase the anti-cancer effects of the *Fluorouracil*. These are still the players. When the infusion is complete, Dixie will reattach her port to an ambulatory infusion pump and continue the chemotherapy infusion process at home or wherever she goes for the next forty-six hours. On Thursday, we will return to SCCA where the pump will be disconnected. By now it seems routine to us. A routine we would not wish on anyone.

The winners? The verdict is still out. Prayers are in the air. We know our Coach and Mighty Healer is watching. This game has gone on for a long time. The score is...well, we just don't know yet. It's close, but we are in overtime. We are hopeful. Those in the stands who have been praying, encouraging, putting their all into their support for us are amazing! Don't leave us too early. These heartfelt prayers are more than 12th-MAN noise. So much more.

The smoke of the incense, with the prayers of the saints, rose before God from the hand of the angel. ~ Revelation 8:4.

There's that incense again; but, you know, the more it mingles with the prayers of God's people, the more I'm beginning to like it.

I know you can't read the scoreboard from where you are standing (no one is left sitting in a game this close). Nor can we. But this much we know. There is One who has the ball right now and holds our times in his hands. That can only mean one thing. It's okay to offer up a shout out for Jesus. Regardless of the final score...WE WIN!

44

The Thing Between God and Us

When pain and suffering come upon us, we finally see not only that we are not in control of our lives, but that we never were.
~ Timothy Keller, *Walking with God through Pain and Suffering*

Super Bowl XLIX is over. Dixie and I enjoyed our own quiet and comfortable Super Bowl party ... except for the final 20 seconds of the game. Ah, life can be cruel, can it not? Seattle grieves the improbable loss of sports history within its grasp. But not for long. Because, you see, it's only a game. Please, don't pelt me with rotten tomatoes. So it's on to baseball and those few days in Springtime when the sun peeks through Seattle's clouds, flowers bloom, and where for 37 seasons Northwest sports fans have wistfully said to one another, "This could be the year. Go Mariners!" For those few of you who don't eat, sleep and breathe

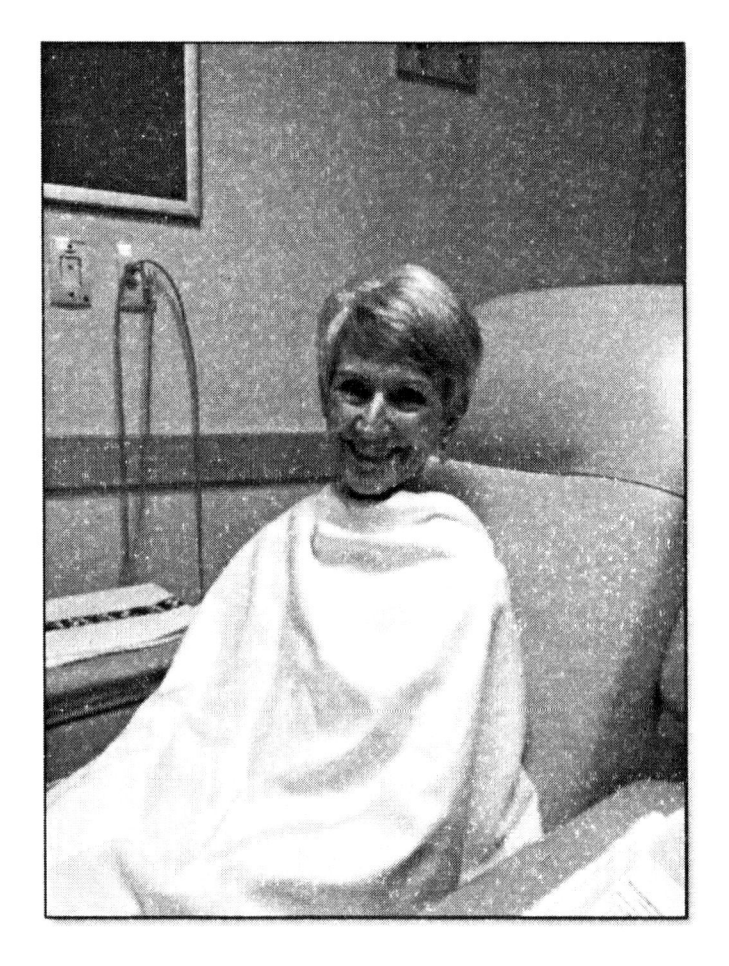

21 Dixie stays warm while waiting for treatment to get underway.

baseball, the Mariners are our team. And they've never sniffed World Series air. Play ball!

Monday 2 February. We are caught up in heavy traffic and arrive twenty minutes late for the 8 o'clock blood draw. No matter. Dr. Chiorean will be behind schedule as well since she lives on the Eastside, too. At 9:40 we are together again in the same small room, listening to the results of Friday's CT scans.

"Your post-Whipple operation shows no evidence of local recurrence," says Dr. Chiorean, "and in the lungs most of the previously seen pulmonary nodules seem to be stable for now. But there is a continuing increase in the size of the hepatic metastasis. In other words, the mass we see on the liver continues to resist chemotherapy."

This is not a game. This is not a winning or losing play in the 4th Quarter. This is not a long fly ball in the ninth inning. This is life and death. It is disheartening news. Dixie asks for a break in treatment. Dr. Chiorean agrees. Dixie has been receiving chemo doses in a strength that patients half her age find difficult. Dr. Chiorean will confer with Drs. Park and Kim to plan for next steps. And so instead of chemotherapy, Dixie undergoes a 2-hour hydration infusion and by 2 o'clock we are home again.

For because he himself has suffered when tempted, he is able to help those who are being tempted. ~ Hebrews 2:18

Tuesday. Weariness in the battle is inescapable. It is a hard day. The past two months of *FOLFOX* chemotherapy have been exhausting. With each infusion it is harder to recover from the side effects of nausea and extreme fatigue. Outside our apartment this morning it is cold, the sky is gray and close over the city, with a light mist falling. One of those Northwest days in which you can walk in the rain forever without an umbrella and never get wet.

A few more days and one year will have passed since we sat together in a doctor's office and were given the news. Pancreatic cancer.

"How should I feel about this?"
"Nervous?"

An understatement, looking back on a year of surgery, biopsies, chemotherapy, radiation, scans, sickness, pain, suffering. And depression. Light at the end of the tunnel this morning seems farther away than ever. She looks up from a breakfast barely touched, her countenance lined with tears and weariness and says simply, "I don't think I can do this," followed moments later with, "Sorry, I don't want to be a complainer."

In the year past, I do not recall ever hearing her utter the "c" word. Until now. After breakfast she sits on the floor near the fireplace and reads. Later in the day she goes to the kitchen, a favorite place to create, to be busy, and prepares the evening meal. Enchiladas. Green beans. Salad. A favorite and it is tasty terrific, though she can eat very little.

Thursday, Michele and I have our regular 5 o'clock "First Thursday" coffee at Starbucks. She tells me how she wishes she could do more, be more involved, more caring. There are tears. From both of us. I can feel how this is eating away at her in so many ways. I tell her, "You are doing it right now, just being here with me. This is caring."

> *By itself suffering does no good. But when we see it as the thing between God and us, it has meaning. Wedged in the crux—the cross—suffering becomes a transaction. The cross is a place of transaction. It is the place where power happens between God and us.*[9] *~ Joni Eareckson Tada and Steven Estes*

At 8:15, Dixie and I arrive at a place new to us in north Seattle, the SCCA/UW Proton Therapy Center, to meet a team that is also new to us, including Kenyan-born clinical nurse, Zippy Mwicigi,

---

[9] *When God Weeps: Why Our Sufferings Matter to the Almighty.* Joni Eareckson Tada and Steven Estes. Zondervan, 1997.

and gastrointestinal specialist, Dr. Apisarnthanarax ("Just call me Dr. A."), a Thai from Texas. We are here today to be introduced to a next-generation radiation treatment that more precisely targets tumors, minimizing radiation to healthy tissue, than is possible with any other instrument. It is the very latest thing.

Seattle's Proton Therapy Center is the newest of ten such facilities in the US, and is built around a giant cyclotron, with four different radiology treatment bays designed for patients with differing types of cancers. We learn that Proton therapy is ionizing, high-energy radiation in which larger doses can be delivered to the targeted area, with fewer side effects and faster patient recovery due to its precise application. The Proton therapy story and the facility is both state-of-the-art and a bit overwhelming.

During a lengthy discussion with Dr. A, we are informed that Dixie is a candidate for such treatment. However, she could also deal with this bad-boy liver tumor surgically with Dr. Park at UWMC. Outcomes are predicted to be 80–90% successful, and pretty much the same whichever way she chooses. Dixie wants Dr. A to discuss the options again with Dr. Park. He agrees to do so and to arrange for us to meet with Dr. Park, before a final decision is made.

This evening is "First Thursday" for Mom and Michele. They go to a nearby restaurant, find a quiet corner and do their favorite thing, sit and talk. It's the first time Dixie has been out like this for some time and it is therapeutic.

The next morning, she tells me that, while reading prayers of Benedictine monks in *The Glenstal Book of Prayer,* she became aware of just how these prayers all seem to focus, not on petition, but rather on praising God in every circumstance. And with that awareness, no matter what the ongoing treatment outcomes might be, she feels her own spirit begin to lift. After days in the Valley of Shadows, her eyes are alight with gratefulness and praise to God.

In the real world of pain, how could one worship a God who was immune to it (suffering)? I have entered many Buddhist temples in different Asian countries and stood respectfully before the statue of the Buddha, his legs crossed, arms folded, eyes closed, the ghost of a smile playing round his mouth, a remote look on his face, detached from the agonies of the world. But each time, after a while I have had to look away. And in imagination I have turned instead to the lonely, twisted, tortured figure on the cross, nails through hands and feet, back lacerated, limbs wrenched, brow bleeding from thorn pricks, mouth dry and intolerably thirsty, plunged in God-forsaken darkness. That is the God for me! He laid aside His immunity to pain. He entered our world of flesh and blood, tears and death. He suffered for us. Our sufferings become more manageable in the light of His. There is still a question mark against human suffering, but over it we stamp another mark, the cross which symbolizes divine suffering.[10] ~ *John R.W. Stott*

Outside our apartment this morning it is still cold, the sky is still gray and close over the city, with a light mist still falling. Another one of those Northwest days in which you can walk forever without an umbrella and never really get wet. But inside, there is a Light in the Valley of Shadows.

We are not alone.

---

10 *The Cross of Christ* by John R.W. Stott. IVP Books, 2006.

45

Happy Valentine's Day

So I ask you not to lose heart over what I am suffering for you, which is your glory. ~ Ephesians 3:13

One year. Our first "anniversary." 365 days. 8760 hours.

When the actual cancer battle was first joined only God knows. When the first bad boy cell met up with another rogue cell, then another and another, until a gang of miscreant cells formed an army of millions, all with the same deadly intent; truly, only God knows. And with this realization, my "Why?" questions, the ones I so often have shaped in words unspoken, almost accusatory, over this last year of impossible days, surface again.

Why, if he knew, did he not do something about it then? As with Job of old, I query God. Why have you not answered? Why do you allow my beloved to suffer? I'm the one who should be suffering, not her. Followed moments later with, "I'm sorry, Lord, I don't want to be a complainer."

Are not two sparrows sold for a penny?

And not one of them will fall to the ground apart from your Father.
But even the hairs of your head are all numbered.
Fear not therefore; you are of more value than many sparrows.
~ *Matthew 10:29–31*

It is one year ago today the Enemy Cancer's behind the lines infiltration was discovered. One year ago that friendly forces launched an all out counter attack designed to destroy the Enemy. One year during which Dixie's body has been a battlefield for Good vs. Bad cellular warfare.

One year in which my heart has broken a little more each day.

Tuesday. We return to UWMC for a visit with Dr. Park, still the soft-spoken youngish gentleman we have grown to respect and in whom Dixie has great confidence. We are joined in the small examination room by a resident physician. We crowd in together as Dr. Park brings up pictures of Dixie's most recent CT scans on the computer screen, explaining in detail what we are seeing.

The spots we observe in the lungs appear to have responded to the chemotherapy for now, but the target of immediate concern is still the liver where the original pancreatic tumor has metastasized. The reason we are here today is to discuss options for the next battle strategies, 1) surgically burning the mass (now 2.4 cm or approximately one inch in size) clearly visible in the scans, or 2) taking the route of proton therapy. I watch and listen while Dr. Park patiently goes over the pros and cons of both procedures with Dixie and then makes his recommendation.

I know Proton therapy is not Dixie's first choice. We have discussed this numerous times. But her countenance expresses clear relief at hearing Dr. Park's recommendation. She trusts him and his argument in favor of proton therapy has made good sense to her. There are no guarantees of success, but the percentages are favorable for a good outcome with far fewer side effects. This is it then.

On Thursday of next week, we will make an early morning stop at SCCA to replace a lost power port identity card. Then it's on to UWMC for a 9 o'clock blood draw, a stop at the admitting office, and then to F1 and Radiation where the surgical insertion of tiny seeds around the tumor attached to the liver will take place. This procedure and follow-up will keep us here the rest of the day. It is the essential first step in Dixie's proton therapy procedure. Nothing comes easy.

And so the battle continues. A year ago, we did not get one another Valentine cards. It was not high on our list of priorities that day. And this year, I forgot to even get cards for our kids. It is something that has never been on my to-do list in the past. Dixie takes care of these things. So my apologies to all. Sorry, kids. And best wishes to everyone. Happy Valentine's Day. You are special. You are loved. Really.

46

Our Family in Christ

> "If God is our father, the church is our mother." The words are those of the Swiss Reformer John Calvin… It is impossible, unnecessary, and undesirable to be a Christian all by yourself as it is to be a newborn baby all by yourself.
>
> ~ N.T. Wright

Thursday 19 February. I awaken Dixie at 4:30 for a small portion of yogurt, water for MEDS, and black coffee. She is not permitted to eat anything solid after 5 o'clock until the surgical procedure later this morning is completed. We arrive at UWMC AT 8:45, for blood draw and admitting, then to F2 and Radiology. After the extensive prep, I kiss her lightly and watch as she is rolled away to the procedure room. It is 12:40 when I accompany her to F4 East Tower where she will remain under observation until 5 o'clock.

I make a latté run for her while she orders a sandwich and snicker doodle cookie and some apple juice. The Plaza Café on F1 is considerably larger than SCCA's Red Brick, and with many more choices. Life is good. The next few hours are spent reading and dozing. At 4:45 she is released, fifteen minutes early. I want to wheelchair her to parking, but she refuses; and so we make the long F3 walk to Pavilion parking slowly, recover our car and make our way back across Lake Washington to Bellevue and home. It's been a long, arduous, but successful day.

The tumor was located by ultrasound and then the skin pierced twice to accommodate the placement of two soft tissue gold fiducial markers in the liver near the mass. The markers will enhance accuracy and efficiency during proton therapy, providing real-time accurate localization of the treatment volumes. These are essential, we are told, whenever the target may move during and between treatments relative to external skin markings.

Next week we will return to the Proton Therapy Center in north Seattle to see what is ahead. We have been told 10–15 treatments will take place, but don't know yet exactly when these will begin, how many for sure, and with what frequency. We are grateful for these good people and their skills, the futuristic equipment, the caring attitudes we meet every day, and that it all exists within a few miles of our home. And most of all we are grateful for our family. Our extended family, yes, but also *the* family, the community we enjoy in Christ.

Now you are the body of Christ and individually members of it. ~ 1 Corinthians 12:27

Life stories are celebrated in the gifts of Word and sacrament, in birth and health, in illness and death. Our new lives, our redeemed lives began in Christ and the church. A small church in a farming/ranching community is where I made a serious life commitment to Jesus and was baptized. For Dixie, it was a church body formed in a large city nearly two thousand miles from my hometown. Church communities very different, very distant. What are the chances we would ever meet?

Dixie and I have served three churches in our lifetimes. Though I've not kept an accurate count, I've preached in more than 200 other churches, plus youth camps, radio, television, marriage seminars, seminary classes and church conferences. Dixie has been at my side, teaching and speaking on many of these occasions. Three churches plus. Weddings. Funerals. Infant dedications. Baptisms. Christ and his community. Our family!

Perhaps you are one of these we have met only once. Others many times over. Some have long since made the final turn, crossing the finish line of their sacred journeys. Many we've simply lost track of through the years. Some we've known only through notes or letters or brief conversations. Still others have come back to us in this past year of shadows; old friends and brand new, again and again, with prayers and encouraging words. The physical body is an amazing thing. The body of Christ more amazing still!

Who could have known so long ago that two scared kids, with no real idea of what was ahead, were about to experience such holy adventures as these?

Actually there is One who knew right from the start.

And all he said was, "Follow me."

I tread no path in life to Him unknown;

I lift no burden, bear no pain, alone;
My soul a calm, sure hiding place has found;
The everlasting arms my life surround.
                ~ *from "God, Thou Art Love," Robert Browning*

47

Don't Breathe

When I am afraid, I put my trust in you. ~ Psalm 56:3

It has been four weeks since Dixie's last chemotherapy infusion treatment. She is feeling considerably better as a result. It was 19 February, when doctors planted the two permanent gold markers into her liver at the site of the tumor. I know diamonds are a girl's best friend, but in this case gold will have to do. It was the first step in proton radiation therapy.

On Thursday this week, Michele joins us for the afternoon at the UW/SCCA Northwest Hospital campus, site of the Proton Therapy Center. We meet again with Dr. A and go over what will happen today. Eventually a technician comes and invites Dixie to follow her into one of the therapy treatment rooms where she is introduced to her team members.

After a few minutes of becoming comfortable with one another, she is placed on a hard-surface table and instructed to move her hands and arms into the surrender position while her pelvis area is locked in so she cannot move. This will be her position during actual radiation treatments. She remains this way without moving for the next two hours while her team works with her.

They find her earlier set of tattoo markers and proceed to add some new ones. I think this would be a great time to get a heart shaped tattoo with an arrow through it and "I love Ward" across it in script lettering. I've suggested this at other times so I don't bother saying anything now. The answer would be the same. She doesn't love me that much.

A breathing coach teaches her how to hold her breath while radiation is administered. Dr. A stops by to assure her that he will be here with the team throughout this prep session. He retires to the control room to watch over the technicians as they work. The precise measurements must be set in advance of the real deal. Dr. A tells us later that she did well, "like a swimmer." Much better than many of his patients. Of course she did.

She is given a handheld control with a thumb button. A mask is placed over her nose and mouth so when the technician chooses, air is removed and she is no longer able to breathe (this process is not for the faint of heart!). She holds it first for 15, then 20, 25, and 30 seconds. Each breath-hold graduation is done five times so it takes awhile. As long as she presses down on the thumb button she's okay. If something happens or there is a glitch of any kind and she needs help, the button is released (that is if she remembers to remove her thumb) and help is on the way.

The breathing coach and two others are in the room with her while she is training. During regular treatments she will be alone. On this first dry run, there are several technicians and others who are also in the control room observing the process with Dr. A. Since UWMC is a teaching hospital everyone is interested in what is going on. Once she and everyone else are confident she can do the treatment format successfully, she undergoes yet another CT scan. Dixie says if cancer doesn't get her, the X-rays may do the job. She has had a lot of them for sure.

Our hope is that the treatment will kill this specific Enemy Cancer mass. It will be a great victory for Dixie and for us all.

48

It Takes a Village!

Lord, my fervent prayer today is, let me touch people in a way that you can bless, or change, or draw them to yourself. Amen. ~ DLT diary, September 1990

⁓

In Dixie's first full year of battling cancer, we guesstimate she has been served by over two hundred dedicated men and women in the medical field who are directly or indirectly part of Bellevue's Overlake Medical Center (OMC), the University of Washington Medical Center (UWMC), and the Seattle Cancer Care Alliance (SCCA), also part of the Fred Hutchinson Cancer Research Center. Now we add the Proton Therapy Center team.

Monday 2 March. We are back at UWMC for another body scan. As Dixie is leaving, she is given a dated yellow card with her name and birthdate and the words, "This patient had a nuclear medicine procedure and may still have small amounts of radiation capable of detection. This amount of radiation poses no danger to the public..." She is advised that these small amounts will slowly disappear over the next three days. We decide it gives the song, *"You Light Up My Life,"* an entirely new meaning.

On another morning, Katy comes to hang out with Gramma. Any day now she will deliver our second great-grandson. Needless to say, excitement abounds.

Thursday. We are carving out new frontiers in Dixie's treatment program. Early this Thursday we are called back to the Proton Therapy Center (PTC) and informed something is showing wrong from her final scan and trial run the day before. She has to be retested. After several anxious moments it is determined the problem is with the machine, not Dixie. Testing with a new machine brings the expected results. The green light is given. After all this, finally, it's a go!

This evening at 7 o'clock, Randal, a member of her tech team, comes to escort her to the changing area and Treatment Room 3. Michele and I settle in near the fireplace in the large and comfortable waiting area as Dixie begins her first real proton radiation treatment. The safety margin sought for in this treatment is impressive and a bit daunting. There is zero margin for error when one steps back and thinks of what is being undertaken.

And so it begins with yet another medical team at the Proton Therapy Center, where the motto is *"It's About Beating Cancer Today. And Every Day After That."*

Dr. A heads the team. He is an Associate Professor of Radiation Oncology at the University of Washington, a board-certified radiation oncologist with expertise in proton therapy, specializing in gastrointestinal cancers, including liver, pancreas and rectal cancers. Zippy is the Care Team Nurse. Other Treatment Team Assistants help Dixie prepare for each session. Radiation Therapists make sure she is positioned properly for her treatment sessions. The same team works with her through every treatment.

Once her clothing is changed, she is placed on a hard table and positioned precisely for the proton beams. Hands over her head in surrender mode. A device to clamp her nasal passages shut. A snorkel tube inserted into her mouth with air flowing through. When everything is ready, a few short breaths to fill her lungs, then the air is shut off. She holds her breath for 30 seconds during the beam shots. Relax. Don't panic. Six times altogether, remaining in the same posture, with intermittent changes of table position. The entire first time process takes two hours.

Many are involved in Dixie's treatment program. The Intake Team coordinates the exchange of records, collects information for evaluating her case, and schedules consultations. A Financial Counselor assists with payment and insurance issues. The Patient Services Team greets us with each visit to the Center. Medical Physicists deliver the radiation and monitor equipment and therapy procedures.

Dosimetrists collaborate with Dr. A to prepare the treatment plan specific to her situation. They calculate the angles and doses of proton energy required to treat the targeted tumor, while ensuring healthy tissue is exposed to as little radiation as possible.

Machinists create a custom mold that matches the shape and form of Dixie's tumor. During treatment, protons are delivered through this mold to guide the exact therapy delivery. Engineers make sure the equipment and systems needed to produce the proton beam are finely tuned. Facilities Staff maintains the building, ensuring it is clean and safe for the patients.

Last, but definitely not the least, are our many friends who continue to offer comments, cards, emails, letters, telephone calls and text messages, meals to feed us, even make long distance trips to visit us, and bend the ear of God so many times in prayers for us.

It really does take a village to fight Enemy Cancer!

49

"Beam Me up, Scotty"

What terrifying teachers we are for that part of creation which loves its eternally childish state. ~ Rainer Maria Rilke / Sonnets to Orpheus II:14

～

You and I are not the first to face the challenges of aging, but at some point we do each face them ourselves for the first time. It is new territory, much of it seems uncharted, some might even view it as the holy wild. So it's good to learn from others in the wilderness.

We listen to children describe what (they think) it is like for their aging parents. We read the not-always-so-accurate wisdom of gerontologists, many of whom have yet to begin journeying through this new territory themselves. But there is nothing like living the adventure. Aging is not an accident. The late Dr James Hillman left us much to consider in his view of the purpose of aging. "The last years," he said, "confirm and fulfill character."

This is another BIG transition week for us.

Our first visit to the Proton Therapy Center was on 05 February. More visits have followed, including the surgical procedure placing the gold markers on the liver at each side of Dixie's bad-boy tumor that so far has been unresponsive to chemotherapy.

~

Wednesday 11 March. Over a month after our initial PTC visit, the first treatment takes place and every weeknight following. On Thursday last we attend the 2nd Anniversary Celebration of the Center, learning more about how the beam works. It has a *Star Wars* kind of feel to it. Patients, families and invited guests attend and are treated to a behind the scenes tour of the treatment rooms and machine shop, the cyclotron and control centers. Just about everything is on display. It is an engineering and medical science marvel.

Friday 27 March. Our second great-grandson, Finnigan Michael, decides to break out into this brave new world at about the noon hour. His brother, Corbin, and parents, Katy and Geoff Peterson are excited, to say the least. Michele and GG are there to witness his birth. Grandparents and great-grandparents are happy, too!

Wednesday 1 April. Graduation Day. The PTC staff holds a luncheon for nine graduates who are completing their therapy. Dixie is one of the nine. Each patient is given a beautiful PTC Medallion. On it is engraved a personal number to honor their brave participation in warring against their respective cancers. Dixie is #429 of the now 450 patients having begun or completed their treatment at the Center these last two years. And tonight, eight weeks after our first introduction to proton therapy, Dixie successfully completes her final treatment.

22 A proton therapy treatment bay

In the process she has become her team's breath-holding star. Most of the patients cannot hold their breath 30 seconds and so require additional help. She holds hers for a minimum 30 seconds at least eight times each night while lying prone on a flat hard surface as the team takes her through the 1 to 1–1/2-hour procedure. After witnessing Dixie's success from the first night, the team members all try holding their breath. Their best time is 26 seconds.

They decide Dixie must be an excellent swimmer. She says, "No, it's not that. It's just that I've been married to Ward for almost 59 years and I've learned to hold my breath a lot during that time... to say nothing about holding my tongue!" A true PTC celeb!

Tonight we are tired, but thankful we will not be crossing the SR 520 bridge into Seattle again until Monday morning. On Monday we return to SCCA for a new blood draw and to discuss next steps with Dr. Chiorean (I still do not call her Gabriela, much less *Gabby*).

We wish all our friends a happy Easter, being confident of this one thing. He is risen. Christ is risen indeed!

Let your steadfast love comfort me, according to your promise to your servant.

~ Psalm 119:76

50

Traits of the Long Distance Runner

> *(I wanted) to make sure I was not running or had not run in vain.*
> ~ Galatians 2:2

In 1962, Alan Sillitoe wrote the book (later a movie), *The Loneliness of the Long Distance Runner*. It is the story of a rebellious young lad who discovers himself in long distance running. It raises the question, "What are the qualities essential in making a mentally tough runner?"

Dr. JoAnn Dahlkoetter, at http://www.DrJoAnn.com, Sports Psychologist, author of *Your Performing Edge*, winner of the San Francisco Marathon and second-place finisher in the World Championship Hawaii Ironman Triathlon, lists seven key traits inherent among runners who succeed:

- **Resilience**: Able to bounce back from adversity, pain or a disappointing performance.

- **Focus**: Able to focus in the face of distractions or unexpected circumstances.
- **Strength**: Mentally tough, strong and flexible, able to respond to any situation that arises.
- **Preparation**: Anticipates situations ahead of time. Feels prepared. Doesn't panic in a crisis.
- **Vision**: Keeps moving forward with the objective, even when there are no immediate signs of getting closer to the finish line.
- **Openness**: Constantly learning, open to all possibilities, listens to the inner voice saying, "I can do this."
- **Trust**: Has faith in oneself, trusts in her training, her plan and her coach, even when there is no one close by to boost her confidence, even when the finish line seems far away.[11]

I see these traits as being similar to those required of the long-distance cancer patient. Or for anyone facing an uphill struggle with no initial guarantee of success. Resilience. Focus. Strength. Preparation. Vision. Openness. Trust.

And one more besides.

Having observed Dixie and others we have met on their long distance run for more than a year now, the difference maker setting some runners apart from the others in attitude and determination is their *clear faith in the Almighty God.* These outstanding souls, running steadily, often painfully on their sacred journey, are running *to*, not *from*. They are not quitters. For them the victor's crown is the prize waiting at the finish line. It is a "Well done, good and faithful runner..." spoken by the Master Runner himself, winner of the greatest marathon of all time, Jesus Christ.

---

11 *Your Performing Edge*, JoAnn Dahlkoetter. Pulgas Ridge Press, 2007.

We are enjoying our son, Stephen, this week, visiting again from Hong Kong. Taking a break from chemo and proton therapy until the end of the month, Dixie prepares Mom's favorite meals for her family in the evenings. And we all enjoy them. Sis and brother-in-law open their guest room and loan a car to Steve during the day. We are together. Life is good. God is good. All the time.

Therefore, since we are surrounded by so great a cloud of witnesses, let us also lay aside every weight, and sin which clings so closely, and let us run with endurance the race that is set before us. ~ Hebrews 12:1

51

More Traits ...

Language... has created the word "loneliness" to express the pain of being alone. And it has created the word "solitude" to express the glory of being alone. ~ Paul Tillich

To the aforementioned traits of the long distance runner, these elements must be added: *loneliness, patience, solitude.* These three are not optional. They are as much required as any part of one's sacred journey. It may seem strange to some, but if these are not engaged in with intentionality the journey will be empty, without true meaning, without the joy of life lived in fullness to the very end.

It is said that long distance runners are a tribe apart. For example, marathoners often choose only runners as close friends. Running is the centerpiece of their lives. They may have other relationships, but believe only runners truly understand their world. They are often introverted, since running long stretches alone requires runners to embrace solitude.

Mother Teresa once said, "Loneliness and the feeling of being unwanted is the most terrible poverty." Loss, dashed hopes, sadness, despair are hungers that gnaw at the human spirit. Still, the "glory of being alone" (Tillich) speaks to another kind of loneliness, a transforming of patient endurance into sacred solitude.

But the fruit of the Spirit is love, joy, peace, patience.... ~ *Galatians 5:22–23 (emphasis mine)*

By its very nature "the glory of being alone" with Christ nourishes the quiet strength of the human spirit.

After he (Jesus) had dismissed the crowds, he went up on the mountain by himself to pray.
When evening came, he was there alone. ~ *Matthew 14:23*

Loneliness. Cancer patients with whom I have spoken affirm this to be true. Especially those with faith in the resurrected Jesus. It is true for long distance caregivers as well. Even while friends and family care for loved ones and cheer them on through their Valley of Shadows, serving them with acts of love and kindness, it is vital to not feel pity or regret, but to acknowledge the essential courage and awesome sacredness of the lonely marathon itself. Those being cared for are on a journey that is, at times, so personal only they can understand it. Theirs is not a *loneliness* expressed in the pain of one's being lonely. It is a *solitude* in which to explore and express the "glory of being alone."

Patience. On Tuesday, late in April, Dixie goes through two full body CT scans, one at UWMC in the morning and another at SCCA in the afternoon. The following Thursday, we visit with Dr. A at the Proton Therapy Center, where he shares with us "some good news and some not so good news."

The "good news" is there are no additional tumors visible in the liver. However, the resistant bad-boy tumor is larger than at the beginning of Proton treatment. He says more time must pass before its size increase is determined to be due to the radiation itself, or something more sinister. We pray for continued success. Killing the liver tumor is key to our cancer battle.

The "bad news" from Dr A is that during recess from chemotherapy, the previously observed spots in the lungs are growing and additional spots are now visible. Also there is new activity showing in two lymph nodes, one close to the heart. This is very discouraging indeed.

Yesterday, Michele and I accompanied Dixie on her return to SCCA for a blood draw and appointment with Dr. Chiorean (who can actually say "Apisarnthanarax" without blinking, though she admits it took practice). She concurs with Dr. A's assessment of the CT scans. We spend time reviewing where we have been and best options for moving forward, including a genome study that is an option requiring further conversation before deciding. Its potential value must be weighed carefully.

Solitude. What Dixie agrees to is a return to chemotherapy. This next Monday, she will resume chemotherapy infusion treatment at SCCA. Long procedure hours that we hope will not be as debilitating as the rounds of *FOLFOX* were in January. This new infusion treatment will take place every three weeks instead of two, plus daily medications.

We ask for a CT scan, but Dr. Chiorean says we must wait until after three more infusion treatments. We want to know more quickly than in nine weeks how things are going, especially given what we've heard today.

Rest and renewal. Reading and prayer. As much activity as energy permits. Quality of life. These are the selections on the menu. Emotionally, we need to recharge. The love, prayers and encouragement of others are what fuel the human spirit in us right now.

52

Chemotherapy Round 4

Question: What are the only man-made things in heaven?
Answer: the wounds in the hands, feet and side of Jesus.

If we have never sought, we seek Thee now;
Thine eyes burn through the dark, our only stars;
we must have sight of thorn pricks on Thy brow;
we must have Thee, O Jesus of the scars.
~ Edward Shillito (written near the end of World War I)

―

Monday 18 May. Michele gets off work early today to join us for the drive across the SR 520 floating bridge. It is a lovely sun-drenched afternoon in the Northwest. The kind of day when everyone moves outside. White sails, fueled by a warm gentle breeze crisscross back and forth across the azure surface of Lake Washington, a pleasant precursor that disappears suddenly once we enter the underground parking levels beneath SCCA.

How quickly reality takes over. Blood draw. Teaching session for a new chemo drug. Meet with Claire Stockhausen, PA-C. And finally, here we are again, this time on F5 Bay 23.

Evening's furtive shadows stretch eastward along city streets. Patios, decks and sidewalk cafes are favorite places to be tonight in Seattle's seventy-five-degree weather. A handful of white clouds dot the sky. It's past six-thirty when Michele and I return from sharing a Caesar salad and a Brazilian something-or-other at a nearby restaurant. Meanwhile, Dixie is drinking water from a plastic bottle, eating cheese and crackers from the nurse's larder, and a health bar she brought with her from home. Proof once more that life isn't fair!

A familiar face enters. Nurse Debbie is serving Dixie again today. A lovely mom with two children at home, she has been our nurse before. Dixie is finishing her anti-nausea meds infusion. A must with the powerful drugs yet to come. We watch as Debbie slips into her protective plastic gown and gloves. She calls for a second nurse, Sarah, and together they begin what has become for us the all too familiar routine of reading aloud to each other the chemotherapy checklist.

At seven o'clock it's a go. Push the on switch, and for the next two hours a clear white substance called *Oxaliplatin* makes its way into Dixie's system.

By this time we grasp how cancerous tumors are characterized by out-of-control cell division. *Oxaliplatin* interferes with cancer cell growth and random spread. That's the good news and we get that.

The problem is it can also lower good blood cells that help fight infections and your blood to clot, making infections or bleeding always potential problems, along with other rather dramatic side effects we must watch for during the days following infusion. Chemo is not for sissies. At last, after two plus hours of chemo online into Dixie's port, we unplug and head for home, arriving at nine-thirty, ready for bed.

This morning she stares out the window from her bed to where flowers are in colorful bloom, doing their best to lift the spirit of the one who planted them there.

While reading silently, I come across these words written by someone known only to God, found on the wall in a Nazi concentration camp after WWII:

I believe in the sun, even when it isn't shining,
I believe in love, even when I feel it not,
I believe in God, even when he is silent.

I look up to see her watching me. I smile, press back tears I do not want her to see. She is so beautiful lying there. And so fragile. Nothing is left that matters that is not in this room. And I am losing her. Slowly, surely, with each day passing I feel her slipping away.

The world outside goes on without me.

I sit with thoughts left unspoken as an unknown prisoner carves his commemorative epitaph of ultimate hope on the walls of my heart.

Today the sun is shining.

Tonight the stars will burn through a Northwest darkness like the eyes of God.

Today I am loved by you.

Tonight I will believe in you, even if you remain silent.

In you O Lord, by you, and for you.

Amen.

53

Icons of Aging

We are the only icons of aging that younger people will ever meet. What we show them as we go, gives them a model of what they, too, can strive for.
We show them the way to the fullness of life. ~ Joan Chittister, The Gift of Years

But I am like a green olive tree in the house of God;
I trust in the mercies of God forever and ever. ~ Psalm 52:8

⁓

I never read this verse in the Psalms without being reminded of the olive tree standing at the center of the patio as you entered the Little Chapel in which we began what, over time, became twenty-three years of pastoral ministry in Dublin, California. It was a beautiful tree. It was full of biblical analogy and symbolic meaning, especially for those who had lovingly planted it sometime prior to my coming on the scene.

It was also filled with messy, allergy producing pollen dust.

Many an early Sunday morning at certain times of the year, you could find me out front on the patio, broom in hand, making

23 Dixie with the Charles River and Boston in background

a clean sweep of green pollen dust from under the olive tree before people started arriving for and sneezing through another worship service.

In spite of this inconvenience, it did serve as a strong symbol to every person who walked beneath it. In any circumstance: hot, dry, cold, wet, rocky, or sandy, an olive tree will live and produce fruit. It is said that you can never kill an olive tree. When cut down or burned, new shoots will emerge from its roots. It is a reminder that no matter what comes your way or how messy life becomes, you can stand sturdy in the presence of God...like the olive tree... always green (faithful) and always bearing fruit in season.

I know of "green olive trees" like this. I have seen them, walked among them, plucked fruit from off their branches. Sometimes they are messy, always strong in spirit, always sturdy in practicing the presence of God, always with the green of faithfulness, always living fruitful lives... "icons of aging," spiritual giants, examples for others of what they, too, can strive for, showing the way to the fullness of life. I believe it is true...

...you can never kill a green olive tree.

Friday 22 May. Early this morning she is very sick. She throws up steadily, one sick bag after another, for several hours until I wonder what can possibly be left for her to give up! At 3 o'clock we make an emergency run to SCCA. Michele confiscates a wheelchair and delivers her through the main entrance while I park the car. She is too weak to walk in on her own. Soon we are assigned a treatment bay. For the next couple of hours, nurses administer hydration infusion mixed with pain-killers. And by 6 o'clock we are home again.

A long Memorial Day weekend follows, stretching out the remaining days of May. Dixie stops taking further infusion or oral chemotherapy. Dr. Chiorean is away at a cancer conference and so we arrange an appointment for her on 08 June, to discuss next options. Dixie continues to grow weaker. Her appetite is almost nonexistent. I ask what sounds good and she thinks awhile before responding. One day it is half a deli sandwich. On another it is tapioca pudding. Then, non-spicy pad Thai noodles. It feels like I'm feeding a pregnant woman.

Except instead of eating voraciously, she eats a bite, maybe two, then pushes the rest aside.

⌒

Monday 01 June. We drive north a couple of hours to a quiet resort with a view across the water into Canada. A place where the maid makes up your room each day, and a chef cooks wonderful breakfasts and dinners, and nice young people who plan to spend the summer in Europe after graduating from college serve your meals and pick up your empty dishes.

Usually when I travel, Dixie packs. This time, being the consummate caregiver, I give her a break and do my own bag. Other than arriving with no deodorant and no underwear, I think I did pretty well. We hang out together, talk, read, take short beach walks, enjoy a lovely dinner at the best table, thanks to Michele and Mark's generous advance dinner reservation.

Under a cloudy sky, we rock alone in a row of twenty outdoor wooden rocking chairs, bask in fresh sea breezes, watch boats and seagulls sail by, and hold one another's hand as we celebrate our 59th wedding anniversary. Creating mind pictures. It's the way we started married life. Just the two of us. Together.

...for richer, for poorer, in sickness and in health, until death do us part.

⌒

Thursday 04 June. By the time we arrive home, Dixie is exhausted. She retires immediately while I unpack our things. I am sad. I make a mental note that while world travelers we have been, we have just experienced our new limits for travel.

Monday 08 June. We arrive at SCCA at 12 noon for blood draw and our appointment with Dr. Chiorean. After the blood draw is done we are informed the doctor has a family emergency and will not be available. I keep my thoughts to myself. We return home.

Once Dixie is settled in, I step outside. I don't want her to see that I am angry. Angry at Dr. Chiorean's family emergency. At medicine that is failing us. At the world for just being the world. At God for not doing his job. It seems a very long time since we've spoken with Dr. Chiorean and this meeting had been important to us. It's been an even longer time since God has spoken and that isn't right either. Doesn't he know how much I love her? How much I need her?

After awhile, I go back inside. We settle in for a quiet evening.

Tuesday 09 June. By 9:30, Dixie, Michele and I are seated in the SCCA F4 waiting room. How many times have we done this drill? At 10 o'clock we are led by a nurse to an examination room. Weight. Blood pressure. Temperature. Had any falls? The doctor will be in shortly. Sure she will. She has served us well and we've learned to adapt to this professional foible. But today I'm on edge. At 10:35, Dr. Chiorean arrives.

Now we are together at last to ask the hard questions and listen to equally difficult-to-hear answers. We understand options are diminishing. Dixie does not want more *Oxaliplatin*. Combined with the daily intake of *Capecitabine (Xeloda)* chemo tablets, the side effects are overpowering to her.

Dr. Chiorean offers the possibility of three infusions with reduced tolerance levels of *Oxaliplatin* and *Capecitabine,* one every three weeks, to see if Dixie can absorb them, and then do a CT scan. We want a scan now so we can see what our status really is. Dr. Chiorean tells us it is too early and that we need to go through the treatments first.

Finally, we come to an agreement. The first treatment in this fourth round is scheduled for Monday, 15 June. This will be followed by two more infusions, each three weeks apart, after which scans will be done and we will know more accurately where we stand. Dr. Chiorean concludes by making it clear, it is our right to call it all off at any point.

Dixie's pain is constant now and increasing. Pain meds are in daily use. Dr. Chiorean says it will only get worse. As our last time together concludes, it has been an emotionally exhausting session for everyone.

Nine more weeks of treatments.

It feels daunting.

Tuesday 16 June. To augment yesterday's *Oxaliplatin* infusion, Dixie begins the morning by taking the first of what will be morning and evening doses of oral *Capecitabine* in pill form. By nine o'clock she is throwing everything up. So much for chemo pills!

Capecitabine (Xeloda) tabs are potent, belonging to a category of chemotherapy called *antimetabolites*. Antimetabolites are similar to normal substances within a cell. When the cells incorporate these antimetabolites into the cellular metabolism, they are unable to divide.

While the first morning with the chemo pills causes Dixie to be ill, after this she is able to keep everything down. Her pain level has increased substantially these last three weeks. She does not complain, but I see it in her eyes and her face. She has always possessed this wonderfully expressive countenance that telegraphs what she may not be saying out loud.

To live with Dixie successfully (let's say as a husband or a youngster, for example), you need to learn to read her face early on. Truth? This is good advice for any husband or child. When Mom's look reaches the you'd-better-not-make-me-come-and-get-you stage, you take note. In the days when our children were young, if Mom's look was accompanied by a snap of the fingers, it mattered not where you were in the church or who you were doing it with, you had just been given your last hope of survival notice! She has always been the best in our family at this. I think it's a gift.

This week, she finally owns up to the pain level she is experiencing. It's been in her eyes and countenance for some time. She agrees it is time to up the pain medication. This helps somewhat. Still, her energy is extremely low and the ability to fight off pain is decreasing.

Wednesday. We spend the morning reorganizing and chronicling all her meds, sorting the out-of-date from the still good. By noon, we are at SCCA again. Dixie's pain level is sufficiently high enough to require an X-ray of her back. The pain in her lower back as well as in her abdominal area is steadily increasing. The medicines make her sleepy so she is resting more. Her energy level remains low.

Soon we are home again. Whether in pain or pleasure, home is still the best place. Her creativity and instinct for comfort, functionality and beauty, has made it so.

... so teach us to number our days that we may get a heart of wisdom. ~ Psalm 90:12

…they say you can never kill a green olive tree. Some live for 1500 years. New shoots will spring up from the roots to ensure that life goes on, passed from one generation to another. Green olive trees in the house of God…

… the only icons of aging that younger people will ever meet.

What we show them as we go, gives them a model of what they, too, can strive for.

We show them the way to the fullness of life. ~ *Joan Chittister*

I realize how amazing it is to live in the shade of a tree like this.

But she is only one.

Many more green olive trees are needed.

54

Attitude and Tenacity

Attitude is a little thing that makes a big difference. ~ *Winston Churchill*

∽

Chris Evert, giving commentary on a tennis match at Wimbledon, said of a young female player: "If she doesn't learn to play beyond herself she won't go very far."

What about life? Should the goal of life be to "live beyond oneself?" I think that is the central message of Christ. To live beyond ourselves. To look beyond the perimeter of our own skin and our own comfort in order to touch the perimeter of others and to enter fully into God's perimeter.

People whose perimeters are closest to mine, who have refused to touch the perimeters of others, remain angry, isolated and unhappy people. Even as I have watched and reached out, their perimeters have shrunk smaller and smaller until those individuals have diminished into a cell of hell. Lord, help me live beyond myself. ~ *DLT diary, July 1997*

∽

Monday 15 June. During the intervening days emotions are at low ebb. Not much of anything positive or encouraging has been heard. It is with this mindset that we arrive at SCCA for a 12:40 afternoon blood draw and a 1:00 medical interview, prior to a 5:00 infusion.

We meet Karl Cristie F Figuracion for the first time. Karl Cristie is a Nurse Practitioner. She is young, attractive, intelligent and prepared. And her attitude is refreshing. Uplifting even. Dixie answers the usual series of update questions. And then asks one of her own. "Tell me what are the physical signs that indicate one's body is beginning to shut down?"

For a moment the nurse is caught off guard by the question. But only for a moment. She focuses in quickly, articulating clear cause and effect issues from a medical viewpoint. Then she asks, "Why the question?" Dixie says she is deliberating the value add reasons before undertaking this next infusion. Since the outcome is more questionable, good reasons are needed for putting oneself through additional pain and suffering.

People may hear your words, but they feel your gratitude. ~ John Maxwell

Nurse Karl Cristie and Dixie make a surprising connection. Not that the information being shared is different. It isn't. Not that anything has changed with what we are facing. It hasn't. We conclude our time together in the tiny exam room. She expresses how much she enjoyed being with Dixie. Gives a couple of assignments. Shakes our hands. Smiles. And as quickly as she has entered our lives, she is gone. We never see her again.

On our way to F5 and the infusion treatment center, we talk about why we are so affected by the interview. One word sums it up. *Attitude.* In addition to the usual professionalism one comes to expect, it is her manner, her disposition, her physical expressiveness, her relaxed attitude. The feeling given that the patient sitting before her and her husband do matter. A lot. That she is in charge, confident, caring and seeking to understand. That she knows hope is sometimes as important as a prescription.

Late that evening, following chemotherapy infusion, we return home.

Tuesday. There is a visit with Dr. Anne, our family physician, for blood work and an assignment for physical therapy. On Thursday, Dixie begins some very limited exercise routines with therapist Magdalena Pertoldova at Overlake Physical Therapy.

Friday. She walks with me ten blocks to have her nails done. It has been a long while since we have done this much physical exercise together. Her hands are too unsteady to do her own nails, so a manicure is a nice reward. Overall, things are going very well.

Saturday 20 June. Suddenly, all the previous day's forward progress is thrown in reverse. Dixie awakens so weak she can hardly get up and move about the room!

There are times in life when people must know when not to let go. Balloons are designed to teach small children this.
~ *Terry Pratchett*

Sunday. It is the same. She sleeps most of each day. Lots of cramping and belly pain. Her digestive system appears to be totally blocked

Monday. We are at SCCA again. More instructions. More meds. More infusion hydration.

Tuesday. Still nothing is better. She has been unable to eat or drink for several days.

Wednesday 24 June. I reach out to Dr. Chiorean's nurse again and insist something more must be done than is being done. All home remedies have failed. She agrees. By 11:30 we are on our way to UWMC's emergency room.

Michele leaves work early to meet us at the ER. Earl and Nancy Heverly, former members of our pastoral team in Dublin California, now pastors at a church in Sacramento, are planning a visit today on their way to a wedding in Boise, Idaho. I reach them by telephone and redirect them to the hospital.

They arrive near the noon hour and spend the day with us in the ER. We have history. They are longtime friends and ministry colleagues who served with us for fifteen years. We laugh and tell stories, catch up on family and give thanks for the privilege it has been to invest years of our lives in theirs and in those of their children.

Late in the evening, Dixie is transferred to F7 SE room 7354. Once she is settled in, I return home. It is so late that the SR 520 bridge toll is turned off. I've never seen that before. For some reason I think the State has missed a huge opportunity. Then I wonder why I am thinking about things so minuscule at a time like this.

Thursday 25 June. Back at UWMC at 9 o'clock the next morning, I find Dixie engaged in a lively conversation with seven white frocked doctors, pharmacists and nurses who are crowded into her room. It's the teaching hospital way. Some teaching, some learning, some observing. She is well medicated today as we await a resolution to her problem. I am told there is still a long way to go, whatever that may mean. I'm just relieved to have her under the watchful care of the medical team.

Cramping and belly pain continues to come and go as her digestive system refuses to cooperate. Her condition is severe. We are informed she must remain in the hospital for another night under the watchful care of the medical team headed up by Dr. Max Cohen, with Dr. Andrew Harris assisting.

The patient has a life-threatening bowel obstruction. It is not caused by her cancer or by any abnormal twisting or blockage. It is an outcome of the morphine medication taken to alleviate pain. One of those side effects we are always hearing about. This has resulted in severe constipation. As the levels of nausea and pain continues to increase, the team recognizes they are in trouble. They call for Dr. Lucille Marchand, UWMC director of palliative care.

Dr. Marchand is told before coming in that I am a "prominent person in the community and so she really needs to step up." In recounting this to me later she said, "Well, I told them I don't really care whether he's prominent or not. My goal is to treat everyone in the same way. I just know this is a family in deep trouble and they need me."

It doesn't take long before we are all in love with Dr. Marchand.

Friday, 26 June. It is a beautiful day outside, but for Dixie it's just another morning at UWMC. Sunshine is a window only experience. Jess, the day nurse is busy administering medications and connecting an infusion hydration line. Dixie has eaten virtually nothing since entering the hospital and for several days prior. Minutes ago she vomited most of her meds before they even had a chance to perform their respective duties.

Dr. Marchand is discussing dietary options with Dixie. Michele sits close by, taking notes.

Early this morning, Dr. Cohen expresses concern at how treatment up to now is having little, if any success. The full assigned medical team joins us to discuss the situation and share evaluations. A decision is made to stop any additional hydration for now. Instead, she is going in for more X-rays to try and find what is making success so elusive.

At every stage of discovery there is shock and new apprehension. After they are gone I try to keep my attitude and conversation with Dixie and Michele on a positive, encouraging tone. But the Valley of Shadows looms dark and long in my heart.

Saturday-Wednesday. For the next several days the struggle goes on. Dr. Marchand is with us in the room once every day for at least an hour. I learn she is fairly new to her position, having come here four months earlier from the University of Wisconsin. I think to myself, maybe she doesn't have all that much going on as yet, so that's how she can spend so much time with us. We are more accustomed to "in and out," like a fast-food drive through. Nothing could be further from the truth as it turns out. She is here to learn who we are, to hear our stories, our concerns and hopes, and to determine how best to support us all.

Dixie had been ten days like this, without eating, constipated and in pain before we came to ER. She has been given nothing to eat since. She has to be starving. When I say something about this, I'm told it will be worse to feed her, even intravenously, in her present state.

The process drags on endlessly. Dr. Marchand and the medical team's angst deepens as the first line of medicines has no desired effect. The first line is comprised of the very best, the newest and most exotic drugs that can be utilized. They try again with a second line, or the second best drugs, on top of the first, to see if things can be broken loose. Nothing. Commencing with the third line, it has become obvious the medical team is very concerned. Dixie's pain level continues to increase Still there is no sign of relief. Nothing they try is working!

When a fourth and final line of drugs is utilized with no results, I observe the staff stealing concerned glances at one another. What are they thinking? What are they saying to one another when they leave the room and huddle together in the hallway? I want to be in that huddle with them, listening, urging them on. Instead I hang back, knowing it is not my place. My place is here with her.

Dixie tells Dr. Marchand she wants to finish well. She wants to be able to go on living, but does not want to be a dead person walking. Quality of life over quantity is a priority. She thinks about her grandchildren and great-grandchildren. She wants to continue creating warm memories of her in their minds, but does not want to be a burden to her family. She is having trouble being the receiver and not in the giving role.

Time passes like a slow moving stream. My tolerance level is shrinking. Too much in-and-out going on. Too many doctors and nurses, too much medicine that isn't working. I want a plan. I am watching, listening, asking questions. What's the plan for today? Do we even have one? What's the plan for tomorrow? I want to be in control, making something good happen, but I am not and it isn't.

I am told later the medical staff realizes they are in a near emergency situation. Nothing they know to do has worked so far. There is a sense of hopelessness and defeat in the air. It is at this point that Dr. Marchand decides to fall back on her nursing background. Small enemas have been tried unsuccessfully, but she recalls doing large volume enemas in the old days.

"I think we should try large scale enemas with mineral oil and soap suds and special positioning to help it work," she declares. She has been talking with Drs. Max and Andrew every day. And every day they laid out a new game plan because Dixie is in such critical condition.

She tells me later, "When I say to them we are going to order high-volume enemas they look at me like, 'Really? I don't think we've ever ordered one of those before.'

"When I was a nurse, we didn't have a lot of fancy drugs, so enemas were a pretty basic thing for us. When you tell this to a doctor or nurse today, they stare and say ... 'wha-a-at?' But if this didn't work for Dixie there was nothing else. She was going to die. She would have ever-increasing pain until the end. It would be a terrible way for her to die.

"So I was always in the room talking it through with the nurse while we did this, telling her what it was we were going to do and how we were going to do it. I would give her explicit instructions on positioning. This is how you do it. I showed her every detail. This is how you give a full enema."

And with that they go to work.

Under the guidance of Dr. Marchand and over the course of several days, the old-fashioned procedure is what at last produces results. She exclaims, "When we finally have success, it's like if I could have danced, I would have danced! Because if this didn't work, there was nothing else."

I express to Dr. Marchand how grateful we are for her *tenacious spirit,* mirroring so well the *tenacity* of Dixie, and how much we have become believers in palliative care during these critical days. We had met earlier with the palliative care team at SCCA, but it was here in this current crisis we came to better understand the essential and effective service this comparatively new addition to hospital medical teams brings to the patient and their family.

55

The Tipping Point

> *The point at which a series of small changes or incidents becomes significant enough to cause a larger, more important change ~ Vulcan Post*

Thursday 02 July. In mid-afternoon of Day 8 in the hospital, the blockage in her digestive tract shows further signs of breaking up. One more night and, nine days after her admittance to ER, Dixie wishes the hospital staff well and returns home. It feels right and good to have her here again, at home, in her nest, even if the next few days will prove to be challenging ones.

We strive to monitor her pain levels, listen to the multiplicity of inputs from doctors and dietitians, and keep up with the ever-changing recovery plan. Her pain fluctuates 24/7 on a scale of 3–10, 10 being "it doesn't get any higher than this!" But this is where she is and what we do.

I praise you, because I am fearfully and wonderfully made; your works are wonderful, I know that full well. ~ Psalm 139:12 (NIV)

Monday 06 July. At 7 o'clock, we check in at SCCA for a routine blood draw. By eight o'clock we are on F4, ready for our appointment with Dr. Chiorean. The window views of life on Lake Union offer their familiar beauty. Sail boats and kayaks, houseboats and seaplanes. They are like living museum pieces on a watery tableau, filling the eye.

Dixie's name is called and we follow a nurse to Exam 4, answer the questions, and check BP counts (130+ in both arms). As the nurse leaves, he tells us the doctor will be with us shortly. We settle in. Michele is with us so we entertain ourselves while waiting. Eventually Dr. Chiorean and nurse Kate join us and undertake a review of what has happened over the previous three weeks and what decisions must be made regarding next steps.

It turns out the partial information resulting from scans performed last week at UWMC hospital is generally viewed as good. There is more discussion. And more indecision. The adverb "*When* I take the chemotherapy" and the conjunction "*If* I take the chemotherapy," is a noticeable part of the intercourse between Dixie and Dr. Chiorean. Dr. Chiorean advises three more treatments in three week intervals, followed by scans after a total of nine weeks. A compromise is agreed upon after further discussion, comprising a chemo infusion today and then three weeks following, a series of scans to further clarify the status of Dixie's cancer.

We move on to F5 Bay 9, where preparations for the chemo infusion are being made. Within minutes a glitch shows up. Once again a reminder that nothing is easy when being treated for cancer. Dixie's blood pressure has shot up more than 70 points during the last hour! The nurse rechecks. Then checks a third time. All three are mutually corroborating. Quickly Plan B is created on the spot and set in motion.

The chemotherapy nurse administers *hydralazine*, an antihypertensive high BP medication, causing a relaxation of blood vessels as they carry blood away from the heart and towards the organs and tissues. The exact mechanism of how *hydralazine* causes arterial smooth muscle relaxation is not understood by medical professionals. It is one of the yet-to-be-solved mysteries of medical science and the human body. But by the end of infusion therapy, her BP is down 40 points from its high. Still, this sudden spike in BP remains another unknown piece of her treatment requiring a close watch.

Speaking of food... well, on second thought, let's not. It remains a major concern. The very thoughts and smells of food often bring Dixie to the point of nausea, not nourishment or pleasure. Food is altogether distasteful. Another one of chemotherapy's unwanted side-effects.

Dixie is visited by a nutritionist specializing in cancer diets, and by nurse Jodie from palliative care. The result is additional information and a commitment to become more directly involved in helping oversee the home medicine schedule, which in and of itself is very challenging. It was so much easier when professionals were responsible during her hospital stay. Here at home base, medicines that once worked, don't work now. Some never worked and are discarded. Some must be taken with/without food, etc.

Saturday 11 July. Thursday and Friday are downhill days for us. Deeper into the shadows. Lots of unrelenting pain. No nourishment intake at all. It is the weekend now. I think every crisis seems to take place on weekends when it is difficult to reach the folk at SCCA. I decide to leave a message for Dr. Marchand at UWMC. Within a few minutes she returns the call. We discuss the situation on speakerphone, so Dixie and Michele can be included. I watch Dixie's countenance during the

15-to-20-minute conversation. Her pain level can be read in her eyes. We conclude with expressions of love and a promise of hugs to be shared again one day. The decision is unanimous. It is time.

The tipping point.

I leave a telephone message informing Dr. Chiorean. We are requesting Evergreen Hospice to assist us with home care. Dr. Chiorean's nurse and the SCCA palliative care team return our call the week following, expressing their concerns and best wishes.

The shadows on life's sundial lengthen further still.

Yet God continues to fill in the gaps with hope and love, goodness and peace. He reinforces these elements as we exercise our faith in the Valley of Shadows. We water them. We cultivate them. They are a portion of the fruitfulness to which we are called.

King David said to Solomon his son, "Be strong and courageous and do it. Do not be afraid and do not be dismayed, for the LORD God, even my God, is with you. He will not leave you or forsake you until all the work for the service of the house of the LORD is finished" (1Chronicles 28:20).

Good words.

Words to finish well by.

56

What I Learned from Dixie

Thank you God for love...for your love. But, Lord, the apathy I feel at times must grieve you. Please replace apathy within me with passion. Passion for the people you are passionate about. Passion for the work you want me to accomplish. Lord, help me model, encourage, and mentor others to seek passion, not apathy in their lives. Show me the way. Amen. ~ DLT diary, April 2004

Hi Dixie,

I pulled out my now very old handwritten copy of the tribute I did at your anniversary celebration at VCC. Not sure why I have saved it all these years, but I am so glad that I did because it is as relevant now as it was then.

Much of what I learned from watching, listening, and serving alongside you through those exciting as well as painful years continues to serve me well through my own good times and hard ones. Because I am naturally an observer and analyzer, I must have been watching you very closely! The result was that God used you to shape me in some very vital ways, and I have been able to build those into my own life. Now I model them to those who watch me! So I pulled out my tribute tonight and typed it up for you.

I love you and thank you from the bottom of my heart for being my friend and mentor. And for continually kicking me forward into places I didn't want to go.

7 *Attributes of a Highly Effective Pastor's Wife*
~ What I learned from Dixie in 15 years of doing life and ministry alongside her ~

Risk. *Risk giving yourself to God.* Let *Him* do *His* work in you no matter how hard or scary it is. Let Him stretch you into becoming who He wants you to be.

Recreate. *Plan the fun times.* Laugh much. Plan come-as-you-are parties, and laugh at what they look like when they show up at your door.

Dream. *Allow God to give you His dreams for your ministry.* They will seem like just that—dreams. But with God's involvement, dreams will become reality.

Persevere. *Sometimes you just have to set your jaw and go forward— but always as you pray.* Whether it be family issues or ministry issues, develop a deep relationship with God in prayer.

Build. *Build strong relationships with those God has placed alongside you.* Invest yourself. Learn to be vulnerable and transparent even if it doesn't come easily.

Trust. *Trust in God no matter what the circumstances are or how things appear to be.* Don't give up. Trust and wait.

Love. *Love is a choice, a decision.* Love with your actions, love with your heart. Love with God's unconditional love. Love in ways that people need to be loved.

Dixie is a highly effective pastor's wife because, first and foremost, she sought to become a woman of God. ~ Nancy Heverly[12]

Some seeds fell on good ground.
They are like people who hear the word and remember it.
Their hearts are honest and good.
These people keep on believing,
and much good comes from them.

~ Luke 8:15 (WE).

---

12 *Nancy is the wife of Earl Heverly, senior pastor of Cornerstone Community Church in Sacramento CA. She is an ordained minister, directs church small group ministry and oversees the Women's Ministry Leadership Team. Earl and Nancy and their three daughters came to us from Illinois to begin their pastoral ministry at Valley Christian Center of Dublin, California.*

57

The Most Important Thing

The Good News of the gospel, therefore, is not that God came to take our suffering away, but that God wanted to become part of it.
~ Henri Nouwen

What's the most important thing? I mean really. What do you think it is? Like Moses of old, you stand on life's mountaintop with God and you see the land of promise just ahead, bejeweled with golf courses and grandkids, fishing trips and sunny beaches. You've dreamed of this. You finally made it. And God is smiling. (That's always a good sign.) After years of trekking through the workplace wilderness, you have arrived. It's retirement reward day!

And then God tells you that others you've led safely through the wilderness will cross over, but you will not. It hits you like a stone from David's slingshot. Your dream bursts like a bubble. You worked hard to nurture your bubble, only to have it poked

24 Dixie's mountain

by your best friend. And the question is still there. *"What's the most important thing?"*

> *Then Moses went up from the plains of Moab to Mount Nebo, to the top of Pisgah, which is opposite Jericho. And the Lord showed him all the land, Gilead as far as Dan, all Naphtali, the land of Ephraim and Manasseh, all the land of Judah as far as the*

western sea, the Negeb, and the Plain, that is, the Valley of Jericho the city of palm trees, as far as Zoar. And the Lord said to him, "This is the land of which I swore to Abraham, to Isaac, and to Jacob, 'I will give it to your offspring.' I have let you see it with your eyes, but you shall not go over there." ~ Deuteronomy 34:1–4

Not all things in life are fair, but God is fair and in control of all things. His sovereignty is never delegated or shared. Not to lesser gods. Not to you or me. Yet he somehow remains intimately involved in our lives. Our days are in his hands.

The Psalmist says all the days of one's life were recorded in God's book, "when as yet there was none of them" (Psalm 139:16). In other words, our Lord knows where you were, where you are now and where you will be later.

Will you look back on life and say, "I wish I had," or "I'm glad I did"?

~ Zig Ziglar

He sees you as you dance with joyfulness along the pathway, or stand perplexed at one of life's crossroads. This way or that? What will it be? He does not make the which-way choice for you. Yet he does know which way you will chose.

He knows the exact number of your days, be they few or many. He knows when your last breath will be taken. He makes certain your life will not be "cut short." You are in his hands. Someone once said, he is more than a Timekeeper who winds up history like a clock and lets it run its course. He is God Almighty, worthy of trust. All of your days...

And still the question remains. *What's the most important thing?*

Life was his against all odds. Forty years in the palaces of Pharaoh. Forty more watching over his father-in-law's sheep and learning the ways of the desert. Finally, forty years of doing his best, most fortuitous work, that of leading a slave nation to freedom through an unforgiving wilderness. So he lost it once or twice along the way. Is it fair that after all this he doesn't get to so much as leave a footprint in the promised land?

Isn't the promised land what life is about? After all the sacrifice and suffering that goes into it? Not even a toe print? Or a gold watch? What about the fruits of your labor? What about those world-class grapes? The grandkids? And the milk and honey. What about that?

Aren't these the most important things?

Monday 20 July. This week Dixie continues to fight the good fight, and we with her. I admit to being weary, a kind of physical and emotional weariness that cuts more deeply than I dare allow just now. Dixie is exhausted, but with the right to be. I can't let myself go down this path. Not yet.

I am weary in spirit as well. I do not question God's seeing our tears, hearing the prayers. Yours. Ours. Everyone's. You can count on him, no matter what. He never fails to listen, never throws away a sincere prayer no matter how poorly stated. On this sacred journey, I have learned he answers in his good time and in his own all-knowing, all-powerful way. I am also reminded his answers are not always those I choose.

On the physical level, Dixie has continued to lose ground since her extended hospital stay at UWMC. Her final chemo infusion is on 06 July. Her choice. No more chemo. The next week, pain and nausea continue to build, coming and going like waves of the sea, crashing against a shore already weakened by the storms. We remind ourselves. Often he waits until we are ready. Not for the answer we choose, but for the one he is preparing to give.

Our days are in his hands.

Tuesday 21 July. For some weeks we've recorded weight in double, not triple digits. Yesterday another pound was lost. The night passes with a grating 10+ pain factor, and this morning two more pounds are gone. Since 11 July, hospice nurses in our home have been doing their best, but meds are either not working or cannot be kept down. This morning an ambulance is requested and at 10:30, Dixie is transported to the Evergreen Hospice Center in Kirkland, our sister city to the north.

The EHC facility is designed to be homelike, much more than a normal medical center; with rose gardens, hummer feeders in windows, and a door from each room leading directly onto the outdoor patio. Room 8 is spacious, as hospital rooms go, and includes a private bath. Before we know it, a new medical team enters our lives. Barbara is a resident physician with nine months of training still remaining toward becoming an OB/GYN; Brynne and Cindi are our RNs. Everyone seems to be at ease and on a first name basis here.

Meredith is our newest medical doctor. She takes time to explain what is going to happen and what the goals will be. As she concludes, she asks if there are any questions.

Dixie speaks up. She asks a question she has asked before, at another time and place, "Do you think the symptoms I'm experiencing are signs that indicate my body is beginning to shut down?"

Dr. Meredith hesitates for a split second. It is not the first question she is expecting from her newest patient. Then she replies forthrightly, "Yes. This is very likely what is happening," and continues on with her explanation. When she is finished, Dixie thanks her for being honest and straightforward.

After everyone is gone and Michele and I are alone with Dixie, she looks around the room and out the window to where three small sparrows are flitting about the hummer feeder, trying to understand why their beaks won't fit in the holes. They see the promised land with its refreshing sugar water, but just can't get to it. I know how they must feel.

Dixie laughs. "I like it here," she says. "If I need to come back again for my final days, I won't mind at all."

Michele and I smile. There is relief in knowing she feels this way. We agree. If home becomes too difficult, this will be a good place.

I have board meetings this week. We have agreed to close CASA 50+ Network after thirty-three years of training and supporting ministry to and through adults in life's second half. An amazing amount of good work has been accomplished. Hundreds of pastors and lay leaders have been exposed to older adult ministry. But it is time. While the need remains for the message, the messenger has concluded its *raison d'être*. This is the final gathering of the board. A time of closure. We have a last dinner together along the banks of Lake Washington in one of our popular Eastside restaurants.

After dinner, while others go to their hotel rooms, I slip away and return to the Hospice Center. To Room 8. To sit for a while with the patient sleeping there, comfortably sedated, free for now from pain. There is no need to awaken her. She does not need to know I am here. Time passes slowly. This is a hard place.

Sunday 26 July. We pack up her few belongings and say goodbye to EHC today. The medications appear to have balanced themselves out under the watchful care of the hospices team. We are going home with a long list of medications and an even longer list of instructions. At 11 o'clock the ambulance returns along the freeway and through the city streets to our home, but no sooner are we there than Dixie has another vomiting spell.

I am anxious. Is it the result of the transition and transport, or did we leave EHC too soon? Eventually, however, she settles into her own bed. At least into the hospital bed that now serves as her own.

And so we wait and offer our own caregiving, along with periodic visits by the home hospice team. Our son, Stephen, is coming to be with us on Tuesday. After the doctors and nurses and specialists of all kinds have given their very finest efforts, perhaps this is the best kind of caregiving of all.

What? What is it you are asking? Oh yes. The question. In the midst of life happening, I had almost forgotten.

What's the most important thing?

The answer is simple really. But profound. Put yourself in your last-day shoes and think carefully. *What's the most important thing?*

When you are standing on top of the last mountain you will ever climb, the most important thing is that God, who gave you your mountain in the first place, is waiting for you there to spend your final day on earth together.

Life doesn't get any better than this!

58

The Journey Ends

Her absence is like the sky, spread over everything.
~ C.S. Lewis, A Grief Observed

Sunday 02 August. Amazing. We were told she would likely be gone in twenty-four to forty-eight hours after we came home. But she is still with us. Michele and I are her round-the-clock caregivers now. At 3 o'clock we awaken to administer her drugs. Michele has been our 24/7 companion and nurse since leaving the hospice center, staying here with us in our home.

Dixie is no longer able to speak. Her last words are to Michele, early in the week, while she is rubbing lotion on her mother's hands. Moving around the bed she becomes aware that Mom is trying to get her attention. Making eye contact she whispers to Michele, "I love you, I love you, I love you." Her final words. She is unable to say anything after that to anyone. We know she hears us speaking to her and conversing around her bed. Her countenance gives the briefest of acknowledgement as I lean into her ear and once again repeat the words I have said to her so often, "I love you, you know."

As I start toward her bed, the room begins to move. I feel a sudden dizziness and nausea. Staggering back against the bed, I reach for somewhere to sit. The room, everything and everyone in it is whirling! I lay down. It's worse. I've not experienced this before. What is happening? Am I having a stroke? I reach for one of Dixie's sick bags, feeling as though I am about to throw up.

Michele is at my side now, asking if she should call 911. I tell her to wait. Maybe this will pass. But minutes later with no letup, I do something I've never done. I tell her to go ahead. Dial 911. Six very long minutes later, two young medics are at the door and soon I am in the ambulance on my way to Overlake Hospital.

Michele tells me later, "You all at once not being here tipped me over. No, it was more than that. It was that now you were sick, too, and I didn't know what was wrong with you. It scared me. I watched you struggle in the bedroom... and suddenly the phone is in my hand and I'm dialing 911. My eyes go from you to Mom and back to you again. It is overwhelming, but I hold it together. I watch from the balcony as you are secured in the ambulance and drive away. I call Mark and Stephen and tell them to go to the hospital. Then I lose it. I can't control the sobbing!"

Mark and Stephen arrive at the ER, where like two bodyguards they assume positions at my side and serve as liaison between Katy and Linda Lenz who are by this time doing the same for Mom and Michele at home.

During the next forty-eight hours, I am wheeled in and out of scans and tests in the hospital while the medical team rules out first one thing, then another. The only thing not cooperating is the room. It is still circling. A CT scan, an ultra sound, an MRI, and something called the Dix-Hallpike maneuver rule out alternating possibilities of stroke or heart attack. Still no letup with the room.

Dr Lam (yes, another newbie in our physician collection) makes a diagnosis of *benign paroxysmal positional vertigo*. The good news is it is not life threatening. The bad news is I can seriously hurt myself by moving around on my own in my present condition.

It is the most common cause of dizziness when balance in the inner ear malfunctions. I am told small crystals in the ear determine the direction of gravity. When these come loose and float around the inner ear, it causes the sensation of vertigo, or spinning. It can be caused by a virus or even be stress related. Well, I don't have a virus. The bad news is, even the walk from bed to bathroom is a dizzying experience for me.

So now I am in a hospital bed with the room continuing to spin round and round with no let up. Outside the open doorway, the hall rushes past like a speeding train. Why is this happening? I need to be home with Dixie and I can't even walk by myself to the bathroom.

Monday 03 August. Michele and Katy arrange for a professional nursing team for Mom. She is pleased, as they settle in, with the way in which they treat Mom and go about their business of giving care.

Tuesday 04 August. Morning. A few minutes after 8 o'clock. I look up to see Stephen standing by my hospital bed, cell phone in hand. He is crying.

"What. What is it?" I ask.

"Mom is gone," he replies through tears.

His words stun me. Take my breath away. *Mom is gone!* The medical team has planned one more hospital day, mainly for my safety in recovery. But I've been here too long. *Mom is gone!* How can this be? This is wrong. She needs me. No, it's the other way around. I need to be there with her. I should have been there. But it makes no difference now. I am too late.

Mom is really gone!

Stephen leans in, wraps his strong arms around me and we hold one another, weeping. Then I push away the sheet and start to get up. This sets off a familiar loud alarm wired to my bed to protect me from injuring myself if I try to walk without assistance. The alarm has gone off several times before during my stay, resulting in voices in the hall, "Someone get in there, he's up again." But the nurse entering this morning quickly realizes today is different.

"What's wrong?" she asks.

The room is still spinning. The hallway is still rushing past my door. It no longer matters. Nothing else matters.

I tell her, "My wife just died. I have to go now! Please help me get checked out of here."

The official time of death: 7:52 am.

Dixie's long, arduous and painful journey is over.

Mom is gone.

And I am not there.

⌒

"Even with all the separation and things that might come our way, I would rather spend my life with you in the work of God than anything else I can think of." ~ DLT letter, 30 June 1955

⌒

∽

This morning, 04 August at 7:52, Dixie slipped quietly and peacefully from earth to heaven. Her long and difficult sacred journey is done.

Surely goodness and mercy shall follow me all the days of my life, and I shall dwell in the house of the Lord. ~ *Psalm 23:6*
~ posted on Facebook and CaringBridge.com ~

∽

A Postscript for Dixie

A desert sunrise... how glorious! How glorious you must be, O Lord, to create such beauty. The changing colors make me realize your creativity is not static, but ever changing, ever revealing and reflecting your beauty.

You not only create the beauty, you give me eyes to see and a heart to appreciate your handiwork. How majestic you are, O Lord! I receive with gratitude your beauty. Create in my eyes the ability to see all the majesty and beauty of your self. Reflect your beauty in my life. Let my family and those around me see the colors of your beauty reflected in me. Take away the darkness of my life so your light can shine through these colors, sparkling like a prism to a dull world that is drab and colorless without you. Let me be warmth to those who can't see your color because they are cold and empty.

Thank you, Lord, for filling my eyes with your beauty... for filling my life with your warmth... for filling my soul with yourself. ~ DLT diary, December 1995

A postscript is any addition or supplement a writer attaches to a book to supply further information. A kind of final word, if you will. This is not the last time I will speak of Dixie, Dix, Mom,

Gramma, or GG. She is all of these and more to us. I will speak of her often, telling her stories to the generations that follow. I will recall her smile at the very end, content in having finished well her sacred journey, anticipating what lay ahead. But this is my last word for now.

How does one fall in love so deeply and stay there for so long? Those who have experienced it may try to describe it, but I cannot. At least not adequately. I only know it happened once and I was there.

Dixie's and my love was at first an *attraction*, a drawing together, physically, emotionally, spiritually. But for attraction to be more than "dry kindling on a hot fire," consuming itself and then dying, requires a *decision* to commit to one another with servant love. It is this kind of true decision to be forever committed to another that remains strong through the tests, temptations and trials of life.

Humility, patience, sexual faithfulness, forgiveness, time, trust, integrity, communication, selflessness. Tears over having hurt or disappointed, spilling from one's eyes in the presence of the other. Suffering and sorrow. Generous portions of laughter with and for one another. Delight and contentment. These are the commitment ingredients that must be mixed thoroughly with attraction if love is to last. Rabbi Barnett R. Brickner says, "success in marriage does not come merely through finding the right mate, but through being the right mate."

Friendship. There are few things on which I see eye to eye with poet, composer and atheist philosopher, Friedrich Nietzsche, but I do agree with this statement attributed to him, "It is not a lack of love, but a lack of friendship that makes unhappy marriages."

I will miss my best friend every day. I will miss hearing her voice, seeing her face, feeling her touch. I will miss bringing her coffee each morning. I will miss reading our out-loud books together: the Bible, books of poetry and prose, theology and philosophy, practical Christianity.

I will miss praying together each morning. Starting busy days this way was oftentimes our only chance to be with one another, intimate in the presence of Redeeming Grace. I most often led in our morning prayers. She liked this. Is there something deep in a woman's heart that longs to be touched this way? To hear her husband pray for her and for those she loves? I believe so.

On occasion I asked her because I, too, so loved listening to her pray, expressing the intimate beliefs of her heart and her inmost depths of longing or concern for those she loved. I've heard her mention many of you by name to our very Best Friend. She could be tender and passionate at the same time. She loved with a fierce love, sometimes standing in the way of blows meant for others. She was a tough lady, and as Pastor Gary, with whom she worked for several years as minister to women, reminded our family at the interment, "she did not suffer fools!"

I will miss all this and more. She honored hers and my relationship by helping us have a happy life with one another, with our children and their children and their children's children, with the family of God and with the many strangers whom we have been privileged to meet along the way.

It seems as though she's still here. Force of habit finds me getting up quietly in the early morning so as not to awaken her. Neighbors respectfully give me space, leave cards expressing sympathy at my door. Candace, the young woman who deep cleans for us once a month cries while she works because "everything I touch reminds me of her ~ the woman who cared enough to talk to me and listen to my story."

My children and their spouses have been rock stars of strength and stability in these days of caregiving. Friends have brought meals. The group of business leaders who meet in our home every Wednesday morning have been a band of brothers to me. So many have sent cards and letters of encouragement, written messages on Facebook and CaringBridge, left phone or text messages. I cannot begin to adequately express what this has meant.

Medical teams have served us well at Overlake Hospital Medical Center of Bellevue, University of Washington Medical Center, Seattle Cancer Care Alliance and Proton Therapy Center, and Evergreen Hospice Center of Kirkland. Well over 200 doctors, nurses, technicians, therapists, and administrators in all.

It is imperative that we view all of life as a sacred journey. From the time we learn to share our toys to the time we learn to share our hearts. The good and the bad. The journey we choose or that is chosen for us is sacred, set apart to be shared unselfishly, secure against violation, offered in the end as a legacy to those who remain after death has at last parted us.

I give you my thanks, as do our daughter, Michele, son, Stephen, and all the members of our family, including you who in one way or another have adopted us on our sacred journey. If you've found the words written here helpful in some way, perhaps you will share them with friends. A gift of *Sacred Journey* to your pastor's wife would bring a huge smile to Dixie's face. I hope you or someone you love will find God's strength and love in your own Valley of Shadows, whatever they may be. My prayer is that you will discover, through your faith and his promises, the ways in which yours will be the sacred journey your Creator/Redeemer envisioned it to be when he saw you for the very first time. It is never too late to begin.

No, this is not my final word about Dixie. I will keep on telling the stories of how she came to us in her youth, touched us, became part of us, loved us, and like a stone cast upon the water, left us at the end with ripples of her love and devotion as our legacy.

I find myself expecting her to walk into the room just now and ask me what it is I am doing. I tell her I am writing the final postscript to a love story.

Her eyes light up, her countenance aglow with knowing.

"It's ours, isn't it?"

"It is," I reply.

With her hands on my shoulders, she leans in until her cheek brushes mine, her gaze resting on the final page. And as she has done so often before, she smiles and says, "So, tell me, what do you think we've learned from all of this?"

It's a good question. One I am sure she would want to ask you, now that you and she have become acquainted.

"What *do* you think you have learned from all of this?"

And now these three remain: faith, hope and love.
But the greatest of these is love. ~ 1 Corinthians 13:1

25 Postscript to a love story

The Beginning

They came from different worlds…

THE SONG SPARROW AND THE HUMMINGBIRD

26 Song sparrow

*The song sparrow made her home on
the ground in scrubby low cover
at the edge of a once very beautiful Garden.
    Beneath her dark eyes and short bill
        she wore a rich, feathery coat of russet-and-gray
        with bold streaks down her white chest.
    Her long tail, cocked and proud,
        pumped up and down on short flights across the Garden.
She was known for her colorful range of songs.*

*She knew twenty different tunes
   with hundreds of improvised variations
   and shared them all with her neighbors.
Favorite among humans in the Garden were what sounded
like the opening four notes of Beethoven's Symphony No. 5.*

*Sadly, those closest to her did not listen.
Mother and father bird seemed always to be fighting,
   too busy tearing their nest apart to hear her songs.
   Like the humans who had once loved their Garden
   and each other but rarely came here anymore.
She felt their anger,
   unloved,
      lonely and ashamed,
         certain it was her fault.
But still she sang her songs.*

One day a charm of hummingbirds flew past, playfully cavorting, dancing in the sun. One hummer heard her singing and abruptly stopped in midair. He circled back. She sat alone on a low branch. Lovely to look at and her songs were... well, they were amazing!

    He landed on a branch in the next tree over. Not too close so as to frighten her away, but close enough to hear her sing. After awhile the song sparrow stopped singing and was quiet. He knew she had seen him. He couldn't hold back. He had to show her how he felt.

He was small, but colorful with iridescent feathers. The humans called him Anna's Hummingbird. An iridescent reddish pink throat and crown. Wings so fast they made a humming noise. He could fly right, left, up, down, backwards, and even upside down.

And so he did. He did it for the song sparrow. Right, left, up, down, backward, and even upside down! He hovered by flapping his wings in a figure-8 pattern. He'd learned this before leaving the nest as a youngster. With his long and tapered bill... he'd learned this by watching his father... he obtained nectar from the center of flowers.

But there were two things he couldn't do. He didn't have a voice for singing and he couldn't walk or hop about. His feet were used for perching only. He was little, but a fighter. One of the fiercest of birds, a warrior! He had successfully repelled much larger birds away from feeders and flowers he liked. Somehow, he wanted her to know that.

At last he got up his nerve. This was it. He swooped in, flared, then lighted on the branch next to her. He waited for what seemed like forever. Waited for her to push him away. To tell him to get lost. To say they were too different, not suited for each other. That they came from different worlds... he from a country farm... she was a city bird.

He had grown up in an open cup nest the size of a golf ball, made up of dandelions, bits of leaves and feathers woven into a dense cup bound together with spider silk and decorated with moss and lichen for camouflage. She, too, had grown up in an open cup, but hers had been low on the ground and made of weeds, grass, leaves, strips of bark, lined with fine grass and rootlets and hidden in tall grass.

She was a solitary bird. He, on the other hand, was part of a charm (a group of hummers). She was monogamous. He was... well, hummingbirds are not so much. Males mate with the female and don't contribute to the care of the eggs or chicks. They defend the territory, but that's about it, and they will pretty much mate with any female in their territory.

But the song sparrow was clear early on about this. If they were to have a lasting relationship it had to be for better or for worse, richer, poorer, in sickness and in health, to love and to cherish; from this day until parted by death. Furthermore, he was going to have to do more than sit on his favorite branch "guarding the territory." He would need to help around the nest and join her in raising any chicks they might conceive.

He was smitten. Sick with love. He did cartwheels, chirping and squeaking, sounding a lot like something was stuck in his throat. He danced over her in the sky. Oh, how he danced...right, left, up, down, backwards, upside down! And as he danced the sparrow lifted her head and sang her love songs.

For many seasons after they flew together. Differences blended over time. They worked at living and loving together and it was good. They were blessed by the Creator of the Garden. The trees and flowers seemed greener and brighter, and birds in the neighborhood found inspiration and encouragement by sharing life together. They liked it when the hummingbird danced in the sky, and they loved the song sparrow's songs.

Each day he would brush against pollen in flower blossoms as he fed with his long bill. Each day with pollen on his head and bill, he transferred it between different flowers to help the plants grow while the songbird built their nests at the ten-foot level instead of on the ground. They called it compromise. And their little family grew, then flew away.

One evening a charm of hummingbirds flew by, on the way to warmer climate. He greeted them with a few rights, lefts, ups and downs, then watched as they disappeared. But something had been different this time. He came to her there in the nest. She was silent. She had not sung her

usual song for the hummingbirds as they passed by. In fact, she did not sing at all.
Not for them.
Not for him.
Not for anyone.

And for a moment...a long breathless moment...the entire garden was silent.

He looked away for an instant, and when he turned back she was gone. The nest was still warm. The scent of her presence still there. But she was gone.

His tiny feet clung to the branch. More tightly than ever before.
His tiny wings fluttered, but he did not lift off.
No left, right, up, down.
No more dancing in the sky.

He gazed at the empty nest for a long while as a cloak of darkness wrapped around him. At last, as dawn began to break, he opened his wounded heart to cry out his sorrow. Instead, he began to sing. Sing like he had never sung before. It was his voice, but they were her songs! Songs he had heard through many seasons. They were his now. Lodged forever in his heart.

His wings fluttered once more as he lifted off.
Right, left, up, down, backwards, and even upside down
he danced and flew over the Garden, singing all the while!

The leaves in the trees were greener again and flowers opened to the sun. Even the humans returned to the Garden to see and to listen

*to the beauty there is in the heart of God
in the magnificent songs of the lowly song sparrow
and the delightful hummingbird dance.*

27 Hummingbird

~ Ward Tanneberg / written in memory of my beloved wife Dixie / 4 August 2015

If you found *Sacred Journey* to be helpful and inspirational, take a moment to write a brief Amazon review, even two or three sentences, and encourage others to experience it as well.

Life is meant to be a Sacred Journey Questions

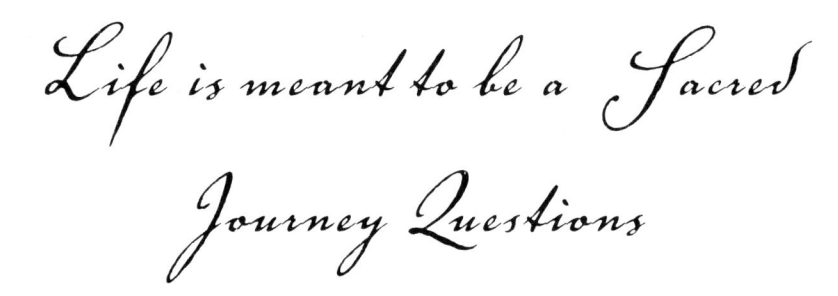

Intended for individual Reflection
and as a Discussion Guide for
Couples, Book Clubs and Small Groups

1. Calm before Storm
   - Some impactful life changes appear suddenly and some can be seen on the horizon. Are you facing a life change at this moment? What do you see on your horizon?
   - Life changes are inevitable. Facing these changes with someone helps balance the fear that comes. To whom or what do you turn when life goes upside down?
2. Valentine's Day
   - Preparing for bad news is challenging; in fact, it may be impossible to be fully ready for it. Sometimes one's only option is to choose how he or she will accept what comes. Describe a time when the news was bad and you had to decide how to move forward.
   - Think of someone you know who has dealt (or is dealing) with extreme challenges in a way that you admire and

respect. Describe what you admire in how he or she handled the situation. What can you do to incorporate these character qualities as your own?

3. Options Are Good
   - During a time of crisis, to whom would you turn for needed support and care?
   - When shadows fall onto your life path, how do you remind yourself that while it may *feel* dark, scary and lonely, you are not alone in the journey?
   - During her illness, Dixie kept a special Scripture passage as a reminder of where she could place herself while considering her options. Read Psalm 131 and consider your own options.

4. Looking for Signposts
   - Every journey requires direction...signposts. Dixie and Ward recognized their signposts of peace, calm, trust, faith and hope as reassurance through the shadows. Define the shadows in your life that keep encouraging signposts out of reach.
   - In spite of the profound relief of a successful surgery Dixie's family still felt the shadow of uncertainty for the things to come. What are some ways you deal with uncertainty?

5. Song Sparrows and Hummingbirds
   - Pain inflicted by others is very difficult to forgive—even more so when the inflictor is someone who should be trustworthy. When forgiveness is required, what holds you back from giving it?
   - Ponder the thought, Worry cannot empty tomorrow of its troubles, it empties today of its strength. In what way has tomorrow's worry robbed you of today's strength?

6. Looking for Warm Places

- Looking for a warm place means looking for comfort. Describe a way you can recognize someone experiencing a need for a warm place and what you could do to offer comfort.
- Stephen Covey says, "Begin with the end in mind." Deciding how one ends is more important than how one began. After reading, "you choose how you will be remembered," what resonated in your heart?

7. Regrets...There Are a Few
   - Is there someone with whom you wish you had made amends before it was too late? If you had it to do again, what would you tell him or her now?
   - Dixie felt she was not wanted or valued by her parents, but over time she deeply understood her value by God. What did she do to find the value God placed on her?

8. Looking for My Father
   - Consider A.W. Tozer's statement, "What comes into our minds when we think about God is the most important thing about us." How would you explain this statement to someone who does not believe in God?
   - What obstacles are in your way of finding the most important thing?

9. The Numbers Game
   - Sitting still on God's anvil, being shaped to His perfection, is the challenge for any Christian. Describe a personal experience in which the results of His handiwork are viewable to you.

10. Waiting and Watching
    - A trait Dixie practiced was listening to people. She drew people out by asking questions, showing interest in them,

and seeking out their story. In the waiting room times of life, how do you stay connected with people?
- What keeps you from sharing your story with others?
11. Love Unexpected
    - Just for the sheer pleasure of the recipient, write a letter to a loved one. To whom you would write? What would be important for you to say and why?
12. A New Normal
    - Difficult outcomes often create what we know as a new normal. Have you had to adjust to a new normal?
    - Do you feel alone in this new life? If you have let go of pleasurable things from the old normal, how can you incorporate those into your new life?
13. Yielding
    - What do you think it means to yield to His work?
    - Is yielding different from simply giving up?
14. Questioning
    - Have you ever just dropped what you were doing and started over?
    - How did you feel God was leading you in this change?
15. The "What If" Question
    - In making a major decision, were you given a clear sense of which way to go? Did the sense of direction occur quickly or after long consideration? Do you sense it was God leading you?
16. The Restless Years
    - Being criticized in a negative, faultfinding way is tough to work through. To deal with negative critique well, one must learn to evaluate which comments to consider as possibly true and which should be tossed out. What was your response the last time someone was critical of you?

17. Success and Sadness
    - While many happy times were enjoyed in California, some of life's experiences would bring each of the Tanneberg family to the brink. For what purpose do you believe God allows both good and bad experiences in people's lives?
    - It can be during the most difficult times that some walk away from faith in God. If God knows this about people, what might be a reason God would allow difficulty at all?
18. Full Circle
    - Describe a time when life took a different direction than you thought it would. Do you look back on that experience with regrets or gratitude? What did you learn about God and yourself?
19. Farewell for Awhile
    - Have you ever felt a sense of divine protection in an uncertain or dangerous situation?
    - What fond memories do you have of absences and returns?
20. Any Port in a Storm
    - Can you look back on a time when God fulfilled His promises and your fears and doubts were forgotten as He answered your prayers?
    - As you think about your own life story, describe as many specific instances as you can of God's faithfulness in difficult times, even the seemingly small ones.
21. Always a Bride
    - What goes through your mind when you think of eternal love?
22. Why Do You Think You're Here?
    - When have you asked God a question and expected an answer?

- Describe how you would know if He was asking you a question.
23. Where Help Comes From
    - Do you think God lets us experience things that cause us to need His help so we would ask Him for it?
    - Think about a need He has allowed for the purpose of bringing you closer to Him.
    - Please read Psalm 22, verses 1- 21. How would you describe verse 21?
24. Left Alone
    - Read the very last sentence of the gospel of Matthew. What do you think when you read this? How does that passage make you feel?
25. Satisfied...Not Settling
    - It is a matter of faith to believe what God provides is always enough. What feeds your faith when hardship overwhelms you?
    - It is a matter of faith to believe that God always answers prayer, even when the answer is not what we hoped. How has your faith grown by all the different kinds of answers God has provided?
26. Seeing with the Eyes of God
    - One of the pleasures of living this American life is enjoying the wide variety of cultures from around the world. Although Jesus said, "Go into all the world and preach the gospel," it might seem that the world has come to us! How do you think God expects us to speak of Him given today's cultural dynamic?
    - Do you think the meaning of the Great Commission is any different today than when Jesus first proclaimed it?
27. Against the Wind

- Disappointment is a great challenge to faith. We hope for and expect certain things but when disappointment creeps in, it can be a point of great sadness. Have you ever been so disappointed in something or someone that you struggled with your trust in God? What do you think God's purpose was in allowing your disappointment?
- If you are still struggling with the results of that disappointment, what would you say to God about how you feel?

28. Lifting Weary Hands
    - It is so easy to help someone who is weak and hurting and almost a joy to feel needed. What makes accepting help so difficult when you are the one in need?

29. Ring That Bell!
    - Take time to recall a moment of sheer joy that emerged after a long, painful struggle. Recall that moment and put on the final movement of Beethoven's 9th. It has a good beat and you can pray to it.

30. Selah
    - His strength, our weakness. Pause to think how you will apply this thought to the biggest problem you have right now. Write down what comes to mind as you ponder.
    - Describe how this exercise helps you realize God's presence.

31. Perspective
    - Recall a time when perspective in a situation allowed you to be more calm and able to cope than the others around you. What was it about the situation that helped you through?
    - Describe how perspective is important to keep in mind when life seems overwhelming.

32. When Setbacks Come
    - Think of a moment when close friends helped you through a difficult situation. What was said or done that you particularly appreciated?
33. Uncharted Territory
    - The significance of Dixie's gift of time at this point should not be lost. What did Dixie do from within to make herself available to the young woman she met? How significant was this action in your view?
    - What is the life message you see from Dixie's example of selfless giving?
34. Midcourse Check
    - Describe something beautiful you have seen in someone who is in the Winter of Life.
    - Reading Ward and Dixie's journey through this particular time, what is clear about where their strength really comes from?
35. My Journey Through the Valley of Shadows
    - Shadows fall at various points in our lives, but when they do, He is there. Read Psalm 23 and underline the passage that is most significant to you.
    - Which passage did you underline and why is it significant to you?
36. Road Trips
    - Ward and Dixie's road trip to the beach was a much-needed respite from the gritty work of cancer fighting. Why do you think it is important to periodically draw away for a time of prayer, refreshment and restoration?
    - Plan a road trip with someone you love. Do it today. Don't wait.
37. The Bad Week

- Are you living as you were designed to live? Dixie described how in her journal when she wrote, *"to glorify God; to drink deeply from His source; to live joyfully, lovingly, richly; to bring pleasure to Him."*
- What habits would you need to incorporate in order to live as you were designed?

38. The Thousand-Year Day
    - If the primary discipline of prayer is waiting, how long should our waiting persevere?
    - If God doesn't dispense answers to prayer like a candy machine, what should we expect from the prayers we pray?
    - What should be our attitude when approaching God in prayer?

39. Doctors Treat...Jesus Heals
    - Treating comes through various methods. Healing comes by various forms. We don't always like the methods doctors use to treat and we aren't often content with the form Jesus uses to heal. What action of faith can we exercise as we participate with both kinds of healing?

40. Merry Christmas!
    - Dixie recognizes that the One whose name is all-powerful intimately knows her name. How does this fact impact your feeling of significance with God, the Almighty?
    - The best gift one can give is an invitation to a personal relationship with God. You are invited at this very moment to know Jesus as your personal Lord, Savior and Friend. Contact your local Christian church if you are interested in more information (or contact Ward Tanneberg Ministries at ward@wardtanneberg.com).

41. The Greatest Small Gift
    - Who, within your church fellowship or neighborhood community, would benefit from your greatest small gift of presence?
42. When Rights Are Not Always Right
    - Describe a time when you were right on principle but the argument was diminished by your attitude.
    - Is there someone with whom you should make peace?
    - Whose forgiveness do you wish for?
43. It's Not Over 'til It's Over
    - In sports, one doesn't leave the game until it's over. Even when a player is benched, he or she still suits up. Why do you think this is important to the team dynamic?
    - Have you ever left a challenge before the end was called? If you had to do it again, what would you change? Say why.
44. The Thing Between God and Us
    - Suffering is a stressful, lonely time that can cause one to really question God's intention and plan. Have you experienced suffering? How did it impact your interaction with God?
    - Does it help to think of suffering as the thing between you and God?
45. Happy Valentine's Day
    - Dixie felt relief at Dr. Park's recommendation, though it was not something she favored. Our ability to give guidance to others at the right time can relieve them of a burden; given at the wrong time it can be counterproductive. How do we know the right time to give guidance to someone in need?
46. Our Family in Christ

- Explain why you believe we are called to participate in a church body.
- Has there ever been a time when you felt God has told you, "Follow Me?"

47. Don't Breathe
    - What is the most difficult medical treatment you have experienced?
    - What did you discover was the best way to endure it?
48. It Takes a Village!
    - Have you ever been a part of someone's village?
    - Describe what you learned from the experience.
49. "Beam Me Up, Scotty"
    - What is the best part of aging?
    - What have you grown to like better about others as they've gotten older?
50. Traits of the Long Distance Runner
    - Recall a time in your life when you were metaphorically running. Did you find that you were running with (or for) someone else?
    - During that time, did you find you became an owner of another's burden, or were you able to run alongside to help carry the burden?
51. More Traits...
    - It is very easy to give into feelings of self-pity and sadness when someone you love is battling illness. As your loved one's caregiver, why is it important to be real, but also encouraging, and fight the desire toward self-pity?
52. Chemotherapy Round 4
    - What does it mean to say God is silent?
    - Do you feel when God is silent that He is also absent?
53. Icons of Aging

- Psalm 52:8 says, "But I am like a green olive tree flourishing in the house of God, I trust in God's unfailing love for ever and ever." The olive tree symbolizes God's faithfulness and steadfastness toward His people. Describe someone who has been a green olive tree in your life.

54. Attitude
    - Sometimes a single person can make all the difference in handling a dire situation. When has this happened in your life?
    - Do you sense there is a person for whom you can make all the difference in the world right now?
    - Have you experienced a crisis in your life in which your attitude and / or tenacity, or that of someone else, made all the difference in achieving a successful outcome?

55. The Most Important Thing
    - Put on your last-day shoes and think carefully. What's the most important thing you can imagine on the very last day of your own sacred journey?

The remainder of the book speaks for itself. There are no more questions.

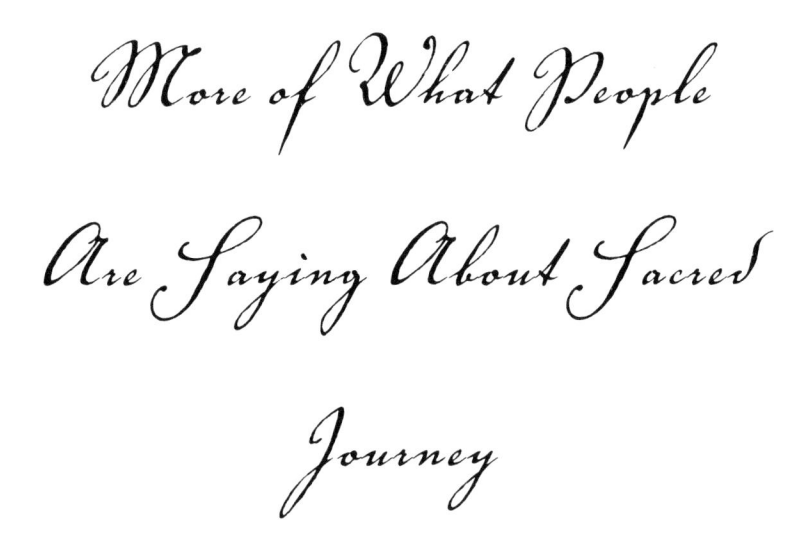

More of What People Are Saying About Sacred Journey

Put on your hiking boots, pick up your trekking stick, load your backpack and join Ward Tanneberg on this extraordinary *sacred journey*. It is a love story, a life chronicle, a handbook, and a psalm of praise to a God who is ever present. Join with Ward and Dixie as they do life together... with the God they love.
Brenda A. Smith, President
Breakfast With Fred Leadership Institute
www.facebook.com/bwfli; BWF Project, Inc., www.breakfastwithfred.com
Breakfast With Fred (Regal Books)

Before we ever knew each other in the '90's, God knew Dixie would be a special influence to carry me forward after those years together in Palm Desert. Her love of Ward and family was a witness to me of this unique, one-of-a-kind friend God had in mind when He created her...a Proverbs 31 Wife of Noble Character living in our present times. *Sacred Journey* is the story of a very special person.

Betty J. Mann
Wife of the late musical composer, arranger and conductor Johnny Mann

As the Tanneberg's pastor for the last sixteen years, reading *Sacred Journey* is like sitting over coffee with two deeply authentic people who know what it means to be on a journey with God, and live what they preach. It is a touching mix of personal stories and sage, heart-filled advice and encouragement for all ages and stages on the journey. Read it and receive fresh and deep perspective into your own life.

Gary Gulbranson, Senior Pastor
Westminster Chapel of Bellevue, Washington

Jacque and I had the honor of knowing and working alongside Dixie and Ward as a couple, both in life and ministry. Death has a way of stopping us in our tracks and when Dixie died, it caused pause: 'Is my faith strong and courageous enough to handle life and death with the same joy, hope and peace Dixie exhibited?' Ward has written many novels but this one is non-fiction, the true love story of a man and woman who genuinely loved, respected and complimented each other in the home, the church and the marketplace. Laugh and weep. Read and learn.

John Coulombe, interGen and Pastoral Ministries Pastor,
EvFree Fullerton, California

Ward Tanneberg's latest book, *Sacred Journey*, comes from the hearts and souls of two who experienced many of life's ups and downs and still held onto their faith in God, who is forever with

us. As you read, you will be inspired and encouraged on your own *sacred journey.*
Dr. Roger E. Bowman
Retired Pastor/District Supt. Church of the Nazarene
CASA Network Board Member, ret.

I just read the beautiful allegory, THE SONG SPARROW AND THE HUMMINGBIRD, included in *Sacred Journey.* Phenomenal. Thank you for singing Dixie's songs. Keep on singing Dixie's songs! One cannot experience you without experiencing Dixie. I experienced Dixie. I heard her songs. One cannot experience Dixie without experiencing God. I felt His Presence.
~ *Ed Germann*
Regional Director, International Students, Inc.

Some touch the surface of your life briefly, others touch more deeply leaving a lasting impact. Ward and Dixie Tanneberg touched us in deeper places, and even the tyranny of distance could not keep us from being drawn into their *sacred journey* of love, courage, faith and hope that springs eternal.
Richard and Shirley Pearce,
Churches of Christ in Queensland
Fresh Horizons Ministry, Australia

Life is a *sacred journey* that needs guides. Ward and Dixie Tanneberg are wise guides that help you navigate the unpredictable minefield of life. In *Sacred Journey* you will receive insight, encouragement, tested wisdom, honesty, and much more for the uncharted course of your own personal journey.
Peter Menconi, author of The Intergenerational Church:
Understanding Congregations from WWII to www.com

C.S. Lewis said, "Aim at heaven and you get earth thrown in. Aim at earth, and you will get neither." Ward and Dixie Tanneberg long ago set their sights on heaven, where Dixie now resides. Their love for Jesus and passion for people made them dearly beloved friends to thousands who have known them as pastors, confidants, and mentors. Ward's telling of their remarkable love story will inspire you to believe that God can do extraordinary things through ordinary people who learn to find strength in weakness, gain in loss, and joy in sorrow.
Don Detrick, D.Min.
Associate Network Leader :: Corporate Secretary/Treasurer
Northwest Ministry Network (NW District Assemblies of God)

Without question, **Sacred Journey** is a courageous and heart-wrenching story. We really do see ourselves best when we see us in someone else. Ward and Dixie give us this chance as we journey with them into a "Valley of Shadows" where surprising discoveries are made. I plan to put **Sacred Journey** in the hands of our 46 chaplains, as a practical pathway companion, articulated with honest passion and vulnerability. A powerful story of faith, hope and love, and the decision to "not waste our cancer."
Rev. Ross Paterson M. Div.
Pastor to Senior Adults and Congregational Care
CrossPoint Community Church, Modesto, California

Dixie was a creative, talented wife, mother and best friend to her husband, Ward. In her lifetime she gave counsel and spiritual help to many. Hers is a story of faith, perseverance and triumph in a valley of dark shadows, helping light the way for us on our own *sacred journeys*.
Bob & Charlene Pagett
Founders of Assist International.

Sacred Journey is authentic, honest, and inspiring—because the life of Dixie Tanneberg is all of those words and more. This book will teach you what real living looks like. Ward's words paint a picture that every reader will want to hang in their home and heart forever.
Jeff Mattesich, Lead Ministry Pastor
Lake Ave Church, Pasadena, California

Sacred Journey is a heartwarming life-and-death saga. Ward Tanneberg wields a pen educated by experience and practical wisdom. Ink flows with grace-filled truth, and joy mingles with sorrow as he comes to grips with one of life's greatest traumas; the impending death of a beloved spouse. The narrative is uplifting and, at times, spellbinding. In a compelling true story, framed by the final eighteen months of a beloved's mortal life, we are introduced to an eternal perspective of light and life, and a Father who loves deeply.
Douglas Anderson, Psy. D.
Owner and CEO, Life Directions Financial

She was and will ever be my spiritual mother, my mentor, and my friend--and so it is. I miss her as spiritual mother. Perhaps because it's possible to have other mentors and other friends, but you only have one mother. There will not be another Dixie in my life.
Bev Beckendorf
Retired in Oregon

Dixie always looked fashionable and lovely, even in jeans and a sweatshirt! She dedicated herself to mentoring women, young and old, and her presence gave the minutes value and purpose. I don't recall ever leaving her without some sort of challenge or

gentle insight. She had a gift for speaking truth in love. She had discovered the sacred and gave it the central place in her life.
Bobbe Evans
Retired in Washington

About the Author

Ward believes story remains our best device for truth telling. The skillful blending of love and hate, inspiration and faith, uncertainty and danger is a daunting challenge. Ward is loved by readers for inviting us to a stage on which compelling characters portray "the God who is there and is not silent," in an irresistible page-turning style.

In fiction, allegory, essay or memoir, his worldview is Christocentric. His stated mission, "listen well, write creatively, speak to influence, stir the glowing embers of my peers and turn the Light on for the next generations" embraces that worldview. When writing or speaking at retreats, conferences and churches, he addresses key questions for every person: *"Who is God in my life right now? Who am I at this powerful season in my life? What shall I do with the years that remain?"*

Ward's literary works include inspirational thrillers **Without Warning, Vanished, Pursuit** and 2015 Illuminations award-winning **Redeeming Grace**. You can also follow his blog, **Perspective**.

He has been an evangelist, denominational youth and men's ministries leader, Christian college public relations director, guest lecturer, adjunct professor, writer, novelist, and pastor in three churches. Ward lives in Bellevue, Washington. A widower, he has 2 married children, 3 grandchildren, 4 step-grandchildren and 2 great grandsons. His interests and ministry have taken him to over 50 countries of the world.

More from Ward Tanneberg:

Without Warning: **When ancient hatreds explode, John Cain is thrust into the middle of a precise, coordinated jihad where he will look straight into the abyss and discover whether or not his God is big enough to see him through.**

Vanished: **This electrifying and heart-pounding sequel to** *Without Warning* **combines a profound understanding of a broken world with realistic portrayals of how Christ can still make a difference in our age of terror. Held hostage by radical Islamic terrorists in Israel, 12-year-old Jessica Cain's survival hangs on a chance encounter with a total stranger and the possibility that her father can save her.**

Redeeming Grace (Illumination Book Awards Winner): Seven years ago, Grace Grafton died in a boating accident while partying on the Georgia, South Carolina coast. Was her death the result of alcohol and drugs or something more sinister? Nobody knows: her body was never recovered. Now years later, a woman reads in disbelief the note addressed to her: Hello Grace, did you think we wouldn't find you? Those nine chilling words end Grafton's self-imposed sanctuary of witness protection. Now she and everyone she loves are in grave danger. Long believed dead, she has a secret that can change the world. She knows the man running for president is guilty of a double murder! But who will believe her? When a murderer moves into the White House no one is safe—not even the dead.

If you enjoyed *Sacred Journey,* **you might like these titles from other Hartline authors:**

Kimberly Rae's *Why Doesn't God Fix It?:* Have you ever wanted to ask, "Where are You, God? Why are You letting this suffering continue? Don't You care?" If you have, you're not alone. Join Kimberly Rae as she struggles through the hard questions about living with illness, and discover truths in God's Word that offer hope, peace, and joy.

Kimberly Rae's *Sick and Tired:* Nearly one out of every two Americans has a chronic health issue, so it's safe to say you either have a health condition, or you care about someone who does. How do you live with the day-to-day struggle? Is it possible to have joy despite saying no to activities/food/opportunities/parties when you'd rather say yes? How do you explain your limitations to people who don't understand? In *Sick and Tired,* author

Kimberly Rae takes you on a journey toward personal peace. With humor and transparency, she offers encouragement and practical tips for the daily struggles. Find out how God's truth will change your perspective, giving you strength beyond yourself and sight beyond your limitations. Come along and enjoy, knowing you are not alone ... and there is hope!